Lessons from the Economics of Crime

CESifo Seminar Series
edited by Hans-Werner Sinn

See http://mitpress.mit.edu for a complete list of titles in this series.

Lessons from the Economics of Crime

What Reduces Offending?

edited by
Philip J. Cook, Stephen Machin, Olivier Marie, and Giovanni
Mastrobuoni

CESifo Seminar Series
The MIT Press
Cambridge, Massachusetts
London, England

MIT Press books may be purchased at special quantity discounts for business or sales promotional use. For information, please email special_sales@mitpress.mit.edu or write to Special Sales Department, The MIT Press, 55 Hayward Street, Cambridge, MA 02142.

This book was set in Palatino by Toppan Best-set Premedia Limited, Hong Kong. Printed and bound in the United States of America.

Library of Congress Cataloging-in-Publication Data

Lessons from the economics of crime : what reduces offending? / edited by Philip J. Cook, Stephen Machin, Olivier Marie, and Giovanni Mastrobuoni.
    pages cm. – (CESifo seminar series)
    Includes bibliographical references and index.
    ISBN 978-0-262-01961-3 (hardcover : alk. paper) 1. Crime–Economic aspects.
2. Crime prevention. 3. Criminals–Rehabilitation. I. Cook, Philip J., 1946–
    HV6171.L47   2013
    364.2'5–dc23
                                        2013004750

10 9 8 7 6 5 4 3 2 1

Contents

III   Feedback and Interactions

Series Foreword

This book is part of the CESifo Seminar Series. The series aims to cover topical policy issues in economics from a largely European perspective. The books in this series are the products of the papers and intensive debates that took place during the seminars hosted by CESifo, an international research network of renowned economists organized jointly by the Center for Economic Studies at Ludwig-Maximilians-Universität, Munich, and the Ifo Institute for Economic Research. All publications in this series have been carefully selected and refereed by members of the CESifo research network.

Crime Economics in Its Fifth Decade

Philip J. Cook, Stephen Machin, Olivier Marie, and Giovanni Mastrobuoni

It is not unusual these days to have a group of economists gather to discuss their research on crime. In Europe and the Americas, a critical mass of academic economists have specialized in the study of crime and its control, and there is now a steady flow of economics doctoral dissertations on this topic. As we near the fiftieth anniversary of Gary Becker's seminal contribution to this field (Becker 1968), it is fair to say that the economics of crime is no longer a "fringe" topic, but part of the standard portfolio that makes up the discipline of economics.

Among some of the markers of progress are the following:

• The National Bureau of Economic Research (NBER) created a working group on crime that has had regular meetings since 2007 and published an edited conference volume in 2011 (Cook, Ludwig, and McCrary 2011).

• A new organization within LACEA (Latin American and Caribbean Economic Association), with the acronym AL CAPONE (America Latina Crime and Policy Network), held its first annual meeting in 2011.[1]

• The Transatlantic Workshop on the Economics of Crime has been running annually since 2009 (Paris 2009, Bonn 2010, Torino 2011, Rotterdam 2012).

• John Jay College of Criminal Justice in New York City recently added an economics department, while US think tanks like the Vera Institute of Justice and the Urban Institute and UK government departments like the Home Office are producing cost–benefit assessments of crime-control programs.

• Leading economics journals in Britain and the United States have been publishing crime papers on a regular basis for forty years, and criminology journals have recently begun publishing articles authored by economists.

• The conference that produced the papers in this volume, sponsored by CESifo as part of its annual meeting in Venice (2011), is one of several similar meetings in Europe in recent years that, like the NBER crime group and AL CAPONE, are helping create an international network of scholars as well as capacity building with junior researchers and doctoral students to produce the next generation of specialists.

Of course, the social-scientific study of crime was well established by the time of Gary Becker's contribution. Prior to that, from the 1920s onward, the dominant disciplines were sociology and psychology, and that continued to be the case as criminology departments and schools were established in the post-war period. Becker chose to bypass rather than engage with that tradition, saying ". . . a useful theory of criminal behavior can dispense with special theories of anomie, psychological inadequacies, or inheritance of special traits and simply extend the economist's analysis of choice" (Becker 1968, p. 170). With this bit of disciplinary imperialism as a guide, subsequent economics contributions tended to adopt the view that crime research was virgin territory, scarcely inhabited. Economists were initially not so welcome in criminology, and for the most part were unconcerned about that fact, feeling that they had little to learn from the "natives." Recently that separation between economics and criminology has begun to break down, a welcome trend that can be traced in part to the growth of multidisciplinary public-policy programs and think tanks in the United States.[2]

What have the economists contributed to the study of criminal behavior and crime control? In what follows, to motivate and describe the contributions to this edited volume, we discuss three domains:

• A normative framework for evaluating criminal law and crime prevention, and the application of sophisticated quantitative methods to analyze the causes of crime and the effects of crime-control measures in this framework.

• The conception of criminal behavior as individual choice, influenced by perceived consequences.

• The aggregation of individual choices to a systems framework for understanding crime rates and patterns.

The chapters in this volume are informed by and contribute to all of these domains.

Part I: Policy Choice and a Normative Framework

During the tumultuous years of the 1960s, with riots in the cities and escalating rates of crime and drug abuse, the US Congress created several high-profile commissions to assess the underlying problems and recommend effective reforms. When these commissions turned to the prominent criminologists of the day, they offered their opinions but had little in the way of relevant evidence. The political scientist James Q. Wilson was a critical observer of criminology at the time and observed that its sociological orientation did not lend itself well to evidence-based policy recommendations (Wilson 1975). Crime was understood to be caused by culture and social structure. An analysis of these "root causes" of crime provided little guidance for policy makers, whose ability to change structural aspects of society was very limited. Moreover the sociologists were highly skeptical of the deterrence mechanism, denying or disregarding a role for the criminal justice system in controlling crime. In Great Britain the disconnect between criminology and policy was perhaps even greater, since the dominant ethos dictated against policy engagement, in part because of its heavier focus on the social context of crime (Muncie 2005).

Among the social sciences, economics tends to be best suited for addressing issues relevant to policy design. The economic model presumes that observed behavior is not the inevitable result of underlying social conditions, but rather results from individual choices influenced by perceived consequences. If government policy can change those consequences, then behavior change can follow. Furthermore, uniquely among the social and behavioral sciences, economic science incorporates a well-developed normative framework that defines the public interest and lends itself to policy prescription.

Indeed Becker's contribution was primarily in the normative realm. He pointed out that the social costs associated with crime are the sum of the direct costs of victimization (and the threat of victimization) and the indirect costs of efforts to control and prevent crime. If the goal is to minimize total social costs, then the optimal amount of crime is unlikely to be zero, since at some point the marginal costs of additional prevention will exceed the marginal benefit of an additional reduction in crime.

This simple and profound insight is relevant today in assessing progress against the crime "problem" in Western countries. Over the last twenty years crime rates have been relatively stable or falling in most European countries and declining in the United States (Buonanno et al. 2011). In the United States the decline has been associated with an increase in public and private expenditure on prevention and control (Cook and Ludwig 2011), notably (but by no means limited to) in the form of the burgeoning prison population. Whether the *total* social costs have been going down is thus an open question, since the increasing costs of control and avoidance may make up for the falling direct costs.

The normative framework also provides guidance for evaluating specific interventions. The economic question is not limited to "what works?" in crime control, but "what is worthwhile?" Cost–benefit analysis provides a set of rules for answering that question, and more generally encourages a comprehensive approach to evaluation. An example in this volume is Emily Owen's chapter (chapter 1) on the COPS program, which provides federal funding in the United States to some jurisdictions for hiring additional police officers. The question of whether the additional officers had an effect on crime rates is surely of interest, but if the answer is yes, there remains the question of whether it passes the cost–benefit test. She expands the discussion to consider the arrest rate, since arrests and subsequent court processing generate public costs. (The fact that she finds that arrest rates actually decline along with crime rates strengthens the case that COPS is cost-beneficial.[3])

The economist's normative framework also provides guidance on the appropriate scope of the criminal law. The tradition of consumer sovereignty, informed by the utilitarian perspective that measures the public interest as the sum of individual preferences, engenders a skeptical view of sumptuary laws of all kinds. The chapter in this volume on drug policy by John Donohue (chapter 2) notes that Nobel laureate Milton Friedman was a passionate advocate for legalization of marijuana, heroin, and other drugs, in part because of his belief that individual adults are the best judge of their own best interests. That perspective does not settle the issue for most observers, including most economists; for one thing, commodities that are both harmful to the user and addictive (e.g., heroin, crack-cocaine, alcohol, and tobacco) pose a particularly stringent test of the utilitarian perspective. Do we really believe that youths who are deciding to shoot up or smoke have their own best lifetime interests in mind? Even starting with a more equivocal view, the economic normative framework helps organize a comprehensive accounting scheme for determining which costs and benefits to consider. Given current practice, the costs of criminalization and enforcement loom large, which motivates a search for more efficient means of controlling use and abuse.

Evaluation and study of criminal activities in this normative framework has recently been greatly enhanced by two phenomena which economists of crime have been the first to fully integrate into their research approach: (1) the significant improvement in data availability and data quality, and (2) implementation of creative statistical methods to directly study causal relations in crime and crime control.

Increased access to high-quality data has greatly improved the potential to study the link between criminal participation and other factors that have theoretically been identified to influence its prevalence. Recorded police crime statistics have historically been one of the main sources of data used by researchers. Such data are very useful for tracking crime rates over time and across areas, for example, as when studying if these have been affected by the introduction of a localized policy initiative. Arrests, and other CJS data, have also been extensively exploited since they have the advantage of providing some basic information on the characteristics of the offenders (e.g., age, gender, and ethnicity). Arrest rates serve as a proxy for offending rates (albeit not necessarily reliable) and allow separate analysis of certain population subgroups. Using arrest data, researchers can also consider how certain policies or exogenous shocks affected the crime rates of particular cohorts.

The latest development in data collection has been the matching of individual administrative criminal datasets with other data sources containing information on offender characteristics such as education and employment of very large samples of the population. Such expanded datasets will, for example, enable research into the complex dynamics between labor market opportunities and criminal participation at the individual level to emerge in the very near future.[4]

The chapters in this volume use or make reference to the very wide array of data sources available across the world today to carry out research into the causes of offending. Over and above data-related advances, they also all emphasize the importance of a solid and coherent methodology to test the validity of the normative framework.

The other important feature of the application of the normative framework has been the contribution by economists of using advanced and innovative statistical methods. The first wave of econometric studies of deterrence using aggregate data (Ehrlich 1973; Sjoquist 1973; Carr-Hill and Stern 1973) utilized complex multi-equation multivariate models estimated by two-stage least squares—at about the same time that criminologists were publishing the results of simple correlations on the same topic. Still, the first wave of econometric research was effectively critiqued by an expert panel of the National Research Council (Blumstein, Cohen, and Nagin 1978) and others (Cook 1977). The essential problem was the lack of plausibly exogenous instrumental variables on which to anchor a causal analysis of nonexperimental data. As economics has increasingly embraced the use of natural and field experiments, economists have produced more robust findings on the causes of crime. One of the leaders in the creative use of plausibly exogenous variation to identify crime causation is Steven Levitt, whose research (and emergence as a celebrity, thanks to his book *Freakonomics*) has done much to inspire subsequent cohorts of graduate students in economics (e.g., see Ayres and Levitt 1998; Levitt 1996, 1997, 2004; Levitt and Dubner 2005).

When it comes to empirical methods, the leading edge for economics and criminology has converged in recent years. "Experimental criminology" is thriving and cuts across disciplines.[5] In this volume chapter 3 by Jens Ludwig, Jeffrey R. Kling, and Sendhil Mullainathan discusses the agenda for policy experiments in crime control. Their theme is relevant to experimental work in criminology as well as economics. The ultimate objective of policy experiments is to discover what works and what is worthwhile. Testing innovative interventions through field experiments is vitally important if we are to have the possibility of evidence-based policy. However, the authors point out that policies or programs are usually quite complex, and their effectiveness may be mediated by a variety of factors specific to time and place.

What we can learn from a policy experiment, then, may be less than meets the eye—even a clear demonstration that a complex program implemented by a particular agency in a given environment is cost effective (in comparison with the status quo) may leave considerable uncertainty about whether a similar policy would be effective, let alone worthwhile, if implemented by another agency in a different jurisdiction. For that reason it is important to focus the empirical research agenda on the basic mechanisms that influence crime rates. For example, if it can be established that the deterrent effect of punishment is more sensitive to the probability of punishment than the severity of punishment (as many of us suspect), then policy innovations that increase the probability of punishment will have a better prognosis than those that increase the severity of punishment. The authors point out that there may be trade-offs in experimental design between whether the intervention is realistic (something that might actually be implemented) and whether it is possible to isolate a particular mechanism. Nevertheless, causal research focused on basic mechanism may produce generalizable knowledge of the sort most needed in policy design.

Part II: Crime as a Rational Choice

A simplistic but common understanding of crime is that the population can be divided neatly into two groups, good guys and bad guys. In this view, the bad guys commit crime unless they are incapacitated and the good guys are reliably law abiding. This view had particular sway as an explanation for the surge of youth violence in the United States during the decade beginning in 1984. The sociologist John DiIulio, together with William Bennett (a member of President Reagan's cabinet), asserted that the surge was due to the growing ranks of remorseless killers, "superpredators" who grew up in poor, violence-ridden neighborhoods and broken homes. In effect, then, the claim was that the surge in murder was the direct result of a surge in the number of bad guys (Cook and Laub 2002). The only recourse appeared to be locking up as many of these superpredators as possible, and indeed most states changed their laws to facilitate sentencing teenage felons to long prison terms (Dodge 2008). As it turned out there was no scientific basis for the "superpredator" claim. Rather, the evidence points strongly to environmental factors, and the leading contender in that regard is the crack-cocaine epidemic. However, the "superpredator" claim was appealing in its simplicity and its veneer of social science.

The economic model of crime shifts the focus from character to the choices that are available to the individual. While certain aspects of character (or "preferences") are surely not irrelevant, criminal activity represents a choice, or set of choices, that is available to everyone. The choice of whether to commit crime is driven by the consequences, which differ among individuals depending on the opportunities available to them. For example, a school dropout will have relatively poor opportunities to earn a legitimate living, but his lack of schooling is no barrier to larceny or robbery. For that reason alone we expect dropouts to be overrepresented among active criminals. One type of formal economic model has treated criminal opportunities as gambles, with a payoff if successful (the "loot") and some probability of failure entailing arrest and punishment. If the threatened punishment includes a prison term, or stigma that reduces access to good jobs, then the effect will be greater for those with good legitimate prospects. An alternative approach has modeled crime as analogous to work, an activity that competes in use of time with other activities (Ehrlich 1973), but with a risky set of consequences.

This rational perspective leads naturally to a presumption of deterrability—that crime rates will be inversely related to the likelihood and severity of punishment. However, the economic model also incorporates the idea that programs to improve legitimate opportunities may have a deterrent effect through increasing the opportunity cost of time spent in criminal activity or in prison. People with something to lose are less likely to view criminal participation as attractive, and crime reductions can therefore be achieved by influencing the life opportunities of potential offenders. Some recent papers, Lochner and Moretti (2004), Machin, Marie, and Vujic (2011) and Hjalmarsson, Holmlund, and Lindquist (2012), have, for example, shown that education has a large crime-reducing effect on cohorts of individuals that were forced to stay longer at school because of changes in minimum school leaving age legislation.

So what happened to cause the epidemic increase in youth violence in the United States during the crack era? As noted, an explanation in terms of the number of "bad guys" does not fit the basic facts.[6] The economic perspective encourages an explanation in terms of an upward shift in the payoff to gun violence. That may indeed have been the case, as the introduction of crack into cities had the effect of disrupting established drug distribution networks and creating new contests over turf that in the United States (unlike other countries) elicited a surge of gun violence.

The economic focus on choices and consequences does not preclude the possibility that character (or what economists are inclined to call "preferences") is also important in influencing criminal involvement. The potential importance of changing preferences is suggested by the very strong relationship between criminal involvement and age; the age profile of crime commission declines steeply after age 20 or so, a pattern that may reasonably be interpreted as reflecting changing preferences (brain development, hormones) associated with the aging process—although aging is not a well-controlled experiment. More specifically, some crime reduction programs focus directly on changing preferences, as for example therapeutic interventions intended to reduce craving for illicit drugs.

Efforts to rehabilitate criminals may focus either on increasing the quality of legitimate opportunities (typically by improving human capital or clearing away barriers to earning a legitimate living), or on changing cognitive processes and capacities, such as self-control, empathy, and rationalization. While there have been myriad evaluations of specific programming intended to reduce recidivism rates, there remains considerable uncertainty about the overall effect of a spell of imprisonment on subsequent behavior. Aurélie Ouss (chapter 4) reviews the contributions of economists to this literature, pointing out that the general consensus emerging that longer prison terms tend to reduce recidivism rates can in fact be somewhat confounded by the effect of age on criminal behavior. Chapter 5, by Stefan Pichler and Daniel Römer, presents new results on recidivism rates by German youths age 18 to 20, finding that those who are sentenced as juveniles tend to have higher recidivism rates than those who are sentenced as adults (with greater use of prison). The mechanism by which prison time affects post-release recidivism rates is not clear. It is possible that the actual experience of incarceration changes perceptions about the likelihood or severity of future sanctions. Nevertheless, there are numerous other ways in which the regimentation and social interactions of prison life might influence character or post-release opportunity.

Crime as a rational choice has recently been applied to understand the behavioral response of an ever wider variety of agents facing criminal participation decisions and of the institutions who aim to prevent offending. In his chapter 6 to this volume, Mikael Priks argues that this framing serves to explain the activities of certain sports fans who are involved in violent activities which may at first appear relatively puzzling. He discusses how his research into what he labels "hooliganomics" shows that people affiliated to sports booster clubs will respond to (dis)incentives influencing crime participation. He argues that the club may provide some check on its members' hooliganism, depending on the composition of membership. If the hooliganism-prone members come to dominate, then the internal regulation of behavior may erode.[7]

Part III: Feedbacks and Interactions

Economics is a social science. The theory of individual behavior serves as a building block for a theory of aggregate outcomes: the wealth of nations, or quantity and price in a specific market. The aggregation of individual choices in the context of a complex system can produce some surprising results—for example, that in a competitive industry the individual producers' pursuit of profit maximization drives down prices to the point where there is no profit to be made. With respect to crime patterns, there can also be counterintuitive results. A case in point is vulnerable population groups that have relatively low crime victimization rates; the "little old ladies" living in the inner city are rarely robbed because they have adapted to the threat by hiding out at home behind locked doors (Cook 1986).

The interacting systems that connect crime-related choices by individuals to aggregate outcomes (aggregate rates and patterns) have not been fully worked out by economists, but the literature provides a start on this project. Criminal activity may be viewed as produced by individuals (active criminals) at a rate that is limited by the activities of the criminal justice system and private security measures.[8] The electorate chooses through the political process how many public resources to devote to the criminal justice system, and private households and businesses make myriad individual choices about how much private effort to devote to crime prevention and avoidance. A further complication is that the effectiveness of the criminal justice system is very much dependent on private (often voluntary) inputs, such as reporting crimes and providing information and testimony during investigations.

There are at least three noteworthy feedback loops in this system. First, the capacity of the criminal justice system to control crime may be diluted by an exogenous increase in crime rates, which then causes a reduction in the likelihood or severity of punishment—resulting in further increases in the crime rate. Second, an exogenous increase in the crime rate may raise the political salience of crime, leading to increased criminal-justice budgets and stricter sentencing, which may then rein in the crime rate. And third, an exogenous increase in crime may induce greater private efforts at prevention and avoidance of criminal victimization, including actions ranging from locking up valuables and carrying a weapon to hiring guards or relocating commercial activity to safer neighborhoods. These private responses can in turn either exacerbate or curtail the crime increase, depending on the specifics. The first two loops of this conceptualization were incorporated in the econometric models of the first wave of modern crime studies (cited above). The third loop, which makes private prevention efforts endogenous, was introduced soon thereafter (Ehrlich 1981; Cook 1986) but has been largely neglected in the economics literature.

Observed crime rates are thus the outcome of a complex interactive system, which may frustrate the goal of making unambiguous predictions, or even keeping track of all the relevant mechanisms. A case in point is understanding or predicting how immigration affects crime rates. The first pass might be to ask "are these immigrants law-abiding people?" (a question that harks back to the notion, discussed above, that crime rates are proportional to the number of "bad" people). A more sophisticated inquiry would attempt to assess the public and private resources available for crime control and prevention in immigrant communities, and the likely spillovers to other communities. (Note that the immigrants are both users and contributors to these resources.) A still more comprehensive analysis would include the effects of the immigrant groups on labor markets (typically at the low-wage end of the spectrum), since immigrants may crowd out natives and reduce their incentive to choose a law-abiding path. In their contribution to this volume, Brian Bell and Stephen Machin (chapter 7) conclude that empirical evidence on the effect of immigration on crime is scanty, and that it proves hard to detect an overall empirical connection between crime and immigration on average. However, they also discuss evidence of variations across migrant groups so that in well-designed spatial panel data studies, immigration by groups that have a weak connection to the labor market may increase the rate of property crime.

In most models of criminal activity, the perpetrators are not organized, and unconcerned about their individual effect on public or private control systems. But, of course, some criminal activity is organized and hence subject to the management by whatever system of control exists within the criminal organization. Economists have not yet paid much attention to criminal gangs, with the partial exception of the Mafia (Reuter 1983). Nobel Laureate Thomas Schelling (1971) was the first to point out that the business of organized crime—the Mafia—is not to provide illicit goods and services to the public, but rather to gain control and extort money from such providers. The resulting cartel position in the provision of vice and other contraband actually creates an incentive to restrict supply in order to preserve prices (Buchanan 1973), which may seem like a good outcome from the public interest perspective, despite the lethal tactics used to acquire and preserve that monopoly. One problem is that the wealth and power of the organization is used to corrupt public officials as well as limit the activities of the private suppliers of vice. In his contribution to this volume (chapter 8) Paulo Pinotti provides empirical evidence that the influence of the Mafia in some areas of Italy extends deep into the political process, affecting the quality of candidates who run for office as well as the amount budgeted for easily corrupted public-works projects.

Among the feedback effects that have figured importantly in crime research is through the political process, which translates public concern about crime into resource allocation to the criminal justice system. The influence of crime rates on police budgets is well documented, as shown in chapter 9 by Paolo Buonanno and Giovanni Mastrobuoni. Interestingly, they find that police hiring in the United States is more responsive to changes in crime than is true in Italy, where hiring and deployment decisions are nationally centralized and subject to perhaps more red tape than in the United States. Another potential mechanism that links policing to crime is the process of learning and innovation. Priks (chapter 6) observes that the police response to hooliganism by soccer fans has evolved in some jurisdictions, where the police have learned that targeting individuals for arrest and prosecution is a more effective strategy than the traditional crowd-control approach (using water cannons, etc.). Despite its evident advantages this selective approach has not yet been adopted everywhere.

The learning and innovation process in policing may well be subject to political pressure brought by public concern about crime, just as is the resource allocation process. Rodrigo Soares and Igor Viveiros (chapter 10) describe the effort to reform policing in Minas Gerais, the second largest state in Brazil, under pressure from a surge in crime rates beginning in the mid-1990s. The police functions in Minas Gerais (as in other states) are divided between the military police, responsible for patrol and the immediate response to crime, and the civil police, which is responsible for investigations and general assistance to the judiciary. The lack of coordination between these two forces reduces effectiveness and efficiency. The government of Minas Gerais was able to overcome bureaucratic inertia and institute a plan of integration and improved communication beginning in 2005. The results for crime control appear to be favorable.

Concluding Thoughts

The economists are here to stay in the study of crime, the criminal justice system, and crime prevention. They have brought with them a strong presumption that criminal behavior can be usefully modeled using the same conceptual apparatus that economic science has developed for risky decision making, labor supply, consumer and firm behavior, and even market structure and performance. Criminal law and crime-prevention programs can be evaluated using the same normative apparatus that is routinely applied to education, health, and environmental regulation. Of course, the rules of statistical inference require no modifications. In short, crime is another choice, as Gary Becker suggested in 1968, and crime research using standard economic methods can be productive.

Our entrance into this arena, led by Gary Becker and Thomas Schelling in the late 1960s, did not lead to immediate assimilation into the field of criminology, and in fact the differences in agenda and conceptual frameworks initially produced a good deal of antagonism. But it is fair to say that the trend is toward greater mutual influence and respect. The topics and references of chapters in this volume reflect the increasingly eclectic approach of economists, and increasing respect for contributions by other social scientists. Those trends are welcome, and offer hope for efficient development of a sturdy base of evidence, derived from carefully implemented empirical work using coherent research designs, that can be used for policy design and evaluation.

Notes

1. The principals in the formation of AL CAPONE had earlier produced an edited collection through NBER (DiTella, Edwards, and Schargrodsky 2010).

2. Most of the US academic economists for whom crime is a long-term specialty have appointments in public policy schools or other interdisciplinary units (including law schools).

3. This is also what Machin and Marie (2011) observed when exploring the mechanisms behind the large drops in robberies they observed after police funding was raised in certain areas of England and Wales (but not in others) to combat street crime.

4. In the past only a couple of papers, Grogger (1995) and Kling (2006), have used individually matched data to explore this relationship and they focused on a relatively small population only composed of offenders. Today researchers in northern European countries are developing national level matched datasets covering a large proportion of the entire population.

5. For example: The *Journal of Experimental Criminology* began publishing in 2005, under David Weisburd's direction. Cambridge University created the Jerry Lee Centre of Experimental Criminology in 2007 under the leadership of Lawrence Sherman.

6. For example, Cook and Laub (2002) show that the cohorts of youths who were caught up in the epidemic of violence between 1984 and 1993 exhibited normal rates of crime

involvement prior to the epidemic, and dropped back toward the normal level following the crest of the epidemic. The extreme volatility of homicide rates for young African-American men during that period also belies an explanation in terms of long-term trends in the conditions of their upbringing.

7. The ability of street gangs in the United States to regulate gun use by their members was exploited by criminal-justice authorities in Boston's Operation Ceasefire (Braga, Kennedy, and Piehl 1997), and has been reported in ethnographic work with gangs in Chicago (Cook et al. 2007).

8. Private actions have great potential to influence crime rates and patterns, and increasing private security expenditures and technology, combined with an extraordinary increase in crime reporting, deserve part of the credit for the crime drop since the mid-1990s (Cook and MacDonald 2011).

References

Ayres, Ian, and Steven Levitt. 1998. Measuring positive externalities from unobservable victim precaution: An empirical analysis of Lojack. *Quarterly Journal of Economics* 113 (1): 43–77.

Becker, Gary. 1968. Crime and punishment: An economic approach. *Journal of Political Economy* 76 (2): 175–209.

Blumstein, Alfred, Jacqueline Cohen, and Daniel Nagin, eds. 1978. *Deterrence and Incapacitation: Estimating the Effects of Criminal Sanctions on Crime Rates, Report of the Panel of Deterrence and Incapacitation*. Washington, DC: National Academy of Sciences.

Braga, Anthony A., David Kennedy, and Anne Piehl. 1997. Controlling niolent offenders released to the community: An evaluation of the Boston Reentry Initiative. *Journal of Research in Crime and Delinquency* 46 (4): 411–36.

Buchanan, James M. 1973. A defense of organized crime?. In Simon Rottenberg ed., *The Economics of Crime and Punishment*. Washington, DC: American Enterprise Institute, 119–32.

Buonanno, Paulo, Francesco Drago, Roberto Galbiati, and Giulio Zanella. 2011. Crime in Europe and the United States: Dissecting the "reversal of misfortunes." *Economic Policy* 26 (67): 347–85.

Carr-Hill, Roy A., and Nicholas Stern. 1973. An econometric model of the supply and control of recorded offences in England and Wales. *Journal of Public Economics* 2 (4): 289–318.

Cook, Philip J. 1977. Punishment and crime: A critique of recent findings on the preventive effects of punishment. *Law and Contemporary Problems* 41 (Winter): 164–204.

Cook, Philip J. 1986. The demand and supply of criminal opportunities. In Michael Tonry and Norval Morris, eds., *Crime and Justice: An Annual Review of Research*, vol. 7. Chicago: University of Chicago Press, 1–28.

Cook, Philip J., and John Laub. 2002. After the epidemic: Recent trends in youth violence in the United States. In Michael Tonry, ed., *Crime and Justice: A Review of Research*. Chicago: University of Chicago Press, 1–37.

Cook, Philip J., and Jens Ludwig. 2011. Economical crime control. In Philip J. Cook, Jens Ludwig, and Justin McCrary, eds., *Controlling Crime: Strategies and Tradeoffs*. Chicago: University of Chicago Press, 1–39.

Cook, Philip J, Jens Ludwig, and Justin McCrary, eds. 2011. *Controlling Crime: Strategies and Tradeoffs*. Chicago: University of Chicago Press.

Cook, Philip J, Jens Ludwig, Sudhir Venkatesh, and Anthony A. Braga. 2007. Underground gun markets. *Economic Journal* 117 (524): 588–618.

Cook, Philip J., and John MacDonald. 2011. Public safety through private action: An economic assessment of BIDS. *Economic Journal* 121 (552): 445–62.

Di Tella, Raphael, Sebastian Edwards, and Ernesto Schargrodsky, eds. 2010. *The Economics of Crime: Lessons for and from Latin America*. Chicago: University of Chicago Press.

Dodge, Kenneth. 2008. Framing public policy and prevention of chronic violence in American youths. *American Psychologist* 63 (7): 573–90.

Ehrlich, Isaac. 1973. Participation in economic activity: A theoretical and empirical investigation. *Journal of Political Economy* 81 (3): 521–63.

Ehrlich, Isaac. 1981. On the Usefulness of Controlling Individuals: An Economic Analysis of Rehabilitation, Incapacitation, and Deterrence. *American Economic Review* 71 (3), June: 307-22.

Grogger, Jeffrey. 1995. The effect of arrests on the employment and earnings of young men. *Quarterly Journal of Economics* 110 (1): 51–71.

Hjalmarsson, Randi, Helena Holmlund, and Matthew J. Lindquist. 2012. The effect of education on criminal convictions and incarceration: Causal evidence from micro-data. Mimeo. Stockholm University.

Kling, Jeffrey R. 2006. Incarceration length, employment, and earnings. *American Economic Review* 96 (3): 863–76.

Levitt, Steven. 1996. The effect of prison population size on crime rates: Evidence from prison overcrowding litigation. *Quarterly Journal of Economics* 111 (2): 319–51.

Levitt, Steven. 1997. Using electoral cycles in police hiring to estimate the effect of police on crime. *American Economic Review* 87 (3): 270–90.

Levitt, Steven. 2004. Understanding why crime fell in the 1990s: Four factors that explain the decline and six that do not. *Journal of Economic Perspectives* 18 (1): 163–90.

Levitt, Steven, and Stephen Dubner. 2005. *Freakonomics: A Rogue Economist Explores the Hidden Side of Everything*. New York: William Morrow.

Lochner, Lance, and Enrico Moretti. 2004. The effect of education on crime: Evidence from prison inmates, arrests and self-reports. *American Economic Review* 94: 155–89.

Machin, Stephen, and Olivier Marie. 2011. Crime and police resources: The street crime initiative. *Journal of the European Economic Association* 9 (4): 678–701.

Machin, Stephen, Olivier Marie, and Suncica Vujic. 2011. The crime reducing effect of education. *Economic Journal* 121 (552): 463–84.

Muncie, John. 2005. The globalization of crime control—The case of youth and juvenile justice: Neo-liberalism, policy convergence and international conventions. *Theoretical Criminology* 9 (1): 35–64.

Reuter, Peter. 1983. *Disorganized Crime: The Economics of the Visible Hand*. Cambridge: MIT Press.

Schelling, Thomas. 1971. What is the business of organized crime? *Journal of Public Law* 20 (1): 71–84.

Sjoquist, David L. 1973. Property crime and economic behavior: Some empirical results. *American Economic Review* 63 (3): 439–46.

Wilson, James Q. 1975. *Thinking about Crime*. New York: Basic Books.

1   COPS and Cuffs

Emily Greene Owens

1.1   Introduction

There is a general consensus among academics that a 10 percent increase in the number of police officers will reduce crime rates by between 3 and 10 percent,[1] and that hiring more police officers is almost certainly a more effective way to reduce crime than increasing punishment severity (Durlauf and Nagin 2011). Knowing that the elasticity of crime with respect to police is negative and relatively large is critical to our understanding of criminal behavior and the criminal justice system, but this knowledge is incomplete; the elasticity of crime with respect to police is necessary but not sufficient to design an efficient policy intervention. Based on the existing literature, the argument that police reduce crime is relatively uncontroversial, but we are still in relative darkness regarding the underlying mechanisms driving this relationship.

Broadly speaking, there are two pathways through which police can reduce crime. First, police officers can induce a change in the behavior of potential criminals. Increasing the number of police on the streets may cause criminals to believe that they are more likely to be caught and punished. This rise in the expected cost of committing a crime will weakly reduce the crime rate, as the return to committing some set of crimes will no longer be viewed as worth the risk. Second, a larger police force will weakly increase the number of criminals that are arrested. If one police officer arrests two people each day, and the number of criminals is large enough, two police officers arrest roughly four people a day. To the extent that incarceration is the ultimate outcome of an arrest, and that most crimes are committed by repeat offenders, arresting more people during time t will reduce the number of crimes that occur during time $t + 1$. These two pathways are formally called deterrence and incapacitation, respectively.

The average budgetary cost of hiring a new police officer is in the range of $50 thousand a year. If police reduce crime through deterrence, then the net social benefit of hiring a police officer is positive if the crimes that officer prevents from occurring would have produced more than $50 thousand worth of harm. Based on conservative estimates of the cost of crime in Miller et al. (1996), this corresponds to roughly two robberies and one assault. Essentially all studies published since 2000 find that hiring a new police officer easily passes this back-of-the-envelope cost–benefit calculation.[2]

If, on the other hand, police reduce crime primarily by apprehending more repeat offenders and causing their incarceration, this "crimes prevented – cost of officer" approach drastically overstates the net benefit of police. If police reduce crime by arresting and incapacitating more people, then the social value of crimes averted must be weighed against not only the cost of hiring the officer, but also the additional costs incurred elsewhere in the justice system, which could include pre-trial detention, trial costs, incarceration, and parole supervision.[3] Given the current policy focus on reducing the cost of administering the criminal justice system (Cook and Ludwig 2011), understanding the implications of hiring more police for the size of court dockets and correctional populations is of pressing importance.

Changes in arrest rates are in large part driven by changes in crime, and as a result estimating the causal relationship of police on arrests is complicated by the same issues that affect estimates of the impact of police on crime. I therefore examine how arrests change in response to an increase in the size of the police force that is arguably uncorrelated with underlying crime rates. Specifically, I exploit changes in the size of the police force due to the Community-Oriented Policing Services (COPS) hiring grants, a federal program that distributed earmarked grants to local law enforcement agencies allowing them to hire new police officers.

Because of the way the grants were distributed, variation in the timing and size of COPS grants was plausibly unrelated to preexisting variation in crime. Using data on crime and policing in the Uniform Crime Reports, Evans and Owens (2007) showed that while cities that received larger COPS grants did not have systematically different trends in crime than cities that received smaller grants, it was the case that cities that got the largest COPS grants had the largest decreases in crime between 1994 and 2001.

In this chapter, I build on the existing literature by asking the question: did the cities that received the largest COPS grants also experience the largest increase in arrests? I find little evidence that this is the case; in fact, hiring more police officers is associated with statistically imprecise reductions in the number of arrests per capita for serious offenses. Part of this reduction is due to a reduced number of crimes, but arrests per crime appear to decline as well. At the same time, however, I do find evidence that cities receiving COPS grants arrested more people for drug offenses, although the precision of this result is sensitive to how I interpret missing data on arrests. I fail to reject the null hypothesis that the overall arrest rate, which incorporates both serious and low level charges, does not change when cities hire more officers. The lack of statistically meaningful change in arrest rates suggests that, at least in some cases, hiring more police can actually change behavior as opposed to simply lead to the incapacitation of a larger number of people.

The chapter proceeds as follows. In the next section, I review the extant literature on police, arrests, and crime rates, as well as provide background information on the COPS hiring grant program. After describing my empirical strategy in section 1.3, I provide a brief discussion of the data I use to estimate the impact of police on arrests in section 1.4. I present my results in section 1.5, and conclude with discussion in section 1.6.

1.2   Cops, Crime, and the VCCA

When the Violent Crime Control and Law Enforcement Act of 1994 (VCCA) was signed into law in January of 1994, it was one of the largest crime bills in American history. The VCCA affected all aspects of law enforcement, from 911-emergency response to juvenile boot camps, and a total of $30.2 billion was allocated to help local agencies invest in new crime-fighting programs and improve existing criminal-justice infrastructure. The VCCA also created a new office in the Department of Justice, the Community Oriented Policing Services (COPS) office. The COPS office was tasked with increasing the number of police on the streets by distributing $8.8 billion to law enforcement agencies across the country.

The COPS office initially offered two types of grants: COPS AHEAD (for agencies in big cities) and COPS FAST (for smaller departments).[4] These two programs provided awardees with 75 percent of an entry-level police officer's salary for three years, up to a total of $75,000 per officer. In 1995, the two programs were merged and renamed the COPS

Universal Hiring Program (UHP). By August 2005, which marked the end of UHP funding, the COPS office had distributed roughly $4.76 billion in grants through the AHEAD, FAST, and UHP programs.[5] The COPS office administered a number of other programs intended to improve the quality of services provided by local police departments, but only one other program, the Distressed Neighborhood Program (DNP), provided salary support for newly hired, regular beat officers. The DNP provided 100 percent of the salary of a newly hired officer for three years and was only available to law enforcement agencies in 18 communities.

The COPS program, and in particular COPS hiring grants (UHP and DNP) were somewhat controversial. Audits by the General Accounting Office (US Government Accountability Office 2003) and Inspector General of the Department of Justice (US Department of Justice 1999), as well as a report by the Heritage Foundation (Davis et al. 2000) argued that UHP grants may have supplanted rather than supplemented new hires. However, Evans and Owens (2007) demonstrated that in medium to large cities, each officer granted by the UHP and DNP program increased the size of the police force by 0.7 officers. Official crime reports further suggested that crime fell in cities that received UHP grants. Using variation in the timing and size of UHP grants, Evans and Owens (2007) estimated that the elasticity of crime with respect to police was approximately −0.3 for property crime and −0.9 for violent crime. Later research on the COPS grants confirmed these results (US Government Accountability Office 2005; Worrall and Kovandzic 2010).

The estimates from Evans and Owens (2007) were consistent with a number of studies estimating the casual impact of police on crime rates. As previously mentioned, the number of police officers employed in any given city during any given year is endogenously determined with crime rates, at least as reported in the Uniform Crime Reports. Studies that did not carefully address this endogeneity typically found either no relationship between police and crime, or a positive one (Fisher and Nagin 1978). In the early 1990s researchers began to figure out ways to break this simultaneity problem, using either high frequency data or econometric techniques suited to causal identification. Marvell and Moody (1996) and Levitt (2002) estimate that the elasticity of crime with respect to police is roughly −0.3 using Granger causality and by instrumenting for the size of the police force with the size of city fire departments, respectively. Lin (2009) demonstrates that localities in states with higher sales tax rates tend hire more police officers and have lower crime; he estimates an elasticity of crime with respect to police of roughly −1. Finally, scholars have also exploited police budgetary policy that allocates officers across jurisdictions in a way that is, in part, independent of local crime rates due to predetermined funding formulas. These types of analyses have estimated that the elasticity of crime with respect to police is as large as −2 (Vollaard and Koning 2009; Vollaard and Hamed 2012).

Corman and Mocan (2000) exploit monthly changes in the number of police officers deployed in New York City and find a larger elasticity of roughly −0.5. Chalfin and McCrary (2012) demonstrate that noise in the measurement of police officers in the Uniform Crime Reports tends to bias estimates of the impact of police on crime upward. Using the Annual Survey of Governments to measure police employment, they estimate that the cost-weighted elasticity of crime with respect to police is roughly −0.4. Other research has noted that crime tends to decline (sometimes dramatically) when terror alerts increase local police presence (DiTella and Schargrodsky 2004; Klick and Tabarrok 2005). Draca et al. (2011) also analyze how crime rates change after a terrorist attack, and estimate that the elasticity of overall crime with respect to police is about −0.3.

Establishing that hiring more police will reduce crime is of first order policy importance. That being said, in some sense this information provides an incomplete picture of the relationship between police and crime as it does not identify the mechanisms through which the reduction in crime occurs. If the presence of police officers reduces the probability that a given individual will engage in criminal behavior, fewer people are arrested, fewer cases are tried, and fewer people are incarcerated. Alternatively, if police reduce crime by making more arrests and incapacitating more repeat offenders, more cases will be tried and more people be incarcerated.

While any interaction with the criminal justice system can have negative impacts on an individual (Fagan et al. 2010), roughly a third of total criminal justice expenditure is dedicated to incarceration (Kyckelhahn 2010). In 2004, approximately 32 percent of all adults arrested for index crimes were eventually convicted in criminal court (excluding larceny), and 25 percent of all arrested adults were sentenced to some period of incarceration, on average roughly one year.[6] Average annual spending on incarceration (expenditure / inmate population) is on the order of $30,000 per year, implying that each additional arrest increases expected correctional expenditure by approximately $7,500. Including the costs imposed on the judicial system, which now must adjudicate additional cases, and the additional costs imposed on the families of arrestees further inflates the cost of hiring new officers. In addition, if it is the case that the marginal person arrested by a new police officer is less criminal than the average arrestee, a point emphasized by Johnson and Raphael (2012), any resulting influx of new prisoners generated by larger police forces may lead to shorter sentences for more serious offenders (Kuziemko and Levitt 2004).

There is currently little direct evidence on whether or not hiring more police will increase the number of arrests that occur, although a small number of studies have indirectly discussed the simultaneous deterrent and incapacitative effects of police officers. Levitt (1998) finds that increased arrest rates appear to have an important deterrence effect, which is consistent with, but not direct evidence of, police doing more than simply arresting individuals. Lee and McCrary (2005) explicitly model and estimate the incapacitative effects of arrests on criminal behavior around the age of majority (18 in most jurisdictions), although their focus is on estimating the amount of deterrence associated with increased sanctions.

1.3   Cops and Arrests

Consider a simple, stylized model of offending, where the number of crimes committed in a jurisdiction is simply

$$Crime_{jt} = Population_{jt}\ f\left(Police_{jt}\left(\Omega_{jt}\right), \Omega_{jt}\right).$$

The total number of crimes occurring in jurisdiction j at time t is determined by the number of people living in the jurisdiction at that time, $Population_{jt}$, and the fraction of the population that offends, $f(.)$. This fraction is a direct function of the number of police officers, as the number of police affects the perceived likelihood of apprehension. By increasing the perceived probability of punishment, larger police forces will reduce the fraction of the population that commits crime.

The size of this change in behavior, the deterrent effect of police, has been the focus on much economic research on crime. The number of police on the street, however, is in part determined by the economic and social conditions, Ω_{jt}, used by local governments in police hiring decisions. These economic and social conditions, which could include the employment rate, number of single mothers, availability of public services, or less precisely defined phenomenon like social disorganization, also have a direct effect on the fraction of the population that chooses to commit crime. Some of these conditions may be easily observed by the researcher, some less so. This simultaneity will produce upward bias in estimates of the impact of police on $f(.)$.

In order for an increase in police to impose additional costs on the rest of the criminal justice system, it must be the case that the total number of people arrested increases when there are more police around. The number of arrests made in this jurisdiction can be defined as

$$Arrests_{jt} = Population_{jt} \, f\left(Police_{jt}\left(\Omega_{jt}\right), \Omega_{jt}\right) a\left(Police_{jt}\left(\Omega_{jt}\right)\right),$$

where $a(.)$ is the fraction of people who engage in crime that are arrested by the police. Note that $a(.)$ is only a function of the number of police officers, although social conditions affect the number of arrests indirectly through its impact on the number of police. The overall impact of police on arrest rates is the sum of two counteracting effects. To the extent that police deter some offenders, $f(.)$ will fall, reducing total arrests per capita. At the same time, increased manpower will tend to increase $a(.)$, as more officers will be able to arrest more people.

Whether or not the overall impact of police on arrests is positive or negative depends on the initial crime and arrest rates. To be more precise, the change in arrests after a change in the number of police is the weighted sum of the deterrent effect (the change in $f(.)$) and the increased probability that criminals are incapacitated (the change in $a(.)$), where the respective weights are the initial fraction of crime cleared by arrest ($a(.)$) and the initial fraction of the population engaged in crime ($f(.)$). For example, in 2001, 21 percent of offenses were cleared by arrest, and at most 4 percent of the population engaged in crime.[7] In this case, if the change in $f(.)$ is greater than 1/5th the size of the change in $a(.)$, increasing the number of police officers will reduce crime and at the same time reduce the number of people who are arrested, adjudicated by the judicial system, and incarcerated in correctional facilities. However, if the deterrent impact of additional police officer is very small relative to the new officer's impact of the probability that a given criminal will be arrested, then total arrests will go up, increasing the strain on the rest of the criminal justice system.

1.4 Empirical Strategy

I estimate the effect of hiring more police officers on arrests using a two-stage least squares (2SLS) approach. The outcome of interest is the change in number of people who are incapacitated after the police force expands – the number of arrests per capita. A direct estimate of this effect could be obtained by estimating the following model:

$$ArrestRate_{jgt} = \alpha_{jg} + \delta_{gt} + X_{jgt}\theta + Police_{jgt}\beta + \varepsilon_{jgt},\qquad(1.1)$$

where $ArrestRate_{jgt}$ is the number of arrests, scaled by population, occurring in city j in year t, and $Police_{jgt}$ is the number of police per capita in the same city and year. In this model, α_{jg} and δ_{gt} are, respectively, city fixed effects and year fixed effects that are unique to cities with similar populations and similar trends in crime and police employment between 1990 and 1994.[8] I include in the matrix X_{jgt} a number of factors that are related to both police and arrests measured at the county level, namely the fraction of the county population that is black, the fraction of the population between the ages of 18 and 24, the average real wage, real per capita income, and the city population.

Even with these control variables, however, it is still unlikely to be the case that $\hat{\beta}$ will be an unbiased estimate of the true relationship between police and arrests. The change in the number of arrests is in part determined by the change in the crime rate. Recall that general social conditions, Ω_{jgt}, affect both police employment and crime. The simultaneous determination of police and crime will create a situation in which the correlation between the number of police and ε_{jgt}, the unexplained component of arrest rates, will differ from zero, even if we were to observe and control for all elements of Ω_{jgt}. Indeed, if places with higher crime rates (and thus higher arrest rates) hire more police officers, then we would expect that corr($Police_{jgt}$, ε_{jgt}) > 0, meaning that $\hat{\beta} > \beta$. In other words, since the change in arrest rates is a function of the change in crime rates, estimates of the causal impact of police on arrests will be biased in situations where the observed change in police is endogenously related to changes in crime.

To address this simultaneity problem, I exploit variation in the number of police generated by the COPS hiring programs. The first stage of my 2SLS approach is to estimate the relationship between the COPS hiring grant program and police.

$$Police_{jgt} = \alpha_{jg}^{FS} + \delta_{gt}^{FS} + X_{jgt}\theta^{FS} + COPS_{jgt-1}\beta^{FS} + \varepsilon_{jgt}^{FS}.\qquad(1.2)$$

Here $COPS_{jgt-1}$ is the number of officers granted to department j in population–crime–employment group g in year $t - 1$. As in Evans and Owens (2007), the grant is lagged by one year to allow time for the granted officer to be hired and trained.[9]

Under the assumption that changes in the size of the police force induced by the COPS grants are conditionally independent of ε_{jgt}, then any correlation between COPS grants and arrests is driven by the fact that police officers hired under COPS are independently affecting the number arrests that occur in a given city. The reduced-form relationship between COPS grants and arrests is as follows:

$$Arrests_{jgt} = \alpha_{jg}^{RF} + \delta_{gt}^{RF} + X_{jgt}\theta^{RF} + COPS_{jgt-1}\beta^{RF} + \varepsilon_{jgt}^{RF}. \qquad (1.3)$$

The central point of this chapter is the estimated value of β^{RF}, which, under the assumption that the size and timing of COPS grants was conditionally independent of arrest rates and that the COPS grants would only impact the number of arrests through its influence on police employment, reflects the causal impact of those COPS officers on the incapacitation of city residents. The political debate surrounding the COPS grants, and intergovernmental grants in general, make the estimates of $\partial Police / \partial COPS$ grants and $\partial Arrests / \partial COPS$ grants of independent interest. Under the assumption that the variation in arrests driven by officers hired through COPS can be generalized to the impact of all changes in police employment, then the ratio β^{RF} / β^{FS} is equal to $\partial Arrests / \partial Police$.

A priori there is no reason to suspect that the marginal effect of an additional police officer on arrests will be constant across crime types. The deterrent effect of police on crime may depend on the opportunistic element of the crime. Crimes that take place in public spaces, like robbery, some sexual assault, and car theft, may be more sensitive to the number of police officers. Similarly criminal acts that take a long time to complete, such as burglary, may be less likely to occur when potential burglars expect police to respond to calls for service more quickly. Incapacitation may be relatively less important for these easily deterred offenses. Further, if crime committed in public spaces imposes larger costs on society, the reduction in social losses due to crime may in fact outweigh the overall reduction in total crime rates.

1.5   Measuring Crime and Arrests

I use three sources of data to estimate the impact of police on arrests. Annual counts of index crimes, arrests, and the number of officers in 2,074 cities are taken from three components of the Federal Bureau of Investigation's Uniform Crime Reports: Offenses Known and Clearances by Arrest; Arrests by Age, Sex, and Race; and Law Enforcement

Officers Killed or Assaulted (LEOKA). The sample consists of cities with an average population of 10 thousand people or more between 1990 and 2001 and reliable crime data for more than four sample years. On the one hand, law enforcement agencies are not required to report to the UCR, but since UCR statistics are used to determine eligibility for federal grants, such as the Byrne Local Law Enforcement Block Grant, most agencies participate by reporting known offenses to the FBI. LEOKA data reports the number of sworn officers employed in each agency in October of each year, which is administratively a low-cost statistic to report.[10] Arrest data, on the other hand, are less reliable, as there is no federal funding attached to this measure, and reporting imposes a nontrivial administrative burden on local agencies.[11] I calculate the total number of arrests made by each agency for each index crime in each year, based the breakdown by age.[12]

As table 1.1 shows, there are fewer valid arrest measures than crime and employee measures. It appears that agencies are less likely to report arrest data in years where there were no reported crimes;[13] the mean murder rate in the overall sample is 0.5 per 10 thousand people, roughly half the mean murder rate in agency/years where any arrests are reported. Similar discrepancies are apparent for rape (3.5 crimes overall versus 4.2) and robbery (14.6 crimes overall compared to 16.2). This disparity suggests that only nonzero arrests numbers are reported, and missing values are probably correspond to no arrests being made. On the other hand, the crime rates for agencies that do and do not report arrests are closer for property crimes, implying that missing arrest values are not necessarily "true" zeros.

In order to control for some of the variables in Ω_{jgt}, the UCR data are merged with county-level data from the Census Bureau and the Bureau of Economic Analysis. Specifically, I use Census estimates of the fraction of the county population that is between 18 and 24 and the fraction that is black, as well as BEA measures of county per capita income and the number of jobs per adult. These variables constitute my control matrix X_{jgt}.

The third data source, measuring the number of full time police officers granted through UHP and DNP grants, was obtained from the COPS office. Because both grants support the hiring of entry level officers, I combine the UHP and DNP grants into a "paid officers granted" variable, which is equal to $0.75 * UHP_{jt} + DNP_{jt}$. On average, there are 19 officers per 10 thousand residents, and 0.4 paid officers

Table 1.1
Police, COPS grants, and arrests, 1990 to 2001

	N	Mean	Standard deviation
Policing measures			
Officers/10,000 pop	23,335	18.9	7.37
Paid officers granted/10,000 pop[a]	8,359	1.09	0.988
Arrest measures			
Murder arrests/10,000 pop	9,878	1.04	1.10
Rape arrests/10,000 pop	16,496	1.60	1.41
Robbery arrests/10,000 pop	19,184	5.29	5.55
Assault arrests/10,000 pop	21,817	17.6	19.4
Burglary arrests/10,000 pop	22,020	14.1	11.6
Larceny arrests/10,000 pop	22,208	73.0	64.6
Car theft arrests/10,000 pop	20,466	5.90	5.82
Crime measures			
Murder/10,000 pop	23,335	0.500	0.858
Non-missing arrest records	9,878	0.981	1.04
Rape/10,000 pop	23,335	3.55	3.30
Non-missing arrest records	16,496	4.26	3.34
Robbery/10,000 pop	23,335	14.6	20.5
Non-missing arrest records	19,184	16.2	21.1
Assault/10,000 pop	23,335	34.1	38.9
Non-missing arrest records	21,817	33.9	44.5
Burglary/10,000 pop	23,335	95.5	69.4
Non-missing arrest records	22,020	95.0	68.6
Larceny/10,000 pop	23,335	336	188
Non-missing arrest records	22,208	334	187
Car theft/10,000 pop	23,335	44.5	45.9
Non-missing arrest records	20,466	46.0	46.1
Demographic measures			
Percent black	23,335	0.102	0.111
Percent 18–24	23,335	0.1400	0.030
Average wage	23,335	30,308	6669
Per capita income	23,335	25,244	7584
Jobs per adult	23,335	0.908	0.984

a. In years with a grant. Wages and Income measured in constant 2000 dollars.

granted in each city in my sample. Between 1994 and 2001 roughly 2 percent of the police force was subsidized by the COPS office.

1.6 Results

1.6.1 Police officers and Arrest Rates

In order to provide some context for the IV results, I first present naïve estimates of equation (1.1) in table 1.2. Conditional on demographics and my full set of fixed effects, cities with larger police forces arrest more people. Indeed, hiring one additional police officer is associated with 0.04 additional arrests for robbery (se = 0.02) and 0.2 additional arrests for assault (se = 0.1). Arrests for nonviolent crimes also increase; each additional police officer is associated with the arrest of 0.1 more burglars (se = 0.05) and 0.9 more thieves (se = 0.32) each year. This is suggestive evidence that hiring more police officers will result in more people interacting with the criminal justice system, but ignores the endogenous positive correlation between police officers, crime rates, and arrest rates.

1.6.2 COPS Grants and Police Officers

In order for COPS grants to be a valid instrument for changes in the size of the police force, it must be first established that COPS grants do cause an increase in the number of sworn officers employed by local police department. In table 1.3, I present my estimates of equation (1.2), replicating Evans and Owens (2007). Conditional on the demographic makeup of the county, the number of local jobs, average local salary, and local per capita income, each paid officer granted by the COPS office increased the size of the recipient police force by 0.69 officers (se = 0.08). As the more common UHP grants paid for 75 percent of a police officer's salary, this means that for every four officers granted by COPS, three salaries were provided by the federal government, and two new officers were hired.

Dividing police agencies by city size, it is clear that larger agencies were more responsive to COPS grants. In police departments serving cities with more than 25 thousand residents, every four paid officers granted increased the police force by between 2.2 and 2.8 officers. In smaller cities, only 1.6 officers were hired for every four granted. This pattern is consistent with reports by the Urban Institute, which found that smaller localities had a harder time raising the matching funds necessary to retain officers hired under the COPS program (Koper et al. 2001).

Table 1.2
Fixed effects estimates of police and arrests per 10,000 residents, 1990 to 2001

	Arrests for violent crime				Arrests for nonviolent crime		
	Murder	Rape	Robbery	Assault	Burglary	Larceny	Car theft
Police officers/10,000 residents	0.0023	0.0054	0.044*	0.19*	0.11*	0.88**	0.047
	[0.0051]	[0.0064]	[0.022]	[0.097]	[0.049]	[0.32]	[0.024]
Fraction black	-1.22	-1.86	5.31	17.7	42.7***	172.7*	22.5**
	[2.24]	[2.22]	[4.98]	[15.1]	[10.7]	[67.8]	[7.22]
Fraction 18–24	1.78	7.47**	3.9	-22.1	-26.4*	-220.4**	-2.87
	[2.13]	[2.28]	[5.80]	[23.2]	[13.0]	[66.9]	[7.66]
Jobs per adult	-0.02	-0.077	-0.1	-0.57	1.25**	-0.78	0.58
	[0.071]	[0.076]	[0.20]	[0.62]	[0.46]	[1.80]	[0.35]
ln(Average salary)	0.17	0.54	-1.8	-9.27*	-5.95*	-12.1	-3.79**
	[0.47]	[0.53]	[1.09]	[3.77]	[2.39]	[11.4]	[1.39]
ln(Per capita income)	0.35	0.13	5.45***	5.61	16.0***	42.0**	8.63***
	[0.48]	[0.52]	[1.35]	[4.48]	[3.08]	[12.9]	[1.67]
Mean of DV, 1993	1.20	1.81	5.87	18.7	16.2	78.3	6.7
R^2	0.73	0.59	0.82	0.81	0.77	0.88	0.72
N	9,878	16,496	19,184	21,817	22,020	22,208	20,466

Note: All regressions include population group by crime growth by police employment growth by year fixed effects, as well as agency fixed effects. Standard errors in brackets allow for arbitrary correlation in dependent variable over time within police agency. *$p < 0.05$; **$p < 0.01$; ***$p < 0.001$.

Table 1.3
First-stage estimates of COPS grants and police per 10,000 residents, 1990 to 2001

	All agencies	>250,000	100,000–250,000	50,000–100,000	25,000–50,000	10,000–25,000
Lag paid officers granted/10,000 residents	0.69***	0.81**	0.74**	0.92***	0.90***	0.56***
	[0.077]	[0.28]	[0.28]	[0.17]	[0.22]	[0.086]
Fraction black	13.6*	67.8*	11.1	3.54	9.19	13.4
	[5.28]	[31.3]	[12.4]	[8.85]	[7.69]	[7.77]
Fraction 18–24	-7.91	-15.2	-26.3*	-8.04	-25.1***	2.66
	[5.24]	[30.9]	[10.4]	[13.4]	[6.11]	[8.45]
Jobs per adult	0.042	-0.57	0.44*	-1.04	-0.32	0.21
	[0.19]	[0.77]	[0.21]	[0.59]	[0.35]	[0.36]
ln(Average salary)	-5.26***	0.06	-6.92*	-7.35*	-5.90***	-4.64**
	[1.03]	[11.3]	[3.49]	[3.04]	[1.67]	[1.53]
ln(Per capita income)	4.61***	-1.05	7.94***	6.22	7.34***	2.61
	[1.02]	[11.1]	[2.33]	[3.29]	[1.66]	[1.47]
Mean of DV, 1993	18.2	24.5	18.5	17.5	17.4	18.4
R^2	0.93	0.98	0.98	0.97	0.96	0.89
N	23,335	713	1,482	3,170	5,828	12,142

Note: All regressions include population group by crime growth by police employment growth by year fixed effects, as well as agency fixed effects. Standard errors in brackets allow for arbitrary correlation in dependent variable over time within police agency. $*p < 0.05$; $**p < 0.01$; $***p < 0.001$.

1.6.3   COPS and Arrests

Evans and Owens (2007) establish that by inducing more police hiring, COPS grants did, in fact, reduce local crime. However, what is still unknown is whether or not these reductions in crime were the result of deterrence or incapacitation. If police officers simply arrested a larger fraction of the population, then the observed negative relationship between police officers and crime is not necessarily due to any behavioral change on the part of potential criminals.

In table 1.4, I present estimates of the change in arrests per capita as a function of COPS hiring grants received last year.[14] This marginal effect will encompass any reduction due to increased deterrence, as well as the ability of more police to apprehend more people. While there is a positive relationship between COPS grants and the number of new officers, I do not find evidence that arrests also increase when the grants were received. In fact there is a statistically significant negative relationship between the number of arrests for rape and the receipt of COPS grants, corresponding to a 5 percent reduction in the number of people arrested for rape with an average grant of one paid officer. The reduction in number of arrests per capita is roughly twice the size of the reduction in reported rapes per capita associated with COPS grants (Evans and Owens 2007).

Using information on the average incarceration rates of arrestees in large counties, I can make rough estimates of the expected change in correctional burden with each additional COPS officer. In 2004, 50 percent of rape arrests resulted in incarceration,[15] implying that the number of people incarcerated for rape fell by 2.5 percent with an average COPS grant. While not statistically precise, the reduction in the number of people arrested for robbery is also large relative to the sample mean, corresponding to a 3 percent decline for each paid officer granted, or, with a 40 percent incarceration rate following arrest, a 1.2 percent reduction in incarceration.

Arrests for both larceny and car theft are positively correlated with hiring grants but are also statistically imprecise and small. Each paid officer granted results in a 1 percent increase in larceny arrests and a 0.5 percent increase in arrests for car theft. It is also worth noting that relative to other offenders, additional thieves impose a small burden on the criminal justice system; roughly 13 percent of arrests for car theft result in incarceration, and in 2004 the median sentence imposed by state courts for larceny and car theft was 16 and 24 months, respectively, compared with 36 months for burglary and assault, and 60 or above for the other index crimes.[16]

Emily Greene Owens

Table 1.4
Reduced-form estimates of COPS grants and arrests per 10,000 residents, 1990 to 2001

	Arrests for violent crime				Arrests for nonviolent crime				
	Murder	Rape	Robbery	Assault	Burglary	Larceny	Car theft	Drug offenses	All arrests
Lag paid officers granted/ 10,000 residents	-0.030 [0.022]	-0.11*** [0.032]	-0.22 [0.14]	-0.097 [0.30]	-0.14 [0.15]	0.77 [0.72]	0.029 [0.089]	1.97** [0.68]	5.82 [5.40]
Mean of DV, 1993	1.20	1.81	5.87	18.7	16.2	78.3	6.7	36.9	560
R^2	0.73	0.6	0.82	0.81	0.77	0.88	0.72	0.81	0.80
N	9,878	16,496	19,184	21,817	22,020	22,208	20,466	22,156	23,335
Implied change in arrests with one additional officer	-0.039 [0.025]	-0.15** [0.044]	-0.315 [0.189]	-0.135 [0.375]	-0.192 [0.184]	1.07 [0.916]	0.042 [0.116]	2.77 [0.78]	8.45 [6.98]

Note: All regressions include controls for the fraction of the county that is black, the fraction between the ages of 18 and 24, the number of jobs per adult, the natural log of real average wage, the natural log of per capita income, population group by police employment growth by year fixed effects, as well as agency fixed effects. Standard errors in brackets allow for arbitrary correlation in dependent variable over time within police agency. *p < 0.05; **p < 0.01; ***p < 0.001.

The decision to make an arrest is in many cases completely subject to the officer's discretion. As the seriousness of the crime in question diminishes, one might expect that, ceteris paribus, individual police officers are increasingly more likely to let potential arrestees off with a warning or citation. In the same way, if hiring more police reduces the demand on any given officer's time, one might expect a relative increase in the arrest rate of less serious offenses. In the second to last column of table 1.4, I show that recorded arrests for drug offenses appear to increase when cities receive additional police officers; a grant of one additional officer per 10,000 people is associated with 2 more arrests per capita. Relative to the average drug arrest rate, the magnitude of the effect is quite large, amounting to a roughly 4 percent increase. In the final column of table 1.4, I find a positive relationship between the overall arrest rate and police officers, but the magnitude of the coefficient is roughly the same size as the standard error.

The estimated relationship between COPS hiring grants, index crimes, and arrests imply that, on average, cities that hire more police officers will benefit from lower crime rates, but not necessarily increase the number of people interacting with the justice system. While there is some indication that cities with more police may tend to arrest more people for minor (drug) offenses, I do not find evidence that, on average, city police departments enriched through the COPS program arrested more people for serious offenses than cities that did not apply for or receive these federal funds.

In the bottom row of table 1.4, I present estimates of the average change in arrest rates that could plausibly result from hiring one additional police officer. This IV estimate is roughly equivalent to the ratio of the presented reduced-form estimates divided by the first stage estimates in table 1.3. Hiring one more police officer will, on average, reduce the number of arrests for rape, and the probability that estimated change in arrests for murder and robbery are different from zero is less than 11 percent. Relative to the average number of police officers and arrest rates in 1993, some these changes are quite large; implied elasticities of arrests with respect to police officers are –0.4 for murder, –0.9 for robbery, and –1.5 for rape. The change in arrests for assault, burglary, larceny, and car theft are all around 0.1 to 0.2.

Evans and Owens (2007) found that the changes in crime associated with COPS hiring grants implied large elasticities of crime with respect to police. Observed patterns of arrests suggest that the bulk of this reduction in crime was driven by deterrence, and that hiring additional police officers will not necessarily increase the demands on the rest of the criminal justice system.

1.6.4 Robustness Tests

I now probe the sensitivity of this conclusion to a number of assumptions underlying my reduced-form model, in the spirit of Durlauf and Nagin (2010). Specifically, I examine the importance of missing arrest values, heterogeneity across states, and changes in the crime rate.

Are Missing Arrests Really "Zero" Arrest Years?

Police agencies do not report arrests for all crimes in all years, resulting in a nontrivial amount of missing data that varies by crime. As previously discussed, it is plausible that missing records of arrests for murder means that no such arrests occur. Under this assumption, I replace all missing values with zero and report the results in table 1.5. Comparing the two sets of results, it is not clear that assuming that missing arrest values are zero changes the analysis. Qualitatively, the estimated coefficients on officers granted are robust for all serious crimes save car theft, which becomes negative when missing city-years are replaced with zero arrests. The estimated standard errors are smaller in this analysis, in proportion to the increase in sample size.

The most striking change in table 1.5 is the impact on arrest for drug offenses. The addition of these zeros cuts the size of the estimated coefficient in half, meaning that the coefficient is no longer statistically different from zero, and there is a 95 percent chance that true change in arrests for drug offenses is between –0.38 and 2.52.

State Heterogeneity

One of the strongest critiques levied by Durlauf and Nagin (2010) against past panel-data studies was the assumption of parameter homogeneity across geographic units. Given variation in police practices and overall crime rates across areas, the mean relationship between police and arrests may mask substantial differences across cities; Pittsburgh police may behave very differently from the Miami police. In order to address potential heterogeneity across states, I re-estimated equation (1.3) for each state in my data. My homogeneity assumption will be supported if estimates in each state are tightly concentrated around the nationwide average. There is obviously a large efficiency loss with this approach, as it may not be the case that I need to estimate each of the model's parameters in each state; for example, average

Table 1.5
Reduced-form estimates of COPS grants and adjusted arrests per 10,000 residents 1990 to 2001

	Arrests for violent crime				Arrests for nonviolent crime				All arrests
	Murder	Rape	Robbery	Assault	Burglary	Larceny	Car theft	Drug offenses	
Lag paid officers granted/10,000 residents	-0.03** [0.012]	-0.089*** [0.024]	-0.26* [0.12]	-0.44 [0.32]	-0.31 [0.16]	0.047 [0.81]	-0.073 [0.095]	0.89 [0.79]	5.82 [5.40]
Mean of DV, 1993	0.44	1.13	4.35	16.4	13.3	69.5	5.18	35.9	560
R^2	0.62	0.56	0.78	0.76	0.73	0.8	0.68	0.76	0.80
N	23,335	23,335	23,335	23,335	23,335	23,335	23,335	23,335	23,335
Implied change in arrests with one additional officer	*-0.044** [0.016]*	*-0.13*** [0.034]*	*-0.38* [0.17]*	*-0.63 [0.42]*	*-0.45* [0.22]*	*0.068 [1.06]*	*-0.11 [0.13]*	*1.29 [1.00]*	*8.45 [6.98]*

Note: All regressions include controls for the fraction of the county that is black, the fraction between the ages of 18 and 24, the number of jobs per adult, the natural log of real average wage, the natural log of per capita income, population group by crime growth by police employment growth by year fixed effects, as well as agency fixed effects. All missing arrest data is treated as zero arrests. Standard errors in brackets allow for arbitrary correlation in dependent variable over time within police agency. *$p < 0.05$; **$p < 0.01$; ***$p < 0.001$.

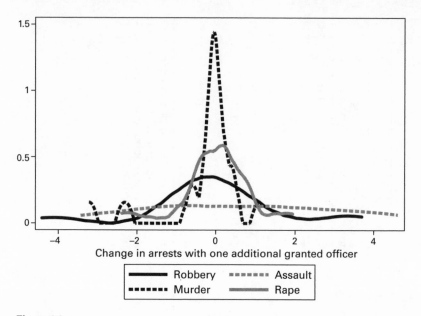

Figure 1.1
Trimmed distribution of marginal effects across states—State-specific estimates of COPS
and arrests for violent crime

wages are theoretically negatively correlated with burglary, but it is
unclear why this relationship should be different in Delaware and
Ohio. It is also not the case that all states have sufficient observations
to estimate equation (1.3). With these caveats in mind, the distribution
of estimated parameters across states is still illustrative of the amount
of effect heterogeneity.

Figures 1.1 and 1.2 display the distribution of effects across states
for violent and nonviolent crime, with the range of reported effects
restricted to ±10 for nonviolent crime, and ±5 for violent crime for the
sake of clarity. With the exception of assault, the range of values for
violent crimes is primarily between –2 and 2, indicating a reasonable
amount of homogeneity in the relationship between extra police and
arrests for violent offenses. The distribution of effects for assault actually has slightly more weight in the left tail, indicating that police
officers may be more effective at deterring these offenses. The "incapacitation" outlier of the distribution for assault is West Virginia.

For most types of crime, the distribution also is unimodal, without
much weight in either tail of the distribution. Two exceptions are car
theft and burglary, which have clear local maximums just below zero,

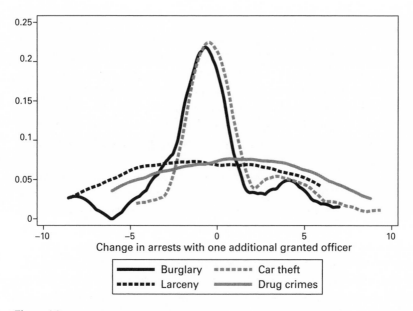

Figure 1.2
Distribution of marginal effects across states—State-specific estimates of COPS and arrests for violent crime

and at around 4 arrests per 10,000 city residents. The fact police appear to increase arrests for these crimes in some states, implies that incapacitation may be of more importance in reducing these crimes.[17] Larceny also has a particularly large right skew, driven by a large positive relationship between police and arrests in Utah and West Virginia. If reducing larceny is considered a low priority for police departments in these states, it is possible that these arrests might be more sensitive to changes in the number of full time police officers. This story is also consistent with the pattern of arrests for drug offenses. The distribution of the impacts of police on drug arrests is centered just slightly above zero, but in many states, some agencies seem to only report drug offenses when more police are hired.

Arrests Conditional on Crime
As a final specification check, I compare changes in the arrest rate to changes in the crime rate. If hiring an additional police officer allowed departments to apprehend more suspects, then it should be the case that in two cities with identical crime rates, the city with the larger police force should arrest, and thus incapacitate, more people. In the

top panel of table 1.6, I include the relevant index crime rate as a right-hand-side variable. The index crime rate is positively correlated with the arrest rate for all crimes, which partially assuages concern that measurement error in the UCR arrest reports renders the data meaningless. It is also apparent that, conditional on the crime rate, COPS hiring grants are positively related to the arrest rate for assault, burglary, car theft, and larceny. Holding the crime rate constant, there is a statistically imprecise negative relationship between hiring grants and arrests for murder and robbery.[18]

Surprisingly, there is a negative and precisely estimated relationship between COPS hiring grants and arrests for rape, conditional on the rate of sexual assault. Recall that there was no statistical relationship between COPS hiring grants and rape rates, only an imprecise negative relationship. This is something of a counterintuitive result, in that more police results in fewer arrests, but potentially the same amount of reported crime. However, consider a hypothetical example in which criminals think there are two types of sexual assault—those with a high risk of arrest and those with a lower risk of arrest. Suppose that more police reduce high arrest-risk sexual assault rates, but at the same time increases the fraction of low arrest-risk sexual assaults that are reported to police. An increase in the rape reporting will tend to bias the estimated relationship between police and crime upward. At the same time, if the presence of more police officers means that rapes that are likely to result in apprehension do not occur, the overall arrest rate may fall (Cook 1979).

In the lower panel of table 1.6, I replace the left-hand-side variable with the number of arrests scaled by the index crime rate. These point estimates are primarily negative, but generally imprecise. Hiring more police appears to reduce the number of arrests for burglary more than it does the burglary rate, but this point estimate is only marginally significant, and arrests per burglary are actually the lowest of all crimes. The lack of a substantive relationship between police and arrests, conditional on crime rates, suggests that hiring an additional police officer "at random" has an important deterrent effect; it does not appear to be the case that more people are necessarily being picked up by police for a given level of crime.

1.7   Conclusion

A statistically precise negative relationship between officers and crime is necessary but insufficient to justify increased police employment.

Table 1.6
Reduced-form estimates of COPS grants, crime, and arrests per 10,000 residents, 1990 to 2001

	Arrests for violent crime				Arrests for nonviolent crime		
	Murder	Rape	Robbery	Assault	Burglary	Larceny	Car theft
Lag paid officers granted/10,000 residents	-0.024 [0.020]	-0.089*** [0.027]	-0.05 [0.10]	0.12 [0.27]	0.027 [0.15]	0.95 [0.66]	0.15 [0.088]
Reported crime/10,000 residents	0.54*** [0.045]	0.20*** [0.011]	0.21*** [0.013]	0.21*** [0.014]	0.073*** [0.0040]	0.18*** [0.011]	0.069*** [0.0044]
Mean of DV, 1993	1.20	1.81	5.87	18.7	16.2	78.3	6.7
R^2	0.78	0.66	0.86	0.83	0.79	0.90	0.75
Arrests per crime							
Lag paid officers granted/10,000 residents	-0.38 [0.22]	-0.1 [0.061]	0.013 [0.052]	-0.016 [0.13]	-0.033* [0.016]	0.025 [0.013]	0.021 [0.023]
Mean of DV, 1993	1.17	0.507	0.483	0.685	0.173	0.216	0.200
R^2	0.5	0.5	0.49	0.38	0.41	0.79	0.58
N	9,878	16,496	19,184	21,817	22,020	22,208	20,466

Note: All regressions include controls for the fraction of the county that is black, the fraction between the ages of 18 and 24, the number of jobs per adult, the natural log of real average wage, the natural log of per capita income, population group by crime growth by police employment growth by year fixed effects, as well as agency fixed effects. Standard errors in brackets allow for arbitrary correlation in dependent variable over time within police agency. $*p < 0.05$; $**p < 0.01$; $***p < 0.001$.

The social costs of crime are high, but if police reduce crime primarily by arresting more people, estimates of the net benefit of more police are possibly an order of magnitude too small. In this chapter, I examine whether hiring more police officers reduces crime by deterring potential offenders, or by increasing the number of criminals who are apprehended and incarcerated. Because most variation in the size of police forces is endogenously determined with crime (and arrest) rates, I focus on changes in the number of sworn officers resulting from the Department of Justice COPS grants. On average, COPS grants increased the size of recipient police forces by 0.7 officers for each paid officer granted, and have also been associated with reductions in both violent and property crime.

I find no evidence that police agencies that received COPS grants arrested more people. This implies that the majority of the impact of police on crime is through deterrence rather than incapacitation. Hiring a new police officer costs roughly $50,000 in terms of salary and benefits, which is a potentially large expense for a cash-strapped local government. If this new officer reduced crime primarily through apprehending more criminals, the total cost of increasing police forces could plausibly be much larger. However, it does not appear to be the case that the actions of this officer will necessarily generate additional costs to the criminal justice system.

Notes

I would like to thank Matthew Freedman, Stephen Machin, Daniel Nagin, Ben Vollaard, an anonymous referee, and participants in the 2011 CESIfo Venice Summer Institute for advice and feedback. This research was made possible in part through the use of Cornell University's Social Science Gateway, which is funded through NSF Grant 0922005. All errors are my own.

1. See, for example, Chalfin and McCrary 2012, Vollard and Hamed 2011, Draca et al. 2011, Lin 2009, Evans and Owens 2007, Klick and Tabarrok 2005, DiTella and Schargrodsky 2004, Levitt 2002, and Corman and Mocan 2000. Durlauf and Nagin (2011) provide a through overview of the current research on police, policing strategies, and crime rates.

2. Note that passing a cost–benefit test is not the same as saying that hiring more police officers is a socially optimal decision, as it may be cheaper to reduce crime by improving police practices.

3. Other possible costs associated with incarceration include social externalities, such as harm suffered by the children of an incarcerated parent.

4. AHEAD and FAST are acronyms for "Accelerated Hiring, Education, and Deployment" and "Funding Accelerated for Small Towns," respectively.

5. In fiscal year 2008, the Obama administration reinitiated many COPS grants, including the UHP, but COPS funding was eliminated in the 2011 Federal Appropriations bill initially proposed in House of Representatives on February 14th, and the amount of funding available in the eventual bill remains in doubt.

6. Sourcebook of Criminal Justice Statistics Online, table 5.0002.2004, http://www .albany.edu/sourcebook/pdf/t500022004.pdf.

7. This assumes that each of the index crimes known to police in 2001 was committed by exactly one person, and that each individual committed at most one crime. The latter assumption is probably less likely to be true than the former.

8. These groups are constructed as follows: for each agency, I regressed the annual crime rate and police officers per capita on a linear time trend between 1990 and 1994. I then divided police agencies into five groups based on the average population of the city in which they have jurisdiction. Within each population group, I first ranked the cities based on the magnitude of the estimated linear trend in crime, and then on the trend in police employment. Each group of cities with the same (1) population size group, (2) crime trend rank, and (3) employment trend rank, has its own year fixed effect. I am therefore identifying the impact of the COPS grants by looking at variation in police employment and crime within similar-sized cities that had similar changes in police and crime prior to the implementation VCCA.

9. Using the contemporaneous number of officers granted per capita does not change the results.

10. A description of which city-years are excluded from the sample due to suspicious crime or police employee reports can be found in Evans and Owens (2007).

11. Agencies report the number of men and women arrested by race and in age categories each month. I exclude agency/offense/year observations where the race-based count was larger than the age-based count. Some agencies report negative arrests for a particular crime in a given month. Following Maltz and Weiss (2006), I assume that any negative arrest count that is less than –24 is a typographical error. Otherwise, negative numbers are assumed to be valid entries intended to correct overcounting in previous months.

12. Using racial breakdowns does not change the results.

13. These missing data are not reported as zeros, but are actually blank data fields in the UCR. In robustness tests, I assume that these missing values are actual zeros.

14. The relationship between control variables and arrests are roughly identical across specifications, and so I omit them for sake of space.

15. The probability of incarceration conditional on arrest is calculated by staff of the Sourcebook of Criminal Justice Statistics, based on data provided by the State Court Processing Statistics. The Sourcebook tables can be found here: Sourcebook of Criminal Justice Statistics Online, http://www.albany.edu/sourcebook/pdf/t500022004.pdf.

16. Sourcebook of Criminal Justice Statistics Online, http://www.albany.edu/source book/pdf/t5602004.pdf.

17. The states in this upper maximum, with between 3 and 9 additional car theft arrests per officer are Arizona, Nevada, Oklahoma, Oregon, Utah, West Virginia, and Virginia.

18. It should be noted that since hiring grants reduce crime, two cities with equal crime rates and different grant levels are not obviously good counterfactuals for each other.

References

Cook, Philip J. 1979. The clearance rate as a measure of criminal justice system effectiveness. *Journal of Public Economics* 11 (1): 135–42.

Cook, Philip J., and Jens Ludwig. 2011. An economist's guide to crime busting. *Wilson Quarterly* 4: 62–66.

Corman, Hope, and H. Naci Mocan. 2000. A time series analysis of crime, deterrence, and drug abuse in New York City. *American Economic Review* 90: 584–604.

Chalfin, Aaron, and Justin McCrary. 2012. The effect of police on crime: New evidence from U.S. cities, 1960–2010. Working paper. University of California-Berkeley.

Davis, Gareth, David B. Muhlhausen, Dexter Ingram, and Ralph Rector. 2000. The facts about COPS: A performance overview of the Community Oriented Policing Services program. Heritage Foundation Center for Data Analysis Report CDA00–10.

DiTella, Rafeal, and Ernesto Schargrodsky. 2004. Do police reduce crime? Estimates using the allocation of police forces after a terrorist attack. *American Economic Review* 94: 115–33.

Draca, Mirko, Stephen J. Machin, and Robert Witt, 2011. Panic on the streets of London: Police, crime and the July 2005 terror attacks. Forthcoming, *American Economic Review* 101: 2157–81.

Durlauf, Steve N., and Daniel S. Nagin. 2010. The deterrent effect of imprisonment. Working paper c12078. NBER, Cambridge, MA.

Durlauf, Steve N., and Daniel S. Nagin. 2011. Imprisonment and crime. Can both be reduced? *Criminology and Public Policy* 10 (1): 13–54.

Evans, William N., and Emily G. Owens. 2007. COPS and crime. *Journal of Public Economics* 91 (2): 181–201.

Fagan, Jeffrey A., Amanda Geller, Garth Davies, and Valerie West. 2010. Street stops and broken windows revisited: The demography and logic of proactive policing in a safe and changing city. In Stephen K. Rice and M. D. White,eds., *Race, Ethnicity, and Policing: New and Essential Readings*. New York: New York University Press, 309–48.

Fisher, Franklin M., and Daniel Nagin. 1978. On the feasibility of identifying the crime function in a simultaneous equations model of crime. In A. Blumstein, D. Nagin, and J. Cohen, eds., *Deterrence and Incapacitation: Estimating the Effects of Criminal Sanctions on Crime Rates*. Washington, DC: National Academy of Sciences, 361–99.

Johnson, Rucker C., and Steven Raphael. 2012. How much does crime reduction does the marginal prisoner buy? *Journal of Law and Economics* 55: 275–310.

Klick, Jonathan, and Alex Tabarrok. 2005. Using terror alert levels to estimate the effect of police on crime. *Journal of Law and Economics* 48: 267–79.

Koper, Christopher, Edward E. Maguire, Gretchen E. Moore, and David E. Huffer. 2001. *Hiring and Retention Issues in Police Agencies: Readings on the Determinants of Police Strength, Hiring and Retention of Officers, and the Federal COPS Program*. Washington, DC: Urban Institute Report to the National Institute of Justice.

Kuziemko, Ilyana, and Steven D. Levitt. 2004. An empirical analysis of imprisoning drug offenders. *Journal of Public Economics* 88 (9–10): 2043–66.

Kyckelhahn, Tracey, 2010. Justice expenditure and employment extracts, 2007. *NCJ Report 231540.*

Lee, David, and Justin McCrary. 2005. Crime, punishment, and myopia. Working paper 11491. NBER, Cambridge, MA.

Levitt, Steven D. 2002. Using electoral cycles in police hiring to estimate the effect of police on crime. [reply] *American Economic Review* 92: 1244–50.

Levitt, Steven D. 1998. Why do increased arrest rates appear to reduce crime: Deterrence, incapacitation, or measurement error? *Economic Inquiry* 36 (3): 353–72.

Lin, Ming-Jen. 2009. More police, less crime: Evidence from US state data. *International Review of Law and Economics* 29: 73–80.

Maltz, Michael D., and Harald E. Weiss. 2006. Creating a UCR utility: Final report to the National Institute of Justice. *NIJ Research Report 215341.*

Marvell, Thomas B., and Carlisle E. Moody. 1996. Specification problems, police levels, and crime rates. *Criminology* 34: 609–46.

Miller, Ted, Mark Cohen, and Brian Wiersema. 1996. *Victim Costs and Consequences: A New Look*. Washington, DC: National Institute of Justices, US Department of Justice.

US Department of Justice, Office of the Inspector General. 1999. Police hiring and redeployment grants: Summary of audit findings and recommendations, October 1996–September 1998. *Office of the Inspector General Special Report #99–14.*

US Government Accountability Office. 2003. Technical assessment of Zhao and Thurman's 2001 "Evaluation of the Effects of COPS Grants on Crime." *Report Number GAO-03-867R.*

US Government Accountability Office. 2005. Community policing grants: COPS grants were a modest contributor to declines in crime in the 1990s. *Report Number GAO-06-104.*

Vollaard, Benjamin, and Joseph Hamed. 2012. Why the police have an effect on violent crime after all: Evidence from the British Crime Survey. *Journal of Law and* Economics 55: 901–24.

Vollaard, Benjamin, and Pierre Koning. 2009. The effect of police on crime, disorder and victim precaution: Evidence from a Dutch victimization survey. *International Review of Law and Economics* 29 (4): 336–48.

Worrall, John L., and Tomislav V. Kovandzic. 2010. Police levels and crime rates: An instrumental variables approach. *Social Science Research* 39: 506–16.

2   Drug Prohibition and Its Alternatives

John J. Donohue III

2.1   Introduction

Illegal drugs, alcohol, and tobacco impose large social costs on society, here and in every major developed country. Interestingly, each of these is estimated—albeit crudely—to impose about $200 billion per year in social costs in the United States (although the costs come in very different forms depending on the nature of the legal regime and enforcement policy). These three substances also share some interesting characteristics: many Americans have a serious attachment to one or more of them, and a sizable proportion of the consumers use one or more of these in a responsible manner, hence imposing little-to-no external costs to society. The bad news is that a nontrivial subset also uses them irresponsibly, and this irresponsible use tends to create very high social costs. This problem is exacerbated by the fact that restricting use of drugs, alcohol, and tobacco to only those who impose minimal social costs is extremely difficult.[1]

Cocaine and opiates first became criminalized at the federal level in the United States in 1914, followed by marijuana in 1937. The criminalization of these drugs has led to the modern "war on drugs," characterized by strict enforcement of drug violations and policing attempts directed at shutting down the drug trade. Scholars and policy makers, however, have questioned whether the "war on drugs" is really the optimal policy, with some suggesting that legalization and regulation may be a better alternative. A remarkable feature of this debate is that strong support exists for almost any position in the drug-policy debate.

The positions of Milton Friedman, Nobel laureate economist, and Robert Weiner, spokesman for the White House National Drug Policy Office from 1995 to 2001, embody the poles of the ongoing debate. Milton and Rose Friedman, famous promoters of free markets and choice, argued for the complete and unregulated legalization of illicit drugs:

> However much harm drugs do to those who use them . . . seeking to prohibit their use does even more harm both to users of drugs and to the rest of us. . . . Legalizing drugs would simultaneously *reduce the amount of crime* and improve law enforcement. It is hard to conceive of any other single measure that would accomplish so much to promote law and order.[2]

Robert Weiner, former head of the White House National Drug Policy Office, on the other hand takes a staunch stand in a favor of the "war on drugs." In a June 14, 2009, address, Weiner[3] said: "Drugs have not 'won the war.'. . . America's overall drug use has declined almost by half in the past three decades. . . . In addition, cocaine use, including crack—the source of much of the former record-high violent crime numbers—is down 70 percent. Want to go back?"[4] Weiner clearly stands by his position, arguing that a "comprehensive anti-drug strategy" has and will continue to produce important social gains. Further Weiner denounced the prospect of legalization in fiery terms:

> Legalization would be a catastrophe. [T]here are an estimated 15 million alcoholics in this country and 5 million drug addicts; do we want the 5 to become 15? Parents, police, and the American people know that taking away the incentive of the normative power of the law would increase drug use and related car crashes, school dropouts, and work absences. That is why the law has remained in place. . . . Hospital emergency rooms would be flooded, and crime would return to the crisis levels of the 1970s and '80s, when drug use was at its highest. Domestic violence and date rape would be substantially higher. The majority of arrestees in 10 major American cities recently tested positive for illegal drugs, a remarkable indicator of a link between drugs and crime.[5]

The difficult task is first to assess if either of the extreme positions championed by Friedman and Weiner is correct or if there is some intermediate position, such as grudging legalization with heavy restrictions or retaining criminalization while pulling back from the "war," that would better promote wise social policy.

2.2   Breaking down the Polar Positions

Both of the polar positions show a degree of theoretical elegance. On the one hand, Friedman's position stems from his ideology that individual choices must be honored, and that societal gains (think in terms of the likely consumer surplus to be gained by rational actors in a framework of neoclassical economics) are to be had from this emphasis on individual choice. Further Friedman draws on evidence from the US experience with prohibition and re-legalization of alcohol to suggest that once legal, the drug trade will become much less violent, saving society from the massive social costs of such violence. And finally, Friedman notes that by legalizing drugs, we would eliminate the massive policing and incarceration costs of prohibition.

On the other hand, Weiner accurately argues that drug consumption alone will produce major social costs if not inhibited by law. From this he argues that drugs should be illegal because the socially optimal level of drug consumption is low or close to zero. Moreover, *given* that these drugs *are* criminalized, Weiner would presumably argue, we develop and propagate *respect for the law* by rigorously enforcing this criminalization.

This fundamental disagreement raises the question of what best promotes *respect for law?* Given prohibition of drugs as the currently established rule of law, theory might suggest that a war on drugs, as suggested by Weiner, would best promote respect for the law. However, if prohibition/criminalization is highly contested, a war on drugs may well breed disrespect for the law, as Friedman argued.

2.3 Applying Further Economic Theory—Externalities and Internalities

Free market and libertarian principles of consumer choice obviously favor the Friedman approach, as these were the theoretical building blocks for his position. The libertarian's case for the Friedman approach, moreover, is dramatically strengthened if one believes the external social costs of drug consumption at the level that would occur under Friedman's laissez faire approach are no greater than the costs of enforcing the criminal prohibition of drug use.

Of course, if the evidence supports the existence of large and unavoidable externalities and internalities, the case for governmental action is strong (although a libertarian might question the possible relevance or existence of "internalities"). Drug use clearly produces *negative externalities*, or social costs that accrue to nonmarket participants, in the form of various harm to the dependents of drug addicts, cost of accidents, missed work, certain costs of medical treatment, and so on. The concept of *internalities*—costs that accrue to drug users but that the users fail to account for in making their consumption decisions—are less frequently discussed, but may be quite large. For example, UCLA Professor of Public Affairs Mark Kleiman argues that a teenager who starts to smoke at age 18 rarely considers that years down the road this choice may hurt the teen's future 12-year-old son when the smoking causes the then-parent's premature death.[6] Yale Professor of Psychiatry Richard Schottenfeld fleshes out this line of thinking and applies it to drug addiction. He stresses that the survival of the human species has depended on love relationships that make a child the special focus of a parent's attention. Drug addiction can supplant that focus as the drug becomes the key love relationship and central focus of the addict's life, much to the detriment of the addict's family.[7] Internalities can result in severe harm for the drug user (potential harmful brain alterations) or to the user's family or even work associates.

Considering these elements, some form of market correction, whether it is high taxes on illegal drugs or prohibition altogether—policies that make the current cost to user of consumption more accurately reflect the long-term and social costs—seems more socially optimal than the free market libertarian policy of Friedman.

2.4 Alternative Approaches

In addition to the polar theories of legalization and a "war on drugs," less extreme alternatives have been suggested. Two intermediate positions might include (1) prohibition without an "all out" war on drugs and (2) legalization coupled with policies of containment via regulation. Prohibition without war would entail less draconian enforcement and more educational programs about the harms of drugs. Containment policies via regulation would likely include taxes, sales restrictions, advertising restrictions, and age-based prohibition, much like the regulations we see in the modern alcohol and tobacco markets (e.g., sales prohibited to those under a given age). Since current alcohol taxes are likely to understate the optimal Pigovian taxes—although concerns about inviting the involvement of organized crime always constrain tax rates—the likely optimal taxation and regulatory regime for cocaine and heroin would likely be far stricter than current alcohol policy. An interesting demand-side alternative policy suggestion is one of legalization followed by targeting of "problem users." Kleiman has discussed the option of identifying "problem users" and presenting them with the choice between immediate sobriety and jail.

2.5   Determining the Costs of Drug Consumption, Addiction, and Incarceration

In a 2007 article published in *The Lancet*, several collaborating medical professors assembled a panel of 8 to 16 scientific, legal, and law enforcement experts to rate 20 substances along 3 dimensions—physical harm, dependence, and social harms.[8] Correlation in scoring between psychiatrists and independent experts was generally high, implying a consensus between the two, and the final averaged scores actually ranked alcohol and tobacco, number three and ten, respectively, in the list of most harmful drugs—both ranking higher than marijuana, which ranked twelfth (see figure 2.1):

The Office of National Drug Control Policy (hereinafter ONDCP) undertook a landmark study in 2002, seeking to estimate the economic cost of illegal drug use in the United States.[9] In particular, the study

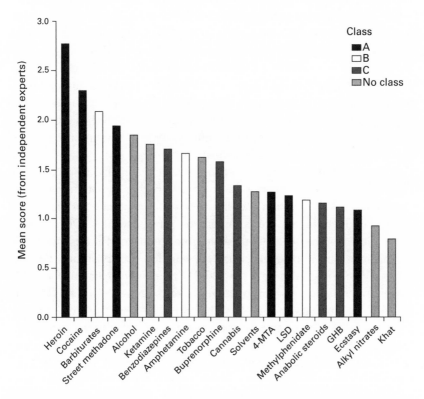

Figure 2.1
Mean harm scores for twenty substances Source: Nutt et al. (2007, p. 1050)

evaluated lost productivity, health effects, and crime-related costs including policing expenditures and incarceration. The study estimates the cost of illegal drug use was $217 billion, in 2008 dollars.[10] Two similar studies estimate the cost of alcohol use at $244 billion and the cost of smoking at $195 billion,[11] again in 2008 dollars.[12]

About 56.6 percent of the estimated cost of illegal drug use was crime related, and over two thirds of these crime-related costs were from lost productivity for those incarcerated on drug charges and from costs related to the criminal justice system. On the other hand, health costs accounted for a very small 8.7 percent of the total estimated cost of drug use. The important point to note here is that there clearly is a tradeoff between enforcement and health-related costs—more enforcement will reduce consumption and thereby reduce consumption-related costs, while simultaneously driving up enforcement costs.

Of course, there are problems with all of these cost estimates. For example, estimates of tobacco-related deaths sum all deaths with tobacco-related causes, whereas estimates of alcohol and drug-related deaths sum only the "death certificate" numbers of these deaths, which often don't take into account deaths or injuries caused by drug use in the distant past, such as strokes caused by prior cocaine use. Hence alcohol and illegal drug-related death numbers may be understated relative to tobacco deaths. Moreover data on drug consumption is fundamentally imperfect. Still the findings of these studies are strong enough to raise concerns about overall US drug policy, and force us to ask whether a "war on drugs" is truly optimal.

If we accept the premise of the *Lancet* article that many drugs, including alcohol, are more harmful and impose higher societal costs than marijuana, a key question moving forward is whether, for example, alcohol and marijuana are complements or substitutes. On the one hand, there is some debate in the academic literature over this question, with researchers finding empirical support for both positions. Pacula (1998a, 1998b) and Williams et al. (2001) find evidence that alcohol and marijuana function as complements using both NSLY and HSPH College Alcohol Survey data.[13] On the other hand, several studies have concluded that drugs and alcohol function as substitutes, including Conlin et al. (2005), Thies and Register (1993), Chaloupka and Laixuthai (1997), and Cameron and Williams (2001).[14] Indeed, since the evidence supporting the substitution hypothesis was on the whole methodologically stronger—particularly the panel data analysis of Conlin et al. (2005)—it is certainly worth considering whether society might benefit from shifting consumption away from alcohol and toward marijuana. But we would need both a sounder estimate of the relative harms and costs of marijuana than *The Lancet* harm rankings and more precise estimates of how consumption of alcohol would be altered by weakening the laws against marijuana consumption before actually adopting a policy to shift consumption from one substance to the other.

2.6   Cross-Country Comparisons of Substance Abuse

A study[15] comparing countries' drug use helps illuminate the US "drug problem." Using *WHO World Mental Health Surveys*, Degenhardt et al. (2008) found that the United States population ranks number one in the world in percentage of respondents ever using cannabis, ever using tobacco, and ever using cocaine. Notably, the US respondents topped other countries in cocaine use by a huge margin—16 percent of US respondents indicated they had used cocaine; the next highest was New Zealand, at just over 4 percent (these results are shown graphically below). The United States is far less of a pathological outlier, however, if one looks at measures of current use rather than the figures for lifetime ever-use, ranking fourth in annual prevalence of cannabis use and third in annual prevalence of cocaine use.[16] Weiner suggests that these numbers showing lower *current-use* than *ever-use* are evidence that the war on drugs is working.

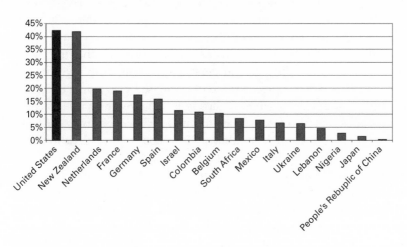

Figure 2.2
Percentage of respondents ever using cannabis in 2001 to 2004, by country Source: Donohue et al. (2011, p. 221)

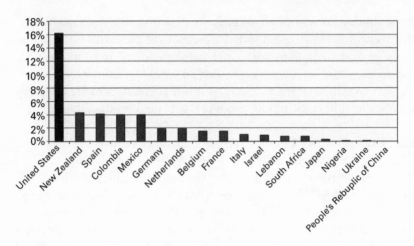

Figure 2.3
Percentage of respondents ever using cocaine in 2001 to 2004, by country Source: Donohue et al. (2011, p. 222)

Indeed illegal drug use in the United States is down substantially from the late 1970s, the height of US illicit drug usage.[17] The trend in reported recent marijuana use for high school seniors does show some interesting trends, peaking in 1978–79, dropping steadily until about 1992, rising from 92 to 98, and then flattening out with a slight downward trend. An important question here is whether these numbers reflect actual use tendencies or reporting tendencies. It seems highly plausible that Reagan's "say no to drugs" campaign in the early 1980s increased the tendency of twelfth graders to simply say "no" when asked if they had recently used drugs, regardless of whether they actually had or not. Still the size and persistence of the drop gives reason to believe that it does reflect a trend of decreased usage over time. The percentage of twelfth graders reporting to have recently used alcohol or cigarettes has also fallen since the mid-1970s, from over 70 to 40 percent for alcohol and from almost 40 to about 20 percent for cigarettes, as shown in figures 2.4 and 2.5.[18]

So, even if Weiner were correct that the all-out war on drugs reduced drug use, the evidence from improvement in controlling consumption of the legal drugs suggests that steps other than prohibition can be effective—apparently, raising the drinking age and increasing tobacco taxes have helped generate equal or greater drops in the usage levels of these respective substances.

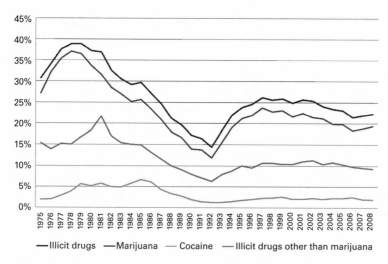

Figure 2.4
Percentage of 12th graders reporting use of various illicit drugs in past thirty days Source:
Donohue et al. (2011, p. 229)

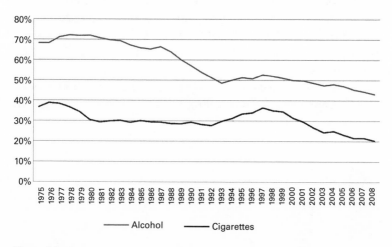

Figure 2.5
Percentage of 12th graders reporting use of alcohol and cigarettes in past thirty days
Source: Donohue et al. (2011, p. 272)

2.7 Other Features of Drug Use and Abuse: The "Top-Heavy" Distribution and Addiction

Across a variety of drugs and substances, it is generally accepted that a small percentage of users account for a very large percentage of the total consumption and/or abuse—this is what we call a top-heavy distribution.[19] Besides this distribution, the nature of addiction presents an interesting caveat in analyzing drug use and the drug market. A study conducted by the Institute of Medicine of the National Academies has published findings on what percentage of those who try a given substance become dependent. Tobacco ranks first at over 30 percent, followed by heroine—over 20 percent; cocaine—over 15 percent; alcohol—15 percent; anti-anxiety drugs and marijuana bring up the rear, each at under 10 percent.[20]

The role of addiction or dependence in this debate is crucial—yet understanding how to conceptualize these ideas with policy-making in mind presents a challenge. A key question that arises here is how much addiction changes behavior and to what extent it alters one's response to incentives. For example, how responsive are addicts to price changes? Are addicts rational welfare maximizers (as decision-makers are generally assumed to be in economic theory), or are they irrational or myopic?

Becker and Murphy (1988)[21] develop a rational addiction model, which lays a framework for reconciling rational decision-making with

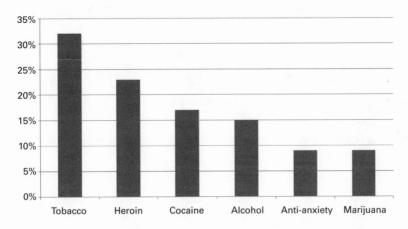

Figure 2.6
Of those who tried, percentage that become dependent by substance Source: Donohue et al. (2011, p. 260)

addiction—they argue that addictions can arise from foresighted welfare maximization, assuming that addicts are better off by starting to consume drugs than they otherwise would have been. This is a very libertarian idea. Based on these assumptions, the model states that demand will be responsive to price, but more so to long-term changes than short-term ones. But is this model really correct? Other models of addiction generally treat addicts as irrational, or at the very least having time-inconsistent preferences. Understanding the nature of addiction and how usage would respond to price changes is very relevant to the legalization debate, as arguments for legalization often hinge on the argument that price mechanisms will be effective measures for reducing use.

2.8   America's Punitive Approach to Illegal Drugs

To give some context for further discussion of the war on drugs, consider the following: In the United States in 2007, there were 1.8 million arrests for drug-abuse violations, compared with 1.4 million DUI arrests, 1.3 assault-related arrests, and 1.1 larceny theft arrests. Possession arrests account for about 82 percent of all drug abuse arrests, with marijuana and heroin/cocaine possession making up 42.1 and 21.5 percent, respectively, of all drug-related arrests.[22] Surprisingly, the rate of US marijuana arrests per 1,000 users, 31, is similar to that of many other countries—34 in Germany, 26 in France, 44 in Austria, 20 in the United Kingdom, and 24 in Australia.[23]

Mark Kleiman provides a nice illustration of the difficulties in trying to curtail consumption through a purely punitive approach. For example, would it be effective simply to deter the drug trade by executing drug dealers? Occupational hazards data show that in a given industry, for each work-related death the industry's wage bill must rise by $1 to $5 million.[24] So let's take the high-end estimate and assume we execute 100 drug dealers—this would raise drug industry costs by $500 million based on the occupational hazard figures. In the $50 billion illegal drug trade industry, this would be a 1 percent cost increase, presumably leading to a 1 percent increase in drug prices. Even 1,000 executions would raise drug prices just 10 percent. Assuming inelastic demand, a generally accepted assumption, this would result in only a minor drop in consumption. An alternative would be to only execute drug dealers who kill. Of course, this may bring about the perverse effect of a higher drug-dealer population if drug dealers who kill tend to kill other drug dealers.[25]

This discussion relates to the "big question" of the US punitive approach to the war on drugs: How did prices for US illegal drugs fall so sharply in the face of such intense enforcement?[26] A portion of the price drop has undoubtedly come from decreases in demand for drugs. Some of the price drop probably reflects better productivity in product distribution. However, the rest of the price drop may reflect efficiency gains in circumventing enforcement—an alarming thought given the high costs of the war on drugs.

On the other side of the debate, another key question arises: How can or could we predict the impact of legalization? Evidence here is mostly impressionistic—there has been little policy variation for the currently illegal drugs in the United States over the past 50 years, and hence there is no panel data to answer the question. Proponents of legalization often draw on anecdotal evidence from the prohibition era to argue that the increase in crime during prohibition occurred directly because of the criminalization of alcohol. Owens (2011), however, offers evidence to the contrary—exploiting state-level variation in prohibition policy, she finds that violent crime trends were better explained by urbanization and immigration, rather than criminalization/decriminalization of alcohol.[27]

Renowned libertarian Jeffrey Miron, on the other hand, draws strong conclusions about the connection between the criminalization of drugs and violent crime using evidence from cross-country comparisons.[28] His logic here is straightforward: homicide rates in Western Europe are just 10 to 20 percent of those in the United States. Miron argues that Colombia, where domestic and international efforts to prohibit drugs are considerable, experiences homicide rates about 8 to 10 times those of the United States. Miron concludes that stronger prohibition efforts lead to more violence, and that more demand-side policies, as used in Western Europe, will reduce violence. But is it fair to attribute differences in crime rates in Western Europe and the United States and in South America primarily to policies toward illegal drugs?

Moreover evidence from the United States in the past twenty years somewhat refutes Miron's suggestion. Since the mid-1990s the "Miron Drug Prohibition Enforcement Index"[29], which measures the aggressiveness of drug enforcement, has risen consistently, yet the homicide rate has fallen over that time. Most qualitative and empirical evidence suggests that this is a result of illegal drug markets becoming more orderly in the 1990s, and this may suggest that the crime drop we

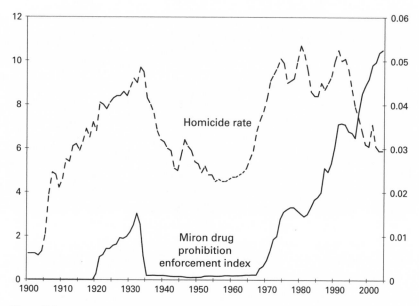

Figure 2.7
Homicide rate versus drug prohibition enforcement index in 1992 dollars Source: Donohue et al. (2011, p. 263)

would get from legalization would be smaller than the one we got, for instance, following prohibition.

2.9 Some Empirical Investigations of the Demand versus Supply-Side Question

Caulkins et al. (1997) presents an important evaluation of the cost-effectiveness of opposite types of drug policy.[30] Overall, the authors find that a demand-side policy—drug treatment—was more effective than the aggressive prohibition policy of minimum sentences. Moreover the authors find the differences in cost-effectiveness to be staggering: each additional $1 million spent on treatment programs reduced net cocaine consumption by 103.6 kg, while an additional $1 million on longer sentences reduced consumption by just 12.6 kg.

Then again, the 1995 drop in supply of methamphetamines generated by the DEA's shutting down of major suppliers allowed for empirical testing of direct supply-side prohibition measures. Dobkin and Nicosia (2009) estimate that the DEA caused an immediate 50 percent drop in supply, leading to a 50 percent drop in meth-related hospitalizations, a short-run tripling of prices, and a drop in purity from 90 to 20 percent.[31] It is important to note, however, that purity recovered to 85 percent of its original level within 18 months, suggesting that enduring supply-side interventions are difficult to engineer. The authors also find that robberies increased about 9 percent in the year following the supply drop, but that no other crime category was affected, and that there was little substitution to other illegal drugs or alcohol. This suggests that the primary contribution of meth consumption to crime came not from consumption (which fell by 50 percent) but likely through the need to steal to maintain a habit as prices rose.

Last, there exists varying evidence on the impact of the decriminalization of illegal drugs, a popular policy in European and South American countries in the past decade. In particular, I would like to call attention to the case of Portugal, which decriminalized drugs in 2001, yet still continues to have one of the lowest rates of cannabis and cocaine use over an entire lifetime, 8 and 0.9 percent, respectively. Moreover the percentage of secondary school students reporting use of common drugs has declined since 2001, the number of new HIV/AIDS cases among drug users has fallen, and the country has not become a destination for drug tourism.

Michael Specter recently profiled the drug situation in Portugal in an issue of *The New Yorker*, summarizing:

In most respects, the law seems to have worked: serious drug use is down significantly, particularly among young people; the burden on the criminal justice system has eased: the number of people seeking treatment has grown; and the rates of drug-related deaths and cases of infectious diseases have fallen.[32]

Specter quotes Miguel Vasconcelos, chief psychiatrist at one of Portugal's major treatment centers, who says of the new decriminalization policy: "this is an alternative that does get people off the streets, reduces the rates of HIV infection, and lowers crime. It is humanistic but also pragmatic."[33]

Critics, however, have argued that the data does not necessarily support the conclusion that decriminalization was the reason for increases in drug users seeking treatment; increases in drug treatment center accessibility coincided with the decriminalization policy. These critics also offer moral arguments in opposition to Portugal's approach to drug use, claiming that decriminalization and easier access to treatment and methadone supplements has decreased incentive to get off

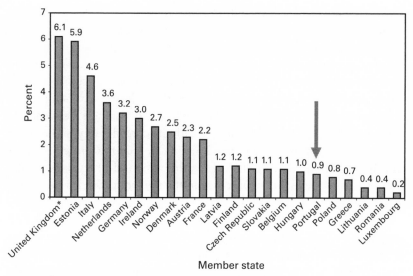

Member state

*Excludes Scotland and Northern Ireland.

Figure 2.8
EU cocaine prevalence by country Source: Instituto da Droga e da Toxicodependência de Portugal (Institute on Drugs and Drug Addiction of Portugal 2007, slide 10)

drugs altogether and increased the portion of population living with managed addictions.[34]

The Netherlands, where small transactions (5g or less) of cannabis are decriminalized, shows somewhat similar evidence to that of Portugal. Lifetime use of marijuana has continued to be lower than in the United States and several other EU member countries. Decriminalization also has had the desired effect of keeping users out of black markets; Abraham (1999) finds that among users over age 18, 48 percent of cannabis purchases occurred in coffee shops and 39 percent occurred between friends or family.[35]

Some US states made steps in this direction in the 1970s, choosing not to decriminalize cannabis, but to depenalize it, downgrading marijuana possession to a misdemeanor. Evidence of the effect of this depenalization has been inconsistent, but most studies find little to no effect. The effect of this type of depenalization is debated: some argue it may help reduce violent crime through a simple economic mechanism: Lesser penalties for drug sales would reduce the risk of engaging in the drug trade, thereby causing new sellers to enter the market, driving down profits, and lowering the stakes of drug-related disputes. Others argue that lower penalties will increase demand and stimulate more illegal activity as gangs vie for the new customers.

On one hand, because Portugal is a smaller, more family-oriented country and the United States is a stressed country as a whole, perhaps Portugal's experience with drug decriminalization cannot offer us much guidance on drug policy because the countries are simply too different. One might think that these cultural differences between the United States and Portugal, coupled with the considerably higher rates of US drug use captured in figure 2.8, indicate that the United States is simply more prone than Portugal to addiction and drug abuse. But a comparison of alcohol consumption in the two countries raises doubts about this explanation.

Since data on alcohol consumption tend to be more reliable (because people are more willing to honestly report legal rather than illegal activity), it is worth investigating the degree of alcohol abuse in the two countries as a possible proxy for how prone to substance use and abuse the two countries are.

In 2003 (the most recent data for which both US and Portugal data are available), Portugal experienced about 30 liver cirrhosis deaths per 100,000 population, 50 percent more than in the United States. Similarly per capita alcohol consumption among drinkers was almost twice as high in Portugal as in the United States at 27.45 liters of pure alcohol per drinker compared with just 14 in the United States.[36] Cortez-Pinto et al. (2010) affirm that high liver cirrhosis mortality is indeed the result of overdrinking, concluding that alcohol is a "heavy economic burden for the health system" in Portugal.[37] The data presented here suggest that Portugal may engage in more heavy drinking than the United States, and that perhaps the United States is not a country inherently more prone to substance abuse than other countries. Of course, it is not known whether a society's predisposition to substance abuse is universal, or whether some factors make Portugal more prone to alcohol abuse and less prone to illegal drug abuse, and vice versa for the United States.

2.10 Moving Forward

It should be clear that the issues presented by America's drug problem are complex. In particular, though evidence from other countries tends to focus on cannabis use, cocaine is the single largest contributor to the social costs of drugs in the United States. Caulkins and Kleiman (2007) estimate that two-thirds of the social costs of illegal drugs in the United States are accounted for by cocaine.[38] However, the most policy-relevant debate today is over legalization/decriminalization of marijuana. These social cost estimates suggest that legalization of marijuana may have less of an upside potential than a broader legalization/decriminalization, but it likely carries far smaller downside risks than, say, a Portugal-style legalization of cocaine.

Still a relevant question is why is there little popular support for legalization of marijuana? Considering the means of drug distribution leads us to one potential answer. Currently the costs of illegal drugs are borne by the government (via spending on enforcement) and by those involved in the drug trade—mostly the poor and minorities. Decriminalization or legalization would probably both reduce the cost borne by the government and increase marijuana usage, thus shifting a higher proportion of the consumption-oriented social costs of marijuana use to the middle/upper classes. Another potential answer, and a very simple one, is the prevalence of moral opposition to drug use in the United States—Specter writes on this point, "It is common in the United States to judge drug addiction morally rather than medically, and most policy flows from that approach."[39]

Further, as discussed earlier, the lack of serious or reliable evidence on the subject prevents accurate estimates of the impact of any radical change in policy. In particular, changes in the market for a particular drug may generate a major cross-substance substitution effect, but we cannot predict this with a significant degree of certainty. This problem is exacerbated by the fact that the implementation of a new policy would be crucial, and again, we have little to no information to point us in the direction of a sound implementation strategy. Hence, any stark change in drug policy would be to some degree a "shot in the dark," despite the considerable research and predictions based on logic or theory.

So, what should we do? I do draw some tentative conclusions and offer some policy suggestions. The evidence suggests that a free market approach to drugs and the US style war on drugs are both suboptimal policies—we would be better off with fewer in prison if nothing else. As for cannabis, eliminating the federal ban would probably produce important gains in terms of lower enforcement costs and fewer unnecessary incarcerations. States should be allowed some policy variation (an added benefit of such variation would be new data with which to analyze the issues surrounding drug control), but the federal government should treat marijuana as it does alcohol in the National Minimum Drinking Age Act of 1984, so that states would at least prohibit young brains (those under 21) from legal access to marijuana. Taxes on marijuana potency would further be set high (and on alcohol ought to be raised), and these tax revenues should be used to enforce prohibition of under-age consumption, discourage use via counter-advertising, and fund addiction treatment.

But what should we do about harder drugs? This is obviously a more difficult question. Before making any serious change here, we should conduct more rigorous evaluations of the new decriminalization of harder drugs in Europe and Latin America. If these policies are in fact successful in constraining consumption to acceptable levels, then perhaps we ought to consider going in the decriminalization direction as well, or even consider legalization and heavy taxation, per the Becker recommendation.

Oddly the war on drugs may be rational in the sense that though it is very costly, it imposes much of these costs on criminals and drug traffickers, as well as on other countries, rather than forcing the average American to bear the social costs of drugs beyond paying tax dollars on enforcement and incarceration. Still the best reading of the current evidence suggests that aggressive prohibition and the war on drugs are suboptimal policies. Even if every element of the war on drugs remained unchanged but we dropped our current prison population of incarcerated drug offenders from 500,000 to 400,000, this would represent a step in the direction of reducing total social costs. How far we would benefit from such retrenchment is an interesting question. We need to pursue additional empirical and qualitative analyses with the ultimate goal of forging a new and more effective approach to drug policy.

Notes

1. Is there "responsible" use of tobacco? Since tobacco may be the most addictive substance and its use causes 300,000 to 500,000 deaths per year, it may be that the scope for responsible use is limited. One could at least imagine that occasional smoking could be possible for some without lapsing into addiction and thereby imposing significant social costs through the elevated risk of premature death. Occasional cigar smoking might fall into this category.

2. See Friedman (2009), appendix B at p. 186.

3. See Weiner (2009). Robert Weiner was then the head of the White House National Drug Policy Office.

4. A possible caveat here is that the numbers may reflect drops only in casual crack use; it is unclear that the number of heavy crack users dropped significantly.

5. Id.

6. See Kleiman (2011).

7. Richard Schottenfeld, via Leckman and Mayes; see Landi et al. (2011).

8. See Nutt et al. (2007).

9. See Office of National Drug Control Policy (2004), https://www.ncjrs.gov/ondcppubs/publications/pdf/economic_costs.pdf.

10. Id.

11. See Harwood (2000, p. 119).

12. The original cost figures as estimated in the respective studies were as follows: illegal drugs—$180.9 billion in 2002 dollars; alcohol—$184.6 billion in 1998 dollars; smoking—$138 billion in 1995 dollars. To ease comparison, I have converted each figure to 2008 dollars using the CPI-based inflation adjustment calculator provided by the Bureau of Labor Statistics, available at http://data.bls.gov/cgi-bin/cpicalc.pl. Figures are rounded to nearest billion.

13. See Pacula (1998a, b) and Williams, Pacula, et al. (2001).

14. See Conlin, Dickert-Conlin, and Pepper (2005); Thies and Register (1993); Chaloupka and Laixuthai (1997); and Cameron and Williams (2001).

15. See Degenhardt et al. (2008), which supplies data on cumulative use of alcohol, tobacco, cannabis, and cocaine.

16. See United Nations Office on Drugs and Crime (2009).

17. See Johnston et al. (2009), pp. 198–99, http://www.monitoringthefuture.org/pubs/monographs/vol1_2008.pdf.

18. Id.

19. See Manski et al. (2001, p. 60). See also Rydell and Everingham (1994).

20. See Kershaw and Cathcart (2009), citing Institute of Medicine of the National Academies.

21. Becker and Murphy (1988, p. 695).

22. See Bureau of Justice Statistics (2011).

23. See Boyum and Reuter (2005).

24. See Viscusi (1991).

25. See Kleiman (1988).

26. See Caulkins, Reuter, and Taylor (2005).

27. See Owens (2011).

28. See Miron (1999).

29. See Miron (2005).

30. See Cauklins (1997, p. 22).

31. See Dobkin and Nicosia (2009).

32. See Specter (2011, p. 36).

33. See Specter (2011) at 38.

34. See Specter (2011).

35. See Abraham (1999, pp. 3–4).

36. See World Health Organization (2011).

37. See Cortez-Pinto et al. (2010).

38. See Caulkins and Kleiman (2007, p. 564).

39. See Specter (2011, p. 45).

References

Abraham, Manja. 1999. Places of drug purchase in the Netherlands. Presented at Conference on Drug Use and Drug Policy, Vienna, Austria, September 1999. http://proxy .baremetal.com/csdp.org/research/places.pdf.

Becker, Gary, and Kevin Murphy. 1988. A theory of rational addiction. *Journal of Political Economy* 96 (4): 675–700.

Boyum, D., and P. Reuter. 2005. *An Analytic Assessment of U.S. Drug Policy*. Washington, DC: AEI Press.

Bureau of Justice Statistics. 2011. *Drugs and Crime Facts*. Available at: http://bjs.ojp.usdoj .gov/content/dcf/contents.cfm.

Cameron, Lisa, and Jenny Williams. 2001. Cannabis, alcohol, and cigarettes: Substitutes or complements? *Economic Record* 77 (236): 19–34.

Caulkins, Jonathan P., C. Peter Rydell, William Schwabe, and James Chiesa. 1997. *Mandatory Minimum Drug Sentences: Throwing Away the Key or the Taxpayers' Money?* Santa Monica, CA: Rand Corporation Press.

Caulkins, Jonathan P., and Mark A. R. Kleiman. 2007. Drug policy. In Peter Schuck and James Wilson, eds., *Understanding America: The Anatomy of an Exceptional Nation*. New York: PublicAffairs Press.

Caulkins, Jonathan P., P. Reuter, and L. Taylor. 2005. Can supply restrictions lower price: Illegal drugs, violence and positional advantage. *Contributions to Economic Analysis and Policy* 5 (1): 1–18.

Chaloupka, Frank, and Adit Laixuthai. 1997. Do youths substitute alcohol and marijuana? Some econometric evidence. *Eastern Economic Journal* 23 (3): 253–76.

Conlin, Michael, Stacy Dickert-Conlin, and John Pepper. 2005. The effect of alcohol prohibition on illicit-drug-related crime. *Journal of Law and Economics* 48: 215–34.

Cortez-Pinto, Helena, Miguel Gouveia, Luís Dos Santos Pinheiro, João Coata, Margarida Borges, and António Vaz Carneiro. 2010. The burden of disease and the cost of illnesses attributable to alcohol drinking—Results of a national study. *Alcoholism, Clinical and Experimental Research* 34 (8): 1442–49.

Degenhardt, Louisa, Wai-Tat Chiu, Nancy Sampson, Ronald C. Kessler, James C. Anthony, Matthias Angermeyer, Ronny Bruffaerts, Giovanni de Girolamo, Oye Jureje, Yueqin Huang, Aimee Karam, Stanislav Kostyuchenko, Jean Pierre Lepine, Maria Elena Medina Mora, Yehuda Neumark, J. Hans Ormel, Alejandra Pinto-Meza, José Posada-Villa, Dan J. Stein, Tadashi Takeshima, and J. Elisabeth Wells. 2008. Toward a global view of alcohol, tobacco, cannabis, and cocaine use: Findings from the WHO World Mental Health surveys. *PLoS Medicine* 5 (7): e141.

Dobkin, Carlos and Nancy Nicosia. 2009. The war on drugs: Methamphetamine, public health and crime. *American Economic Review* 99 (1): 324–49.

Donohue, John J., Benjamin Ewing, and David Pelopquin. 2011. Rethinking America's illegal drug policy. In Phillip Cook, Jens Ludwig, and Justin McCrary, eds., *Controlling Crime: Strategies and Tradeoffs.* Chicago: University of Chicago Press, 215–81.

Friedman, Milton. 2009. Crime. Reprinted in Timothy Lynch, ed., *In the Name of Justice.* Washington, DC: Cato Institute.

Harwood, H. 2000. *Updating Estimates of the Economic Cost of Alcohol Abuse: Estimates, Updating Methods, and Data.* Bethesda, MD: National Institute on Alcohol Abuse and Alcoholism.

Instituto da Droga e da Toxicodependência de Portugal (Institute on Drugs and Drug Addiction of Portugal). 2007. The National Situation Relating to Drugs and Dependency, 2006 Annual Report.

Johnston, L. D., P. M. O'Malley, J. G. Bachman, and J. E. Schulenberg. 2009. *Monitoring the Future: National Survey Results on Drug Use, 1975–2008.* Vol. 1: *Secondary School Students.* NIH publication 09–7402. Bethesda, MD: National Institute on Drug Abuse.

Kershaw, Sarah and Rebecca Cathcart. 2009. Marijuana is gateway drug for two debates. *New York Times*, July 19.

Kleiman, Mark. 1988. Executing drug lords is absurd. Dead wrong. *New Republic* 199 (13): 14–16.

Kleiman, Mark. 2011. Rethinking the "war on drugs" through the US–Mexico prism. *Talk at Yale University*, May 12.

Landi, Niole, Jessica Montoya, Hedy Kober, Helena J. V. Rutherford, W. Einar Mencl, Patrick D. Worhunsky, Marc N. Potenza, and Linda C. Mayes. 2011. Maternal neural responses to infant cries and faces: Relationships with substance abuse. *Frontiers in Psychiatry* 2 (32): 1–13.

Manski, Charles, John Pepper, and Carol Petrie, eds. 2001. *Informing America's Policy on Illegal Drugs: What We Don't Know Keeps Hurting Us.* Washington, DC: National Research Council/National Academies Press.

Miron, Jeffrey. 1999. Violence and the U.S. prohibitions of drugs and alcohol. *American Law and Economics Review* 1 (1): 78–114.

Miron, Jeffrey. 2005. *The Budgetary Implications of Marijuana Prohibition.* Washington, DC: The Marijuana Policy Project.

Nutt, David, Leslie A. King, William Saulsbury, and Colin Bakemore. 2007. Development of a rational scale to assess the harm of drugs of potential misuse. *Lancet* 360 (9566): 1047–53.

Office of National Drug Control Policy. 2004. *The Economic Costs of Drug Abuse in the United States, 1992–2002.* Publication 207303. Washington, DC: Executive Office of the President.

Owens, Emily. 2011. Are underground markets really more violent? Evidence from early 20th century America. *American Law and Economics Review* 13 (1): 1–44.

Pacula, R. 1998a. Does increasing the beer tax reduce marijuana consumption? *Journal of Health Economics* 17 (5): 557–85.

Pacula, R. 1998b. Adolescent alcohol and marijuana consumption: Is there really a gateway effect? Working paper 6348. NBER, Cambridge, MA.

Rice, Dorothy. 1999. Economic costs of substance abuse. *Proceedings of the Association of American Physicians* 111 (2): 119–25.

Rydell, C. Peter and Everingham, Susan. 1994. *Controlling Cocaine: Supply versus Demand Programs.* Santa Monica, CA: Rand Corporation Press, RAND Drug Policy Research Center.

Specter, Michael. 2011. Getting a fix. *New Yorker* (October): 17.

Thies, Clifford, and Charles Register. 1993. Decriminalization of marijuana and the demand for alcohol, marijuana and cocaine. *Social Science Journal* 30 (4): 385–99.

United Nations Office on Drugs and Crime. 2009. World Drug Report 2009. Available at: http://www.unodc.org/documents/wdr/WDR_2009/WDR2009_eng_web.pdf.

Viscusi, Kip. 1991. Toward a proper role for hazard warnings in products liability cases. *Journal of Products Liability* 13: 139–63.

Weiner, Robert. 2009. Address in Washington, DC, June 14.

Williams, J., R. Pacula, F. Chaloupka, and H. Wechsler. 2001. Alcohol and marijuana use among college students: Economic complements or substitutes? Working paper 8401. NBER, Cambridge, MA.

World Health Organization. 2011. *Global Status Report on Alcohol and Health.* Available at: http://www.who.int/substance_abuse/publications/global_alcohol_report/msbgsru profiles.pdf.

3 Mechanism Experiments for Crime Policy

Jens Ludwig, Jeffrey R. Kling, and Sendhil
Mullainathan

3.1 Introduction

Randomized controlled trials are increasingly used to evaluate policies, including in the area of crime policy research. For example, solicitations for research proposals from the US Department of Justice's (DOJ) National Institute of Justice now regularly prioritize studies that randomize people to treatment or control conditions. This trend has been spurred in part by numerous independent groups—the Coalition for Evidence-Based Policy, the Campbell Collaboration, an international network of researchers hosted by the Norwegian Knowledge Center for the Health Services, the Poverty Action Lab, and Innovations for Poverty Action—that promote policy experimentation. Others however question the wisdom of this trend. A vigorous debate has arisen around the value of experimental methods for informing policy (e.g., Angrist and Pischke 2009, 2010; Banerjee and Duflo 2009; Deaton 2010; Heckman 2010; Imbens 2010). We argue this debate has often been framed too narrowly on experimental versus nonexperimental methods. An important distinction *between* experimental methods has been overlooked.

Suppose that a policy maker has already decided on using an experiment. She faces a design problem. Given a fixed budget, how should she design her experiment to maximize policy-relevant information? The answer seems obvious: replicate the policy as it would be implemented at scale, and randomly assign units (people or sites of the sort that would be targeted by the policy) to treatment and control conditions. The design challenges involve selecting the most cost effective units of randomization and the data collection strategies. We call the resulting experiments *policy evaluations*. In practice, most policy experimentation involves policy evaluations. Yet in some (practically relevant) situations these are not the best experiments to use—even if the sole goal is to help inform policy decisions.

A simple example illustrates our point. Suppose that DOJ wanted to help local police chiefs decide whether to implement "broken windows" policing, which is based on the theory that police should pay more attention to enforcing minor crimes like graffiti or vandalism because they can serve as a "signal that no one cares" and thereby accelerate more serious forms of criminal behavior (Kelling and Wilson 1982, p. 31). Suppose that there is no credibly exogenous source of variation in the implementation or intensity of broken windows policing across areas, which rules out the opportunity for a low-cost study of an existing natural experiment (Meyer 1995; Angrist and Pischke 2009). To an experimentally minded economist, the most obvious next step goes something like: DOJ should choose a representative sample of cities, randomly select half of their high-crime areas to receive broken windows policing (or perhaps randomly assign half the cities to get citywide broken windows policing), and carry out a traditional *policy evaluation*.

Now consider an alternative experiment: Buy a small fleet of used cars. Break the windows of half of them. Park the cars in a randomly selected subset of neighborhoods, and then measure whether more serious crimes increase in response. What might seem like a fanciful example is actually the basic research design used in the 1960s study by Stanford psychologist Philip Zimbardo that helped motivate the broken windows theory (Kelling and Wilson 1982, p. 31),[1] which in turn led to the implementation of broken windows policing at massive scale in New York City during the 1990s. One could, of course, perform variants, such as cleaning up (rather than adding) disorder to randomly selected neighborhoods, or focusing on other small crimes; or one could even hire young men to wear the standard-issue uniform for drug distribution (plain white t-shirt, baggy jeans, Timberland boots) and have them loiter at randomly selected street corners. This *mechanism experiment* does not test a policy: it directly tests the causal mechanism that underlies the broken windows policy.

Which experiment would be more useful for public policy? Partly it's an issue of staging. Suppose that the mechanism experiment failed to find the causal mechanism operative. Would we even need to run a policy evaluation? If (and this is the key assumption) the mechanism experiment weakened policy makers' belief in broken windows policing, then we can stop. Running the (far cheaper) mechanism experiment first serves as a valuable screen. Conversely, if the mechanism experiment found very strong effects, we might now run a policy evaluation to calibrate magnitudes. Or, depending on the costs of the policy evaluation, the magnitudes found in the mechanism experiment, and what else we think we already know about the policing and crime "production functions," we may even choose to adopt the policy straightaway.

Mechanism experiments more carefully incorporate prior knowledge and can be designed to maximize information in the places where the policy maker needs to know the most. In our broken windows example, suppose that there is general agreement about the list of minor offenses that might plausibly accelerate more serious crimes (i.e., the list of candidate mediating mechanisms M in figure 3.1). Suppose (from previous work) that we also know the elasticity of minor offenses with respect to policing ($P \to M$ in figure 3.1). What policy makers do not know is the accelerator: by how much will reducing minor offenses cascade into reducing other offenses. The mechanism experiment estimates the parameter about which there is the greatest uncertainty or disagreement ($M \to Y$ in figure 3.1). In contrast, a policy evaluation that measures the policy's impact on serious crimes, $P \to Y$, also provides information about the crime accelerator, but with more noise because it combines the variability in crime outcomes with the variability in the impact of policing on minor crimes in any given city/year combination. With enough sample (i.e., money), one could recover the ($M \to Y$) link. In a world of limited resources, mechanism experiments concentrate resources on estimating the parameters that are most decision-relevant.

We argue that mechanism experiments should play a more central role in the policy process. The broken windows example is not an

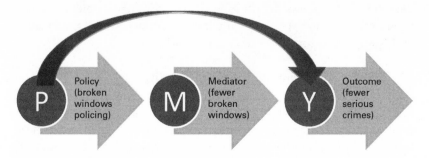

Figure 3.1
Logic model for broken windows policing

isolated case: many policies have theories built into them, even if they are sometimes just implicit. Often these theories can be tested more cost-effectively and precisely with experiments that do not mimic real (or even feasible) policies. Our argument runs counter to the critique leveled by some economists against the large-scale government social experiments of the 1970s and 1980s for "not necessarily test[ing] real policy options" (Harris 1985, p. 161). We argue that some of these experiments, because they highlight mechanisms, could have far-reaching *policy* value. Social scientists already value mechanism experiments because they contribute to building knowledge. Our argument is that *even if the sole goal were informing policy*, mechanism experiments play a crucial, underappreciated role.

This distinction between mechanism experiments and "policy evaluations" could also change the debate between about the use of experimentation to guide policy. We feel many of the criticisms of experimentation are really criticisms of policy evaluations—particularly "black-box" policy evaluations where the mechanisms through which the policy may affect outcomes are numerous or unclear. Deaton (2010, p. 246), for example, fears experimentation generates information that is too "narrow and local" to be of much use for policy. While this can also be true for mechanism experiments, because of their emphasis on *how* programs work, the knowledge gained can extend to a broader range of situations.

The next section of the chapter provides a brief review of how economists have thought about experimentation and the problem of forecasting the effects of different types of policies in different settings—that is, the challenge of external validity. We then discuss what mechanism experiments can teach us, focusing on a variety of different crime-policy applications. We then suggest a framework to help think about the conditions under which the most policy-relevant information comes from a mechanism experiment, a policy evaluation, or both, and close with suggestions for future research.

3.2 Policy Experiments and External Validity

Policy-making is inevitably about prediction. What is the effect of some existing policy when implemented in the future, or in some new setting? Or what is the effect of some entirely new policy? A useful way to think about the types of research activities that help answer these questions comes from Wolpin (2007) and Todd and Wolpin (2008). They distinguish between *ex post policy evaluation*—understanding what happened as the result of a policy or program that was actually implemented—and *ex ante policy evaluation*, which DiNardo and Lee (2010, p. 2) describe as beginning "with an explicit understanding that the program that was actually run may not be the one that corresponds to a particular policy of interest. Here the goal is not descriptive, but instead predictive. What would be the impact if we expanded eligibility of the program? What would the effects of a similar program be if it were run at a national (as opposed to a local) level? Or if it were run today (as opposed to twenty years ago)? It is essentially a problem of forecasting or extrapolating, with the goal of achieving a high degree of external validity."

The challenge in making policy forecasts from *ex post* evaluations stems from the possibility that treatments may interact with characteristics of the policy's setting—including the target population, time period, or other contextual factors. The effects of broken windows policing in Evanston, an affluent North Shore suburb of Chicago, may differ from the policy's effects when implemented in distressed neighborhoods on the south side of Chicago. Those features of a policy's setting (or of the policy itself) that may influence the policy's impacts are what the research literature outside of economics calls *moderators*. We argue that the type of experiment that is most useful for addressing this challenge and informing policy forecasts depends on what researchers believe they know about a policy's mechanisms, which noneconomists sometimes also call *mediators*.

At one extreme are situations in which researchers do not know very much about a policy's candidate mechanisms—the list of plausible mechanisms might be overwhelmingly long, or we might have little sense for whether the mechanisms potentially interact or even work at cross purposes, or what (if any) aspects of the relevant causal chain operate in ways that are invariant across policy settings. The standard approach has been to carry out policy evaluations in as many settings as possible of the sort in which the policy might actually be implemented. As Cook and Campbell (1979) note, "tests of the extent to which one can generalize across various kinds of persons, settings and times are, in essence, tests of statistical interactions. . . . In the last analysis, external validity . . . is a matter of replication" (pp. 73, 78). Angrist and Pischke (2010, pp. 23–24) argue "a constructive response to the specificity of a given research design is to look for more evidence, so that a more general picture begins to emerge . . . the process of accumulating empirical evidence is rarely sexy in the unfolding, but accumulation is the necessary road along which results become more general."

As mentioned above, there is an active debate within the economics profession about the value of this type of research program, focused largely on issues of external validity. Under this approach we forecast a policy's effects in some setting using previous tests of the policy in similar settings—that is, we try to match on the policy's candidate moderators (e.g., see Hotz, Imbens, and Mortimer 2005; Cole and Stuart 2010; Imbens 2010; Stuart et al. 2011). One challenge is that without some understanding of a policy's mechanisms, how do we decide which aspects of the policy or its setting is a potentially important moderator? Another challenge comes from the fact that policy evaluations are costly, and so we will never be able to carry out evaluations of ever candidate policy of interest in every potentially relevant setting. We have nothing new to add to this debate, which we view as largely orthogonal to the main argument we advance in this chapter.

The type of situation to which our chapter is relevant arises when researchers have some beliefs about the mechanisms through which a policy influences social welfare. One way researchers currently use such beliefs is by interpreting the results of randomized experiments through the lens of a particular structural model (Wolpin 2007; Todd and Wolpin 2008; Heckman 2010; Imbens 2010). This approach takes the policy experiment that is run as given, imposes some assumptions after the fact about the policy's mechanisms, fits the model, then forecasts the effects of a wide range of policies and settings. This approach can make sense when we have sufficiently sharp prior beliefs about the way the world works to be confident that we have the right structural model, and that the key structural parameters really are structural (i.e., invariant across settings). The structural model substitutes assumptions for data, traded off against the risk that our assumptions are incorrect.

But, if we believe we know something about the mechanisms through which the policy might operate, why limit ourselves to using this information only after a policy evaluation has been designed and carried out? Why not use this information to help inform the design of the experiment that is being run? Why not design experiments that are explicitly focused on isolating the effects of candidate mechanisms? Once our focus shifts to identifying mechanisms, the importance of having close (or even any) correspondence between the interventions we test and the specific policy applications we seek to inform is diminished. The change that this way of thinking implies for the design of our policy experiments is not just cosmetic. The change can be drastic, as we illustrate in the next section.[2]

Mechanism experiments can help with the policy forecasting or external validity problem in two ways. First, improved understanding of a policy's mechanisms can help us predict what aspects of the policy or its setting may moderate the policy's impacts. Second, by taking advantage of what researchers believe they already know mechanism experiments can be less costly than policy evaluations. This means that we can carry out relatively more mechanism experiments in different settings, and help prioritize the types of policies and settings in which we should carry out full-scale policy evaluations.

3.3   Mechanism Experiments

In what follows we illustrate some of the ways in which mechanism experiments can help generate policy-relevant information. Depending on our prior beliefs, mechanism experiments could be useful for guiding crime policy by helping us: (1) rule out candidate policies, (2) expand the set of policy options for which we can forecast effects, (3) prioritize available research funding, (4) concentrate resources on estimating parameters about which we have the most uncertainty or disagreement, and (5) strengthen causal inference with either randomized or natural experiments.

3.3.1   Ruling out Policies

There is growing concern among probation department officials that access to (distance from) social service providers may be a key barrier to participation by probationers living in economically disadvantaged communities, given the limited access to many low-income probationers to private transportation and concerns about excess demand for services in high-poverty areas.

This concern has led to interest in the possibility of creating community-based "one-stop-shopping" centers for probationers that co-locate social service providers and probation officers. Carrying out a policy evaluation of this type of intervention would be expensive because the unit of randomization is the community, the cost per community is high, and the number of communities needed to have adequate statistical power is large.

Now consider the following mechanism experiment that could be carried out instead: Enroll a sample of probationers living in high-poverty neighborhoods, and randomly assign some of them to receive a free (to them) subscription to a car-sharing service (e.g., Zipcar or I-GO) that would reduce the costs of accessing social service providers located throughout the metropolitan area. By using individuals as the unit of randomization, rather than communities, this mechanism experiment would be much less expensive than the more "realistic" policy evaluation. Randomizing people rather than neighborhoods also lets us test a "treatment dose" that is much more intensive than what could be obtained with any realistic policy intervention, since a free car-sharing subscription would enable probationers to access a far wider range of social services across the metro area than could ever be hoped to bring into a single neighborhood.

Imagine we found that a free car-sharing subscription had no effect on the outcomes of probationers such as recidivism or (legal) earnings. Suppose that we also believed that social interactions are not very important in shaping the willingness of people to utilize social services, and that reducing the effective price of accessing social services never *reduces* the chances of utilizing them (i.e., there is a monotonic relationship between the treatment dose and the treatment response). In that case null results from our mechanism experiment would lead us to predict that *any* sort of policy that tried to improve access to social services would (on its own) be unlikely to improve key probation outcomes such as recidivism and employment.

If we had more uncertainty about the role of social interactions in affecting social service utilization rates, then different mechanism-experiment designs would be required. If we believed that social interactions might be important determinants of people's willingness to utilize social services, then we would need a more costly experiment with three randomized arms, not just two—a control group, a treatment arm that received a free car-sharing subscription service for themselves, and a treatment arm that received a car-sharing subscription for themselves and for a limited number of other friends whom the probationer designated ("buddy subscriptions").[4] If we thought that preferences about social service utilization were determined at a still larger macro level, we would have to randomly assign entire communities to receive car-sharing subscriptions. A community-level test of access to shared cars could still wind up being less expensive than a policy evaluation of community-based social services, because of the large up-front costs associated with establishing new social service providers in potentially underserved neighborhoods. But if we thought that attitudes about social service utilization changed very slowly over time, and at the community level, then we would have to commit to providing free car-sharing subscriptions for entire communities for extended periods of time—at which point there might be little cost advantage compared to a policy evaluation of community-based social services.

The possibility of using a mechanism experiment to learn more about community-based social service provision is not an isolated example. Consider the question of whether smaller high schools improve student achievement, relevant to economists interested in crime given the established link between schooling and criminal involvement. Possible mechanisms through which this might occur include stronger relationships between students and school staff, having students spend more time around peers who share their interests, and providing school administrators with more autonomy (Bloom et al. 2010). Instead of immediately carrying out a full-scale, very costly policy evaluation of small schools, why not first carry out a mechanism experiment focused on bonding instead? Take a representative sample of charter schools, which already provide administrators with autonomy. Randomly assign some teachers to be offered the chance to earn overtime pay by working after school and weekends with small, randomly selected groups of students in an effort to promote faculty-to-student and student-to-student bonding. Evidence that this intervention was capable of promoting student engagement and academic outcomes would suggest the value of carrying out a large-scale policy evaluation. But evidence that even what H. L. Mencken (1946) would call a "horse-doctor's dose" of extra bonding did not affect student outcomes would greatly reduce the motivation to carry out a large-scale policy evaluation of smaller schools.

3.3.2 Expand the Set of Policies and Settings for Which We Can Forecast Policy Impacts

Ruling out entire classes of policy interventions is easier when our experiments test interventions that are as intensive (or more) as anything that could be accomplished by actual policies. Testing unrealistically intensive treatment arms also has the benefit of letting us forecast the effects of a wide range of more realistic policy options in those cases when, despite Rossi's Iron Law[3], our policy experiments do identify successful interventions. As Hausman and Wise (1985, p. 194–95) noted a quarter-century ago: "If, for policy purposes, it is desirable to estimate the effects of possible programs not described by treatments, then interpolations can be made between estimated treatment effects. If the experimental treatments are at the bounds of possible programs, then of course this calculation is easier."

Consider, for example, the US Department of Housing and Urban Development's Moving to Opportunity (MTO) demonstration, which was launched in the 1990s to help learn more about the effects of neighborhood environments on low-income families—including the involvement of youth in delinquency and violence. Since 1994, MTO enrolled around 4,600 low-income public housing families with children and randomly assigned them into three groups: (1) a *traditional voucher group*, which received a standard housing voucher that subsidizes them to live in private-market housing; (2) a *low-poverty voucher group* that received a standard housing voucher similar to what was received by the traditional voucher group, with the exception that the voucher could only be redeemed in Census tracts with 1990 poverty rates below 10 percent; and (3) a *control group*, which received no additional services.

Assignment to the low-poverty voucher group led to more sizable changes in neighborhood poverty and other neighborhood characteristics than did assignment to the traditional voucher group (Ludwig et al. 2008). The traditional voucher treatment did not have many detectable impacts on the outcomes of MTO parents or children 4 to 7 years after baseline (Kling, Ludwig, and Katz 2005; Sanbonmatsu et al. 2006; Kling, Liebman, and Katz 2007; Fortson and Sanbonmatsu 2010). The low-poverty voucher treatment generated a more complicated pattern of impacts. For adults, the low-poverty voucher treatment did not product detectable changes in labor market or other economic outcomes, but did have important effects on mental health and some physical health outcomes, including obesity and diabetes (Ludwig et al. 2011). The low-poverty voucher did not affect children's schooling outcomes, perhaps because MTO moves wound up generating only modest changes in school quality, and had effects on risky behavior that for the most part differed by gender—with girls doing better and boys doing worse as a result of these moves (see also Clampet-Lundquist et al. 2011). However, the one youth outcome for which there were sizable MTO impacts 4 to 7 years after baseline even for boys was violent-crime arrests.

Two of us (Kling and Ludwig) have worked on MTO for many years, and have often heard the reaction that the traditional voucher treatment is more policy-relevant and interesting than the low-poverty voucher treatment, because only the former corresponds to a realistic policy option. But it was the low-poverty voucher that generated a sufficiently large "treatment dose" to enable researchers to learn that *something* about neighborhood environments *can* matter for important outcomes like youth violence. For this reason, findings from the low-poverty voucher have been very influential in housing and criminal-justice policy circles.

3.3.3 Prioritize Research Funding

If a mechanism experiment tested the most intensive imaginable intervention to improve access to social services for probationers living in high-poverty areas, and found no effect on recidivism or other outcomes, we would rule out not only the value of policies to address social-service access but also, obviously, the value of policy evaluations to test those types of policies. Null results from a policy evaluation of a more realistic but less-intensive intervention would not let us shut down an entire line of research inquiry in the same way, since it would always be possible to imagine that a slightly more intensive intervention might yield more promising results.

Encouraging results from a mechanism experiment would help us decide where to invest additional research funding, and might also help shape the types of policies that we subjected to full-scale policy evaluations. Suppose, for example, that we found that a free subscription to a car-sharing service only changed the utilization of, say, education programs. (This might occur because education programs often require participation over extended periods, so that geographic distance is more of a barrier than with services that require fewer visits.) This finding might lead policy makers to conclude that the right policy to evaluate is not just a costly effort to move a comprehensive set of social services into high-poverty areas but also (or perhaps instead) a lower cost program to focus more narrowly on improving educational services in distressed neighborhoods.

3.3.4 Concentrate Resources on Estimating Parameters about which We Are Most Uncertain

At the start of this chapter we noted that mechanism experiments can help us concentrate resources on estimating parameters about which we have the most uncertainty or disagreement. As another example along these lines, suppose that policy makers are concerned about the secondary consequences of psychosocial stress on poor families, including health impacts. For families in poor urban areas, one of the most important sources of stress is crime—particularly gun crime (Cook and Ludwig 2000; Kling, Liebman, and Katz 2005; Kling, Ludwig, and Katz 2005). Policy makers could sponsor a full-scale evaluation of targeted police patrols against illegal guns in high-crime areas, and then test the impacts on obesity and other health outcomes. But previous work already tells us something about this intervention's effects on crime (Cohen and Ludwig 2003), and perhaps also about the effect of crime on stress (Buka et al. 2001). The new information from this experiment is primarily about the stress $\rightarrow$ obesity link. But for a given budget we could learn more about the stress $\rightarrow$ obesity pathway (and how that might vary across settings) by carrying out a mechanism experiment that enrolled residents of high-crime areas and assigned some to, say, a meditation-based stress-reduction program (Kabat-Zinn et al. 1992).

In other situations we might be most uncertain about the link between our policy levers and key mediating mechanisms ($P \rightarrow M$). For example, we might think that the MTO experiment described above tells us about the link between neighborhood conditions and youth violence involvement, or $M \rightarrow Y$ (Kling, Ludwig, and Katz 2005). But we might not understand the effects of policies like mixed-income developments to change the socioeconomic composition of communities, given uncertainty about the housing subsidies that would be necessary to get middle-income families to live in planned mixed-income developments. In situations like this, measures of community socioeconomic composition become what medical researchers call "surrogate clinical endpoints," which then become the dependent variables of interest for our experiments. The idea of focusing selectively on testing individual links in a causal chain also raises the possibility of using mechanism experiments to compress the timetable required to learn about the long-term effects of some policy, by testing different sequential links in a causal chain simultaneously.

Perhaps less obvious is the value of carrying out multiple experiments that use different policy levers to manipulate the same mechanism, given the great difficulty of determining what is the true mediating mechanism that links a policy to an outcome, rather than just a proxy for the mediating variable that really matters.[5] Showing that the effects of reduced stress on obesity is the same regardless of whether stress levels are modified through a meditation program or by some sort of anti–gun policing program would be informative about whether the mediating mechanism of stress is "nonimplementation specific," to use John DiNardo's term, or what Heckman (2010) calls "policy invariant."

A final example about the ability of mechanism experiments to focus research resources comes from the possibility of avoiding the need to carry out full-blown "synergy" (or "kitchen sink") experiments of the sort that the federal government regularly sponsors, like Jobs Plus. This experiment tested the combined effects of providing public housing residents with financial incentives for work (relief from the "HUD tax" on earnings that comes from setting rent contributions as a fixed share of income), employment and training services, and efforts to improve "community support for work," and so is relevant for crime policy given longstanding interest in the potential connection between labor market outcomes and criminal involvement. Previous studies have already examined the effects of the first two program ingredients when administered independently, while the potential value of community support for work is suggested by the work of Wilson (1987, 1996) among others. The key program theory of Jobs Plus is that these three mechanisms interact, and so have more-than-additive effects on labor market outcomes (Bloom, Riccio, and Verma 2005). Across six cities, Jobs Plus randomly assigned entire housing projects to either a control group, or a program group in which residents received the bundle of Jobs Plus services.

We could have instead carried out a mechanism experiment that enrolled a slightly less disadvantaged (and hence slightly less directly policy-relevant) study sample that needed one or two but not all three of the mechanisms the Jobs Plus theory suggests are needed for labor market success. Imagine enrolling people who applied for means-tested housing assistance, which in some cities is rationed using randomized lotteries (Jacob and Ludwig 2011), and are already living in neighborhoods with high employment rates. Then we randomly assign some of them to receive employment and training services. A test of the Jobs Plus "synergy" theory comes from comparing the response to these services for those who were versus were not lucky enough to be randomly assigned a housing subsidy. Our proposed mechanism experiment conserves resources by reducing the dimensionality of the experimental intervention.

3.3.5   Help Strengthen Causal Inference

Mechanism experiments can help us interpret the results of policy evaluations, including null findings. Once we know that some mechanism is linked to an outcome, the first thing we would check upon seeing a zero impact in a full-scale policy evaluation is whether the policy successfully changed the mediator. Evidence that the mediator was unchanged would suggest the potential value of testing other policies that might generate larger changes in the mediator. Without the mechanism experiment, we wouldn't be sure whether it would be worth following up a null impact from a policy evaluation with more research in that area.

Mechanism experiments can also strengthen the basis for causal inference with natural-experiment policy evaluations. Imagine a simple pre-post study of aggregate US level data of a change in Medicaid policies that reduced out-of-pocket costs to poor adults from having, say, tattoo removal. Suppose that the study found that after the policy change, tattoo removal rates among high school dropout minority men increase, and arrest rates for this group decrease. Absent any additional information, this study design would not provide compelling evidence about the link between the Medicaid policy change and crime, given the large number of other factors that are changing over time that influence crime rates. But there would seem to be far fewer confounding threats to estimating the effect of the policy on tattoo removal rates (the $P \to M$ link) from a simple pre-post comparison. Additional evidence about the mechanism (the $M \to Y$ link between tattoo removal and criminality) would enable us to infer how much of the time trend in crime rates was due to the Medicaid policy change.

New mechanism experiments could even be designed with the explicit goal of better understanding existing natural experiment findings. For example, numerous studies of compulsory schooling laws document the causal relationship of educational attainment with earnings, crime, health, and other outcomes (Oreopoulos and Salvanes 2009). Less well understood are the mechanisms behind this relationship. Is it that schooling affects academic skills? Or specific vocational skills? Or social-cognitive skills? The answer is relevant for thinking about how we should deploy the $485 billion the United States spends each year on K–12 public schooling (US Census Bureau 2011, tab. 258). Why not spend a few million dollars on a mechanism experiment that assigns youth to curricula or supplemental activities that emphasize different specific skills, to better understand the mechanisms behind the effects of compulsory schooling laws?

3.4   When Can Mechanism Experiments Be Useful?

The purpose of our chapter is *not* to argue that economists should *only* carry out mechanism experiments, or that mechanism experiments are "better" than policy evaluations. Our main point is that given the current paucity of mechanism experiments designed to help answer policy questions, on the margin we think that economists should be doing more of them.

Table 3.1 presents a framework for thinking about the conditions under which mechanism experiments can help inform policy decisions. Under a very particular set of conditions, mechanism experiments may by themselves be sufficient to guide policy decisions. More common are likely to be scenarios in which mechanism experiments and traditional policy evaluations (which could include natural as well as randomized experiments) are complementary. Under some circumstances mechanism experiments might not even be that helpful, and a more useful approach would be to just go right to running a black-box policy evaluation.

3.4.1   When Mechanism Experiments Can Be Helpful

In order for a mechanism experiment to make any sense at all, we need to believe that we know at least something about the candidate mechanisms through which a policy might affect the outcomes of ultimate policy concern (the right-hand column of table 3.1).

Under some circumstances mechanism experiments might be sufficient to guide policy design. We need to believe that the list of candidate mechanisms through which a policy might affect outcomes is fairly short, or that the long list of potentially relevant mechanisms do not interact or work at cross purposes (a short list of candidate mechanisms that could interact would not by itself preclude a mechanism experiment). Depending on the application, we might need to know something already about other parts of the causal chain. At the very least we would need to be confident that existing systems are capable of reliably delivering the policies that activate key mechanisms. Even then, if the cost of carrying out a policy evaluation were low enough relative to the policy stakes, we would probably still wish to carry out

Table 3.1
Policy experiment checklist

	Prior beliefs/understanding of mechanisms	
	Low	High
Implications for experimental design	Run a policy evaluation OR Do more basic science; multiple methods to uncover mechanisms	Run a mechanism experiment to rule out policies (and policy evaluations) OR Run mechanism experiment to help rule in policies Either follow with full policy evaluation (depending on costs of policy evaluation, and potential program benefits/scale), or use results of mechanism experiment for calibration and structural estimation for key parameters for benefit–cost calculations
Implications for policy forecasting/external validity	Run multiple policy evaluations; carry out policy forecasting by matching to estimates derived from similar policies and settings (candidate moderators) Debate: Which characteristics to match on? Where do these come from?	Use mechanism knowledge to measure characteristics of policy and setting (moderators) for policy forecasting Can run new mechanism experiments to test in different settings prior to carrying out policy evaluations in those settings

a policy evaluation to improve our policy forecast. We would settle for just a mechanism experiment if the costs of carrying out a policy evaluation were prohibitive, or the policy stakes were low.

3.4.2   Do Mechanism Experiments plus Policy Evaluations

One reason it would make sense to follow a mechanism experiment that had encouraging results with a full-blown policy evaluation would be to learn more about other parts of the causal chain, such as when there is implementation uncertainty. For example, medical researchers distinguish between "efficacy trials," which are small-scale research trials of model programs carried out with high fidelity, and "effectiveness trials" that test the effects of some intervention carried out under field conditions at scale. Efficacy trials can be thought of as a type of mechanism experiment, since having a bespectacled, laptop-toting professor loom over the program's implementation is not usually standard operating procedure. Compared to efficacy trials, larger-scale effectiveness trials often have more program attrition, weaker training for service providers, weaker implementation monitoring, and smaller impacts (Lipsey et al. 2007).

As noted above, prior evidence from mechanism experiments can enhance the efficiency of our portfolio of policy evaluations by helping us figure out which evaluations are worth running. This includes carrying out mechanism experiments in different settings to determine where it is worth trying a policy evaluation.

Learning about the mechanisms through which a policy affects outcomes can also help predict which aspects of the policy or its settings will moderate the policy's impacts, although it is worth keeping in mind that the correspondence between mechanisms and moderators is far from perfect. For example, the well-known Tennessee STAR experiment found that reducing class sizes in elementary school improved learning outcomes (Krueger 1999; Schanzenbach 2007). Lazear (2001) argues that a key mechanism for these class-size effects is the reduced chance that instructional time in a given classroom is diverted by disruptive students, which helps explain why in the STAR experiment lower income and minority students seemed to benefit the most. But when California had to hire a large number of teachers to enact class-size reduction statewide, average teacher quality seemed to decline, particularly in those schools serving disproportionately low-income and minority students (Jepsen and Rivkin 2009). Thus teacher quality turned out to be a surprising mechanism (at least to California policy makers). Student background wound up being a moderator that influenced different parts of the causal chain in different ways.

3.4.3   Do Some Combination of "Basic Science" and Policy Evaluation

In some situations researchers do not yet know enough to narrow down the list of candidate mechanisms through which a policy operates, or worry that a policy's long list of candidate mechanisms might interact (or if some might work at cross purposes)—represented by the first column of table 3.1. The debate within the economics profession is about whether it is best under these circumstances to carry out "basic science" studies or to carry out policy evaluations. The extreme position is that policy evaluations can *never* be useful for policy purposes, which strikes us as unlikely to be correct.

In the case of Moving to Opportunity, for example, observational studies going back to the 1920s had shown that neighborhood attributes are correlated with behavioral outcomes, even after controlling for individual- and family-level factors. Policymakers need to know whether such correlations reflect an underlying causal relationship, which is relevant to decisions like whether to whether to devote resources to building public housing or to private-market rent subsidies, or whether to allow suburban townships to limit zoning approval for low-cost housing. Given the large number of potentially interacting mechanisms through which residential location might affect behavior and well-being, it is not clear that anything short of a black-box policy evaluation would have much value in guiding these policy decisions.

One common criticism of black-box policy evaluations is that we cannot understand the characteristics that explain heterogeneity of treatment effects (i.e., a policy's moderators) without understanding the policy's key mediating mechanisms. While there is no question that evidence about mechanisms is tremendously valuable, we believe that it is not correct that black-box evaluations are never useful.

Consider the example of statins, which have been used since the late 1980s[6] and shown in numerous randomized clinical trials to reduce the risk of heart disease and overall mortality (Ross et al. 1999; Gotto 2003). Statins were originally thought to prevent heart attacks by lowering cholesterol levels in the blood, which in turn reduced the chance of plaque buildup. But meta-analyses of black-box clinical trials showed that statins improved health outcomes even among people who already had relatively low levels of blood cholesterol at baseline (Golomb et al.

2004; Wilt et al. 2004; Thavendiranathan et al. 2004). Moreover these meta-analyses showed that the cardiovascular benefits of statins seemed to occur too rapidly after onset of treatment to be explained by the effects of statins on plaque accumulation (Golomb et al. 2008). The leading hypothesis—at least for now—is that statins reduce heart attacks partly by reducing inflammation (Zhang et al. 2010) or blood pressure (Golomb et al. 2008).

The key point for present purposes is that right now we don't really know exactly why statins reduce heart attacks. Yet meta-analyses of black-box clinical trial studies show that they clearly do improve health, and can also tell us something about how their effects on health are moderated by patient characteristics such as age, gender, and baseline health status. Our limited understanding of the mechanisms through which statins work has not prevented them from becoming one of the world's top-selling drug classes, to the extent that some medical experts have suggested that they should be "put into the water supply" (Golomb et al. 2004, p. 154).

A similar point was made during congressional testimony in 1971 by Sidney Farber, the "godfather of cancer research," who argued (as quoted in *Fortune*, 2007): "We cannot wait for full understanding; the 325,000 patients with cancer who are going to die this year cannot wait; nor it is necessary, to make great progress in the cure of cancer, for us to have the full solution of all the problems of basic research. . . . The history of medicine is replete with examples of cures obtained years, decades, and even centuries before the mechanism of action was understood for these cures—from vaccination, to digitalis, to aspirin."[7]

This is not to say that later understanding of mechanisms does not generate tremendous benefits to society. For example, learning more about how chemotherapy works has dramatically increased the benefit–cost ratio of such treatments over time. But evidence that an intervention works, even if we don't understand why, is better than not having access to that intervention at all. Repeated black-box experiments can eventually help us learn something about the policy's moderators and, as in our statins example, can also inform our theorizing about candidate mechanisms as well.

3.5 Conclusions

It seems like common sense that the best way to use experiments to inform policy is to test policies. However, we argue here for increased use of randomized experiments that identify behavioral mechanisms that are central to clearly specified policy questions, even if the specific interventions that are tested (or their settings) do not correspond exactly to what policy makers would implement in practice. While our suggestion might seem obvious once articulated, mechanism experiments that are designed to help answer specific policy questions remain rare. We hasten to add that mechanism experiments and traditional policy evaluations are as a general proposition best thought of as complements, rather than substitutes. We need to make greater use of mechanism experiments, on the margin, without fetishizing mechanisms.

The larger question of how to structure experiments to maximize the ability to apply the findings more generally in other contexts opens up a number of potentially fruitful lines of additional research beyond what we have considered here. For example, many people seem to have the intuition that evidence about either the link between policy levers and mechanisms ($P \to M$ from figure 3.1) or between mechanisms and outcomes ($M \to Y$) is more generalizable than evidence about the link between policies and ultimate outcomes of interest ($P \to Y$). It is not hard to think of situations where this is true, but this need not be true in all cases.[8] It would be useful to learn more about how the causal links from $P \to M$ and $M \to Y$ co-vary across contexts, and the extent to which those links reinforce each other or may tend to offset each other.

A second line of investigation that seems worth exploring more is the benefits and costs of policy field experiments (both mechanism experiments and policy evaluations) versus natural experiment studies. On the one hand, sometimes natural experiment studies have designs that are as good as random assignment of treatment because they actually involve random assignment (e.g., see Angrist 1990; Kling 2006; Jacob and Ludwig 2012). More often natural experiment studies must rely on research designs that generate information that is more local than that obtained from randomized experiments (e.g., regression discontinuity), or that is more vulnerable to omitted variables bias. Nevertheless, natural experiment studies circumvent the external validity concerns raised by either randomization bias (the self-selection of people willing to sign up for a randomized experiment; see Heckman 1992; Malani 2006) or selection-partner bias (the willingness of organizations to participate in experiments; see Alcott and Mullainathan 2011). But, with few exceptions, little is currently known about the extent of randomization or selection-partner bias in practice. Alternatively, policy field experiments and natural experiments may be complements in a broader program of research on an issue that involves multiple stages (Kling 2007).

A final question worth considering is the issue of when and how to export results across contexts. While statistical matching of estimates obtained from similar interventions and contexts is fine, as far as it goes, a broader framework would let us incorporate behavioral models, parameters, and prior beliefs into the policy-forecasting exercise. This type of policy forecasting, or *ex ante* policy evaluation, will inevitably require more assumptions, theory and guesswork than *ex post* studies of previous policies (see also Harrison and List 2004, p. 1033). But policy forecasting is in the end at least as important for public policy. As the distinguished physicist Richard Feynman (1964) once argued, "The moment you make statements about a region of experience that you haven't directly seen, then you must be uncertain. But we always must make statements about the regions that we haven't seen, or it's no use in the whole business."

Notes

This is a revised and updated version of a paper previously published by the same authors under the title "Mechanism experiments and policy evaluations," in the *Journal of Economic Perspectives* (Summer 2011), substantial portions of which are reprinted here with permission of the copyright holder, the American Economic Association. For excellent research assistance we thank Laura Brinkman and Michael Reddy. We thank Nava Ashraf, David Autor, Iwan Barankay, Jon Baron, Howard Bloom, Lorenzo Casaburi, Philip Cook, Stefano DellaVigna, John DiNardo, Elbert Huang, Chad Jones, Lawrence Katz, Supreet Kaur, John List, Stephan Meier, David Moore, Steve Pischke, Harold Pollack, Dina Pomeranz, David Reiley, Frank Schilbach, Robert Solow, Tim Taylor, and conference participants at the University of Pennsylvania's Wharton School of Business, the American Economic Association, the America Latina Crime and Policy Network, and the CESifo Venice Summer Institute for comments. For financial support we thank the Russell Sage Foundation (through a Visiting Scholar award to Ludwig). Any errors and all opinions are our own. The views expressed here are those of the authors, and should not be interpreted as those of the Congressional Budget Office.

1. The same design was used more recently by a Dutch team for a study published in *Science* (Keizer et al. 2008).

2. Another relevant observation here is that if we really believe that the key structural parameters in our model are structural, then there is no intrinsic reason that we would need to test a real policy to identify their value.

3. Rossi's Stainless Steel Law of Evaluation holds that "the better designed the impact assessment of a social program, the more likely is the resulting estimate of net impact to

be zero." Rossi's Zinc Law of Evaluation is somewhat less pessimistic in its way: "only those programs that are likely to fail are evaluated" (Rossi 1987).

4. Duflo and Saez (2003) discuss a cleverly designed experiment that used individuals as the unit of analysis but was designed to identify spillover effects. In their experiment, some people in some departments within a company received incentives to visit a benefit fair to learn more about savings plans. They assessed both direct effects of the information, and effects of information spillovers (from comparisons of the outcomes of the nonincentivized individuals in incentivized departments to individuals in nonincentivized departments). The information diffused through the experiment had a noticeable impact on plan participation.

5. Some simple notation suggested to us by Steve Pischke helps illustrate the problem. Let P be the policy, M be the mediator, Y be the outcome (with $P \to M \to Y$ as in figure 3.1), with $M = U + V$, $cov(U, V) = 0$, $cov(U, Y) = 0$, and $cov(V, Y) > 0$. That is, only the V part of M is causally related to Y. In population data we see $cov(M, Y) > 0$. In this example, M is an implementation specific mediator because policies that change the V part of M will change Y, but policies that change only the U part of M will not influence Y.

6. Thanks to Elbert Huang and Harold Pollack for this example.

7. Thanks to Harold Pollack for suggesting this quotation. At the risk of overemphasizing the point, one more example comes from two of the most important mental health drug discoveries—lithium, which is used to treat bipolar disorder, and Thorazine, which is used to treat psychosis. Modern medicine has very little understanding of why either medicine works in helping patients (Harris 2011).

8. Imagine a case with a single candidate mediator and outcome of interest. Whether either of the individual links in this causal chain ($P \to M$ or $M \to Y$) is more stable across contexts than is the total effect of the policy on the outcome, $P \to Y$, depends in part on how $P \to M$ and $M \to Y$ co-vary across contexts. It is not hard to imagine cases in which the two relationships negatively co-vary, so the effect of the policy on the outcome is more stable across situations than the link between the policy and mediator or the mediator and outcome. Suppose that in neighborhoods where adoption of broken windows policing leads to relatively larger increases in arrests for minor offenses, the stigma of arrest declines, and so the deterrent effect of the prospect of being arrested goes down. Or, suppose that in areas where local residents are not very easily deterred by the prospect of being arrested, policy makers respond by implementing this policing strategy in a way that leads to relatively larger numbers of minor arrests.

References

Angrist, Joshua D. 1990. Lifetime earnings and the Vietnam era draft lottery: Evidence from Social Security administrative records. *American Economic Review* 80: 313–35.

Angrist, Joshua D., and Jorn-Steffen Pischke. 2009. *Mostly Harmless Econometrics*. Princeton: Princeton University Press.

Angrist, Joshua D., and Jorn-Steffen Pischke. 2010. The credibility revolution in empirical economics: How better research design is taking the con out of econometrics. *Journal of Economic Perspectives* 24 (2): 3–30.

Banerjee, Abhijit V., and Esther Duflo. 2009. The experimental approach to development economics. *Annual Review of Economics* 1: 151–78.

Bloom, Howard S., James A. Riccio, and Nandita Verma. 2005. *Promoting Work in Public Housing: The Effectiveness of Jobs-Plus.* New York: MDRC.

Bloom, Howard S., Saskia Levy Thompson, and Rebecca Unterman. 2010. *Transforming the High School Experience: How New York City's Small Schools Are Boosting Student Achievement and Graduation Rates.* New York: MDRC.

Buka, Stephen L., Theresa L. Stichick, Isolde Birdthistle, and Felton J. Earls. 2001. Youth exposure to violence: Prevalence, risks, and consequences. *American Journal of Orthopsychiatry* 71 (3):298–310.

Clampet-Lundquist, Susan, Kathryn Edin, Jeffrey R. Kling, and Greg J. Duncan. 2011. Moving at-risk youth out of high-risk neighborhoods: Why girls fare better than boys. *American Journal of Sociology* 116 (4): 1154–89.

Cohen, Jacqueline, and Jens Ludwig. 2003. Policing crime guns. In Jens Ludwig and Philip J. Cook, eds., *Evaluating Gun Policy.* Washington, DC: Brookings Institution Press, 217–50.

Cole, Stephen R., and Elizabeth A. Stuart. 2010. Generalizing evidence from randomized clinical trials to target populations: The ACTG 320 trial. *American Journal of Epidemiology* 172 (1): 107–15.

Cook, Philip J., and Jens Ludwig. 2000. *Gun Violence: The Real Costs.* New York: Oxford University Press.

Cook, Thomas D., and Donald T. Campbell. 1979. *Quasi-experimentation: Design and Analysis Issues for Field Settings.* Boston: Houghton Mifflin.

Deaton, Angus. 2010. Instruments, randomization, and learning about development. *Journal of Economic Literature* 48: 424–55.

DiNardo, John, and David S. Lee. 2010. Program evaluation and research designs. Working paper 16016. NBER, Cambridge, MA.

Duflo, Esther, and Emmanuel Saez. 2003. The role of information and social interactions in retirement plan decisions: Evidence From a randomized experiment. *Quarterly Journal of Economics* 118 (3): 815–42.

Feynman, Richard. 1964. The great conservation principles. The Messenger Series. Quotation starts at 38:48. Available at: http://research.microsoft.com/apps/tools/tuva/index.html#data=4|84edf183-7993-4b5b-9050-7ea34f236045||.

Fortson, Jane G., and Lisa Sanbonmatsu. 2010. Child health and neighborhood conditions: Results from a randomized housing voucher experiment. *Journal of Human Resources* 45 (4): 840–64.

Fortune, Clifton Leaf. 2007. Why we're losing the war on cancer (and how to win it). CNN Health, January 9. Available at: http://articles.cnn.com/2007-01-09/health/fortune.leaf.waroncancer_1_gamma-rays-testicular-cancer-national-cancer-act/6?_s=PM:HEALTH.

Golomb, Beatrice A., Michael H. Criqui, Halbert White, and Joel E. Dimsdale. 2004. Conceptual foundations of the UCSD statin study. *Archives of Internal Medicine* 164: 153–62.

Golomb, Beatrice A., Joel E. Dimsdale, Halbert L. White, Janis B. Ritchie, and Michael H. Criqui. 2008. Reduction in blood pressure with statins. *Archives of Internal Medicine* 168 (7): 721–27.

Gotto, Antonio M. 2003. Safety and statin therapy. *Archives of Internal Medicine* 163: 657–59.

Harris, Jeffrey E. 1985. Macro-experiments versus micro-experiments for health policy. In Jerry Hausman and David Wise, eds., *Social Experimentation*. Chicago: University of Chicago Press, 145–85.

Harris, Gardiner. 2011. Federal Research Center will help to develop vaccines. *New York Times*, January 23, p. A1. Available at: http://www.nytimes.com/2011/01/23/health/policy/23drug.html.

Harrison, Glenn W., and John A. List. 2004. Field experiments. *Journal of Economic Literature* 42 (4): 1009–55.

Hastings, Justine. S., and Jeffrey M. Weinstein. 2008. Information, school choice, and academic achievement: Evidence from two experiments. *Quarterly Journal of Economics* 123 (4): 1373–1414.

Hastings, Justine. S., and Lydia Tejeda-Ashton. 2008. Financial literacy, information, and demand elasticity: Survey and experimental evidence. Working paper 14538. NBER, Cambridge, MA.

Hausman, Jerry A., and David A. Wise. 1985. *Social Experimentation*. Chicago: University of Chicago Press.

Heckman, James J. 1992. Randomization and social policy evaluation. In Charles Manski and Irwin Garfinkel, eds., *Evaluating Welfare and Training Programs*. Cambridge: Harvard University Press, 201–30.

Heckman, James J. 2010. Building bridges between structural and program evaluation approaches to evaluating policy. *Journal of Economic Literature* 48 (2): 356–98.

Hotz, V. Joseph, Guido W. Imbens, and Julie H. Mortimer. 2005. Predicting the efficacy of future training programs using past experiences at other locations. *Journal of Econometrics* 125: 241–70.

Imbens, Guido S. 2010. Better late than nothing: Some comments on Deaton (2009) and Heckman and Urzua (2009). *Journal of Economic Literature* 48 (2): 399–423.

Jacob, Brian A., and Jens Ludwig. 2012. The effects of housing assistance on labor supply: Evidence from a voucher lottery. *American Economic Review* 102 (1): 272–304.

Jepsen, Christopher, and Steven Rivkin. 2009. Class size reduction and student achievement: The potential tradeoff between teacher quality and class size. *Journal of Human Resources* 44 (1): 223–50.

Kabat-Zinn, J., A. O. Massion, J. Kristeller, L. G. Peterson, K. E. Fletcher, L. Pbert, W. R. Lenderking, and S. F. Santorelli. 1992. Effectiveness of a meditation-based stress reduction program in the treatment of anxiety disorders. *American Journal of Psychiatry* 149: 936–43.

Keizer, Kees, Siegwart Lindenberg, and Linda Steg. 2008. The spreading of disorder. *Science* 322: 1681–85.

Kelling, George L., and James Q. Wilson. 1982. Broken windows. *Atlantic Monthly* (March). Available at: http://www.theatlantic.com/magazine/archive/1982/03/broken-windows/4465/.

Kling, Jeffrey R. 2006. Incarceration length, employment and earnings. *American Economic Review* 96 (3): 863–76.

Kling, Jeffrey R. 2007. Methodological frontiers of public finance field experiments. *National Tax Journal* 60 (1): 109–27.

Kling, Jeffrey R., Jeffrey B. Liebman, and Lawrence F. Katz. 2005. Bullets don't got no name: Consequences of fear in the ghetto. In Thomas S. Weisner, ed., *Discovering Successful Pathways in Children's Development: New Methods in the Study of Childhood and Family Life*. Chicago: University of Chicago Press, 243–81.a

Kling, Jeffrey R., Jeffrey B. Liebman, and Lawrence F. Katz. 2007. Experimental analysis of neighborhood effects. *Econometrica* 75 (1):83–119.

Kling, Jeffrey R., Jens Ludwig, and Lawrence F. Katz. 2005. Neighborhood effects on crime for female and male youth: Evidence from a randomized housing voucher experiment. *Quarterly Journal of Economics* 120 (1): 87–130.

Krueger, Alan B. 1999. Experimental estimates of education production functions. *Quarterly Journal of Economics* 114 (2): 497–532.

Lazear, Edward. 2001. Educational production. *Quarterly Journal of Economics* 116 (3): 777–803.

Lipsey, Mark W., Nana A. Landenberger, and Sandra J. Wilson. 2007. *Effects of Cognitive-Behavioral Programs for Criminal Offenders*. Oslo: Campbell Systematic Reviews.

Ludwig, Jens, Jeffrey Liebman, Jeffrey Kling, Greg J. Duncan, Lawrence F. Katz, Ronald C. Kessler, and Lisa Sanbonmatsu. 2008. What can we learn about neighborhood effects from the Moving to Opportunity experiment? *American Journal of Sociology* 114 (1): 144–88.

Ludwig, Jens, Jeffrey R. Kling, and Sendhil Mullainathan. 2011. Mechanism experiments and policy evaluations. *Journal of Economic Perspectives* 25 (3): 17–38.

Malani, Anup. 2006. Identifying placebo effects with data from clinical trials. *Journal of Political Economy* 114 (2): 236–56.

Mencken, H. L. 1946. CHRISTMAS STORY, illustated by Bill Crawford. New York, Knopf, 1946..

Meyer, Bruce D. 1995. Natural and quasi-experiments in economics. *Journal of Business and Economic Statistics* 13 (2): 151–61.

Oreopoulos, Philip, and Kjell G. Salvanes. 2009. How large are returns to schooling? Hint: Money isn't everything. Working paper 15339. NBER, Cambridge, MA.

Ross, Susan D., I. Elaine Allen, Janet E. Connelly, Bonnie M. Korenblat, M. Eugene Smith, Daren Bishop, and Don Lou. 1999. Clinical outcomes in statin treatment trials: A meta-analysis. *Archives of Internal Medicine* 159: 1793–1802.

Rossi, Peter H. 1987. The Iron Law of Evaluation and other metallic rules. *Research in Social Problems and Public Policy* 4: 3–20.

Sanbonmatsu, Lisa, Jeffrey R. Kling, Greg J. Duncan, and Jeanne Brooks-Gunn. 2006. Neighborhoods and academic achievement: Results from the Moving to Opportunity experiment. *Journal of Human Resources* 41 (4): 649–91.

Schanzenbach, Diane Whitmore. 2007. What have researchers learned from Project STAR? *Brookings Papers on Education Policy* (May): 205–28

Stuart, Elizabeth A., Stephan R. Cole, Catherine P. Bradshaw, and Philip J. Leaf. 2011. The use of propensity scores to assess the generalizability of results from randomized trials. *Journal of the Royal Statistical Society* series A 174 (2): 369–86.

Thavendiranathan, Paaladinesh, Akshay Bagai, M. Alan Brookhart, and Niteesh K. Choudhry. 2006. Primary prevention of cardiovascular diseases with statin therapy. *Archives of Internal Medicine* 166 (21): 2307–13.

Todd, Petra E., and Kenneth I. Wolpin. 2008. Ex ante evaluation of social programs. Working paper. Department of Economics, University of Pennsylvania.

US Census Bureau. 2011. *Statistical Abstract of the United States*. Available at: http://www .census.gov/compendia/statab/.

Wilson, William J. 1987. *The Truly Disadvantaged: The Inner City, the Underclass, and Public Policy*. Chicago: University of Chicago Press.

Wilt, Timothy J., Hanna E. Bloomfield, Roderick MacDonald, David Nelson, Indulis Rutks, Michael Ho, Gregory Larson, Anthony McCall, Sandra Pineros, and Anne Sales. 2004. Effectiveness of statin therapy in adults with coronary heart disease. *Archives of Internal Medicine* 464: 1427–36.

Wolpin, Kenneth I. 2007. Ex ante policy evaluation, structural estimation, and model selection. *American Economic Review* 97 (2): 48–52.

Zhang, Lei, Shuning Zhang, Hong Jiang, Aijun Sun, Yunkai Wang, Yunzeng Zou, Junbo Ge, and Haozhu Chen. 2010. Effects of statin therapy on inflammatory markers in chronic health failure: A meta-analysis of randomized controlled trials. *Archives of Medical Research* 41: 464–71.

4   What Works in Reducing Re-Offending?

Aurélie Ouss

4.1   Introduction: What Can We Learn from Re-Offending?

In the 1990s, 26 different laws, informally known as "three strikes laws," were passed in the United States. These laws imposed long and mandatory sentences on repeat offenders for the purpose of reducing recidivism. The special treatment of recidivism in the criminal-justice system was expressed in *Ewing v. California Supreme Court*.[1] Ewing had appealed a lower court's sentence of 25 years for a "third strike" burglary offense[2] as disproportionate, but the Court denied his appeal on the ground that "[his] sentence is justified by the State's public-safety interest in incapacitating and deterring recidivist felons, and amply supported by his own long, serious criminal record." The opinion continued to state that "recidivism has long been recognized as a legitimate basis for increased punishment and is a serious public safety concern in California and the Nation. Any criticism of the law is appropriately directed at the legislature, which is primarily responsible for making the policy choices underlying any criminal sentencing scheme." This decision and accompanying commentary point to the distinction made for repeat offenses: had Ewing committed all three strikes simultaneously, he likely would have received a smaller sentence.

The logic behind the three strikes law, as phrased in the Court's opinion, has received little attention in the economics of crime. To date, recidivism rates have been used as a barometer to measure the effectiveness of penal policies, while the actual causes of recidivism have remained a black box. Understanding these causes is important for several reasons. First, it would help researchers refine economic theories of crime and, in particular, make sense of the relative roles in reducing crime of general deterrence (resulting from the existence of potential sentences), specific deterrence (resulting from the actual experience of sentences), and incapacitation (crime prevented by removing offenders). Additionally it would help policy makers understand whether laws punishing re-offenders differently from first-time offenders have the intended effect. Finally, a good theory of recidivism would help improve the criminal-justice system's ability to rehabilitate prisoners.[3]

Sociologist David Garland (2001) analyzes the way in which criminal-justice systems in the United States and the United Kingdom have moved from rehabilitation to zero tolerance and mandatory sentencing. The 1970s were characterized by a feeling that "nothing works," in the criminal-justice system in general and in prisons in particular[4]. Interestingly, this analysis came just after first works in the economics of crime and punishment. When Gary Becker wrote his seminal theory of crime and punishment in 1968, he mentions the "trend during the twentieth century toward relatively smaller prison terms and more use of probation and therapy." A few decades later, with the rise of massive incarceration rates in the United States, the 1989 case *Mistretta v. United States*[5] directly confirmed federal skepticism in this regard. In his confirming opinion, Justice Blackmun states: "Rehabilitation as a sound penological theory came to be questioned and, in any event, was regarded by some as an unattainable goal for most cases." Thus research in economics of crime started at the end of an era of rehabilitation attempts, and interest in deterrence and incapacitation resonates with this political context. In more recent years the empirical analyses have focused more on understanding how different ways to carry out sentences might influence recidivism differentially.

The aim of this chapter is to explore the existing economic research on institutions and recidivism. This literature is related to a long line of studies in clinical psychology, criminology,[6] and sociology that have discussed how social context, life events,[7] or particular policies can affect career criminals. Here I take a different view and discuss how experiences within different institutions might affect recidivism, with a focus on prison settings and sentencing strategies.

International comparisons are used in exploring how different sentencing strategies affect recidivism. Most of the international comparisons will be between the Unites States and France, where there has not been a wind of skepticism on the effectiveness of rehabilitation in France.[8] Section 4.2 presents the basic frameworks used in studying recidivism and the institutional differences between the US and French criminal-justice systems.

The question of how different sentencing strategies might influence rates of re-offending has many dimensions, and there are considerable trade-offs. On the one hand, harsh sentences may be thought to have more deterrence effect, since there are fewer post-release opportunities for the prisoners and legal access to intervention services. On the other hand, rehabilitation programs (addiction treatments, therapy, general education, job training, etc.) could improve the prospects of released prisoners, and thus reduce recidivism. This question is discussed in the context of a formal model in section 4.3. Sections 4.4 and 4.5 investigate the relationship between recidivism and length of incarceration or prison conditions, respectively, and section 4.6 discusses alternatives to incarceration.

4.2 Recidivism: Measure and Facts

4.2.1 What Is Recidivism?

In doing quantitative analyses of recidivism, there are two main difficulties to bear in mind: first, definitions vary by administration, country, and literature; and second, even more so than crime in general, recidivism is difficult to measure. At its most basic level, recidivism is the act of repeating a criminal activity. However, in a judicial sense, not all repetitions are treated in the same way. For example, in the United States, mandatory minimum sentences are defined based on whether the repetition is a felony or a misdemeanor. Legal recidivism is even more narrowly defined in France: in the case of misdemeanors (*délit*), a repeat offender will only be considered legally recidivating if the same offense was committed.[9]

Beyond these definition differences, there is another measurement difficulty: although one could get an idea of criminal activity by looking at victim reports, or get an idea of the number of newly committed offenses through self-reporting, one must rely on re-arrests, and re-convictions, to get a proxy for recidivism. Because some crimes go unreported, this measure represents a lower bound to the number of re-offenses. In addition recidivism rates depend on the observation window, which varies across studies. Because of these measurement disparities, researchers must be careful in comparing recidivism rates across studies, and even more so across countries using national statistics.

4.2.2 Sociodemographic Analysis of Recidivism in France and the United States

Many studies have investigated both the levels and determinants of recidivism. The common methodology employed in such studies is following cohorts of released inmates and their rates of re-offending over certain time periods. In the United States, Langan and Levin (2002) from the Bureau of Justice Statistics analyze recidivism rates in a cohort three years after release from prison in 1994. They find that 67.5 percent of the prisoners were re-arrested for a new offense, 46.9 percent were re-convicted for a new crime, and 25.4 percent returned to prison with a new sentence. These recidivism rates vary by age (people released younger tend to recidivate more), by type of initial offense (recidivism rates are highest for property crimes), and by the number of prior offenses.

The French Prison Administration runs similar cohort analyses, as described by Kensey (2007). Kensey and Benaouda (2011) present the latest results of recidivism for a cohort of inmates, five years after their release from prison between June and December of 2002. The recidivism rates proved to be higher than those for the United States: 59 percent of released inmates were convicted for new offenses, and 46 percent received a new prison sentence.[10] As in the United States, recidivism rates decrease with age at release, are highest for property crimes, and three times as likely for inmates having had at least one other prior arrest. Men are also twice as likely to recidivate than women. The Kensey and Benaouda study also includes analyses of how sentences were carried out: when controlling for observables, inmates getting early, supervised release (*libération conditionnelle*) were 60 percent less likely to recidivate, and half as likely to get a new prison sentence, than inmates released with no parole.

However, the Kensey and Benaouda sociodemographic analyses of recidivism simply present correlations between ex-inmates' characteristics and recidivism. Likewise in the meta-analyses carried out to study recidivism by Martinson et al. (1974) and Gendreau, Little, and Goggin (1996), probable counterfactuals to the different analyzed interventions are not available. Few studies use experimental or quasi-experimental settings to identify causalities regarding different incarceration (or alternative) strategies, as Levitt and Miles (2007) point out in their *Handbook of Law and Economics* chapter. The remainder of this chapter will go over existing experimental and quasi-experimental studies of the determinants of recidivism, with emphasis on how this informs the theory of delinquent behavior, and as commensurate with policy-making.

4.3   Economic Theory of Crime and Recidivism

The economic theory of crime initially did not model recidivism. In his seminal paper, Becker (1968) used expected utility to model an individual's decision to participate in a crime, as given by the following equation:

$$EU_j = p_j U_j(Y_j - f_j) + (1 - p_j)U_j(Y_j),$$

where p_j is the probability of the offender being caught, convicted, and sentenced, Y_j the gain from the offense, and f_j the monetary equivalent of the punishment, which is defined as the discounted sum of earnings forgone and the value placed on restrictions in consumption and freedom. Taking this model in its simplest form, it is unclear why re-offenders should be punished at different levels from first-time offenders. That is, if we assume that individuals are well-informed about the different components entering in a cost–benefit analysis, this model does not predict different optimal levels of punishment for different criminal histories. In fact, having been punished could plausibly push would-be re-offenders toward a high estimate of p_j,[11] thus a lower f_j, and deter their committing repeat offenses.

Taking Gary Becker's model one step further, Ehrlich (1973) directly modeled the trade-offs when facing illegal opportunities. Imprisonment, or even having a felony on one's criminal record, might enter in the decision-making, be it through the monetary equivalent of the punishment or through the prospective gains from illegal activities. Indeed, because of the stigma attached to imprisonment or felony, illegal activities may afterward be relatively more attractive than legal activities. If p_j and f_j are kept constant, then Ehrlich points out that recidivism could be expected, given the lower expected gains of the alternative. That is to say, harsher sentences (or a high probability of getting caught) for repeat offenders are necessary to keep recidivists at the same level of offense as first-time offenders. One could think of some reasons why, after incarceration, the expected value of crime *relative* to legal activities might increase:

Legal barriers to employment   In many US states, certain jobs are barred to former felons, often times in low-qualified sectors, such as security guards and transportation. Likewise, in France, people with criminal records are not allowed to work in the French Civil Service, which represents 22 percent of total jobs in France as of 2010.

Bad signals to employers   Employers might use past felonies as a proxy for unobservable characteristics, and sort people (especially with low credentials) using felony history. Pager (2007) and Pager, Western, and Sugie (2009) describe the difficulties of ex-felons in finding jobs, due to both employer preferences and legal barriers, all the more so for black men.

Civil society barriers   Housing, banks, and voting are other areas where non–labor market institutions bar access to former felons. Disenfranchisement will lessen an ex-felon's adjustment in a civil society that prohibits housing or access to banks.

Learning in prison   Meeting more experienced criminals can increase Y_j, if one considers that criminal skills are sharpened in prison. We explore the evidence for this potential in prisons a little further in this chapter.

Thus, while Gary Becker's model of the economics of crime in its barest form does not directly show how different punishment might affect recidivism, Ehrlich's simple expansion of the model provides a good baseline framework for thinking about how prior sentences can change an at-risk recidivist's expected utility in contemplating criminal versus legal activities. More recently Lochner (2004) has formally modeled how incarceration can change the opportunity cost of work relative to crime, for individuals of different ages, skills, and education. Keeping in mind these components of crime theory and recidivism, let us now turn to empirical estimations of different sentencing strategies.

4.4   Sentence Length and Recidivism

Economists have mainly focused on sentence length when studying the effects of incarcerations on post-release behaviors, for two possible reasons. First of all, incarceration length directly relates to Gary Becker's model of criminal behavior: cost of punishment, f_j, is assumed to be directly proportional to number of days spent in prison. Even though in this model recidivism is not directly treated, the model can be used to measure the relative effects of incapacitation, deterrence, and specific deterrence. Second, incarceration lengths are fully recorded in administrative data, and there are additionally several quasi-natural experiments where differences in incarceration lengths are not directly related to potential future crimes.

4.4.1 Incarceration Length

Specific deterrence is the main feature of sentencing policy studied using variations in sentence length: Conditional on having been incarcerated, do longer prison spells decrease recidivism? Two main strategies are used to investigate this question: the first uses plausibly exogenous variations in the length of sentence; the second focuses on length of incarceration conditional on a given sentence. The mechanisms are not quite the same, as in the latter case, realized incarceration is different from the sentence pronounced by a judge. Surprises relative to pronounced sentences could in themselves modify one's perception of the punitiveness of the criminal-justice system, for example, in a Kahneman et al. (1993) framework.

Most quasi-experimental and experimental estimates in the literature find that more time spent in prison is associated with lower recidivism rates. Kuziemko (2007) exploits two sources of variation in incarceration length. The first one is the mass release of prisoners that took place in the state of Georgia in the early 1980s in the United States, under the governor's order to release 900 inmates from overcrowded local jails. The nondangerous inmates with dates closest to release dates were released early; conditional on sentence length, inmates served different amounts of time in prison solely based on incarceration date. Her second source of variation comes from the fact that the state of Georgia uses strict sentencing grids to determine eligibility to parole, and discontinuities in parole eligibility, depending on one's score. She finds that inmates who benefited from early release recidivate more: a one month increase in time served is associated with a 1.5 percentage points decrease in the rate of return to prison, three years after release. Ganong (2011) studies another feature of Georgia's sentencing guidelines, namely the radical change in sentencing guidelines that took place in 1993. The differences in time spent in prison are now much larger than the few month reductions studied by Kuziemko (2007) and can go up by half a year to a year. He finds that for these large increases in time served, on average, each extra month in prison is associated with a reduction of 0.3 to 0.7 percentage point in the recidivism rate, which is a smaller point estimate.

Ganong (2011) takes this analysis one step further; he shows that a substantial increase of time spent in prison confounds aging, incapacitation, and specific deterrence effects, and that age at release is strongly correlated with recidivism. Over a long time horizon it appears that incapacitation and aging explain half of the difference in recidivism usually attributed to specific deterrence. Using the random assignment of public defenders, which leads to a lot of variation in sentence length, Abrams (2010) finds that long sentences may reduce recidivism compared to short sentences but that the effect rapidly diminishes with incarceration length. This is a result that counters the simple OLS model of a strong relation between incarceration length and recidivism.

Yet an earlier experimental estimate of the effect of time spent in prison on recidivism is that by Berecochea, Jaman, and Jones (1981).[12] They find a 4.3 percentage points difference in recidivism rates (26.8 vs. 22.5 percent) between inmates randomly granted six months' early release versus a control group.[13]

All of the papers mentioned above focus on the intensive margin (variation in time spent in prison). Hjalmarsson (2009) looks at the extensive margin of incarceration (prison vs. no prison), also using discontinuities in the sentencing guidelines for juveniles in Washington state. She finds similar instances of individuals going to prison based on small differences in their sentencing scores as being less likely to recidivate than their non-incarcerated peers. Even though she makes the argument that a cost–benefit analysis should round out this result to lead to policy recommendations, all in all, this observation would indicate local, negative effects of incarceration on recidivism for juveniles.

4.4.2 Collective Remission versus Suspended Sentences

Clearly, from the above-mentioned results, the mechanisms in the relation between incarceration length and recidivism are quite complex: the effect of incapacitation, especially as mediated by aging, is particularly difficult to distinguish from specific deterrence. Furthermore the way in which sentences are reduced could affect recidivism directly. In general, case-based reductions in incarceration length could be assumed to have different effects on recidivism; in particular, estimates of recidivism enter into parole decisions. For example, French sentence judges[14] take into consideration an individual's penal past, family support, and behavior while incarcerated in order to determine whether or not to grant a suspended sentence. This practice is in part due to the idea that people from different social backgrounds and with or without penal histories have different recidivism rates. As will be shown later in this chapter, such targeted sentence suspensions do seem to lead to lower recidivism rates.

Collective remissions present clear-cut cost advantages when states are faced with mandates to reduce the prison population, as was the case in Georgia in 1981, and now is the case in several states, such as California. Pardons, or sentence reductions based on remaining sentences, take much less judicial time and effort than individual demands for pardon. Then again, the evidence indicates that this means of sentence reduction leads to higher recidivism rates. An alternative, as discussed in Drago, Galbiati, and Vertova (2009), is the Italian 2006 Collective Clemency Bill, which commuted prison sentences to suspended sentences. The 2006 Italian Clemency Bill presents an interesting contrast to a French law when, in the recent past, on Bastille Day collective pardons were granted each year, as studied in Maurin and Ouss (2010).

Yearly between 1990 and 2006 the sitting French president issued a collective pardon in honor of Bastille Day (a French national holiday celebrated on July 14), whereby sentences were proportionally reduced to the residual sentence on the date of the pardon.[15] Two discontinuities emerged from this law: depending on their sentencing date, inmates would serve less time in prison, and the amount of sentence suspended would depend on the prison time remaining to be served on Bastille Day. This practice is used by Maurin and Ouss (2010) in a regression discontinuity design framework to see how it affected recidivism: inmates benefiting from collective sentence reductions were more likely to recidivate than those who did not.

By contrast, in Italy, upon approval of the Collective Clemency Bill, 22,000 inmates were released from prison. Then, if these released inmates were to recommit a crime within five years, the residual sentence suspended by the Bill would be added onto any new sentence. Drago, Galbiati, and Vertova (2009) find that released inmates were less likely to commit new offenses if the fraction of their suspended sentence was large: they associated each additional month of the residual sentence with a 0.16 percentage point rise in recidivism. With this natural experiment they capture the joint effect of the reduction of time spent in prison (as was the sole objective of Bastille Day presidential pardons) and of a corresponding increase in expected sanctions. Coupled with a very salient addition to one's expected sentence, such a collective sentence reduction could indeed be effective in reducing recidivism, and could overcome the negative effect of simple collective sentence reduction. From these findings we can deduce that collective sentence *suspensions*, which are only slightly more costly than collective sentence reductions in reducing prison overcrowding, do reduce recidivism.[16]

4.4.3 Incarceration Length and the Economic Theory of Crime

As all the foregoing studies suggest, beyond general deterrence, specific deterrence is operating through variations in sentence length. It is unclear, however, why this might be the case in the most basic version of the Beckerian model of crime, unless expectations of recidivism are changed with regard to incarceration. The Italian experiment hints at a promising way to model sanctions, allying both saliency and the deterrent effects of suspended sentences.

4.5   Experiences in Prison

4.5.1   Prison Conditions

Prison conditions can have different effects on criminal activity in general, and recidivism in particular, and this factor enters indirectly in the variable f_j. Incarceration experiences vary widely, since prisons have different rehabilitation programs, amenities, rules, levels of overcrowding, composition of inmates, and so forth. Prison conditions are then one domain where general deterrence may differ remarkably from specific deterrence if there is poor information about prison life,[17] or more convincingly, about a prisoner's direct experience rather than secondhand narrations.

The difficulty in investigating this phenomenon is twofold. First of all, inmates are not randomly assigned to facilities. A naïve comparison of recidivism rates across prisons would confound composition and prison conditions effects. For example, minimum security facilities have higher recidivism rates, but they also mainly house property offenders, who tend to have higher recidivism rates, thus limiting causal inference in the absence of quasi-experimental variations.

Another component that makes analyses of prison conditions less prevalent in the economics literature is that there are many dimensions in which prison conditions can vary, as opposed to length of incarceration; determining which of these dimensions matters most is difficult. This difficulty translates to establishing elasticity measures of crime with respect to living conditions, as opposed to time spent in prison. Finally, since a prison affects similarly all inmates, lack of variation will limit analysis opportunities.

Katz, Levitt, and Shustorovich (2003) consider the general deterrence effect of prison conditions as proxied by the number of deaths per facility. They find that a strong negative correlation exists between number of offenses committed and number of deaths in prison, based on state and time variations of both indicators. One could nevertheless suppose that there are other factors affecting crime rates and death rates in prisons, such as prison gang dynamics, different law enforcement concerns across states, and basic human rights of prisoners. Finally, the authors insist that their contribution cannot suggest policy regarding other prison conditions such as access to television or sport facilities, which could have more direct effects on recidivism.

Chen and Shapiro (2007) explore discontinuities in the security levels of federal prisons. Comparing inmates above and below the different security thresholds, they find that being incarcerated in a tougher prison significantly increases recidivism after release, all other factors kept constant. Nevertheless, there are many differences between maximum- and low-security facilities (which are hereby compared): living conditions, number of interactions with other inmates, and contact with the outside world all depend on type of prison experience. Drago, Galbiati, and Vertova (2011) attempt a similar study of prisoners in Italy. Although their study does not produce a clear allocation directive, it is clear that prison assignments are more random in Italy than in the United States, and that more overcrowding and more deaths do not lower recidivism; thus these authors question the relevance of these specific deterrence factors.

The mechanism by which incarceration conditions affect recidivism has yet to be fully analyzed by economists. It is unclear how much imprisonment is understood to be a cost of crime, and how that cost could be factored in an individual's life after release from prison. Beyond prison conditions, one could also consider the lack of control inmates have over their lives while in prison, as in other institutional-izations; Goffman (1961) showed, that a long period of time spent in an institution can make re-adaptation to daily routines outside institutional walls challenging.

4.5.2   Gaining Criminal Capital behind Bars

With the development of the literature on peer-group influences, more attention is being paid to how interactions among inmates might affect recidivism. Studies of felons connecting with other felons in prisons feature prominently in the literature, as it has in fiction.[18] In the "prison as a school of crime" hypothesis, encounters with other felons while imprisoned might increase Y_j from G. Becker's model after release. For example, inmates may share information about criminal techniques, or gangs may recruit new members among convicts, for example, knowing their lack of alternatives post-release.

Two recent papers explore this phenomenon. Bayer, Hjalmarsson, and Pozen (2009) study peer-group influences in juvenile facilities in Florida, taking into consideration various differences in the overall composition of the prison population. They find that the probability that an individual will commit a certain type of crime relates to the type of inmates that individual would have encountered while incarcerated. For example, the probability that a released juvenile offender will be arrested for car theft is proportional to the number of car thieves among inmates at the time of incarceration. They find similar evidence of peer influence for a number of other types of crimes, all the more so if the released juvenile already has experience in that category of crime. For example, inmates skilled in car theft might share information about how they could steal cars and get away without being caught.. So, for released juveniles who have information on how not to be re-arrested, these estimates would be lower bounds. If the same effect is considered for small prisons, where there are fewer inmates, it may be easier to observe which prisoners frequently interact.

Ouss (2011) obtains finer granularity in the analysis of learning in prison by using cell-level data from French prisons. In French short-term prisons,[19] cells are small (accommodating 2 to 6 inmates at most), and inmates spend most of the day in their cell. They eat their meals inside their cells, and leave only for specific activities such as work assignments, schooling, sports, or time in the court-yard. The law only requires that they be offered a minimum of 2 hours a day outside of their cell. Therefore in this setup it is possible to clearly identify a small group of people with whom most interactions behind bars take place. The median number of cellmates is 5, and 75 percent of inmates have less than 10 cellmates during their incarceration. Furthermore 78 percent of inmates are incarcerated in only one cell, which suggests little association with prisoners in other cells. On average, inmates spend about 32 days together. Conditional on recidivism, this paper finds that drug and theft offenses are more likely when one has been exposed to cellmates having committed these offenses. A new direction that this paper takes is to investigate "in-group biases" of peer effects in prison by considering prisoners of similar age among whom interactions might be natural. As in other studies of peer effects, there does seem to be an in-group bias in both theft and drug-dealing.

These two papers weigh in favor of the prisons as school of crime hypothesis, conditional on the type of recidivist crime. The fact that these peer effects are stronger for inmates close in age suggests that to limit learning in prison, inmates of different ages should be incarcerated in a cell. It also suggests a potential advantage of single-cell incarceration, though isolation can have negative psychological effects on the prisoner: inmates on suicide watches in France are not put in solitary confinement.

4.5.3   Cost of Incarceration

A review of the evidence on how imprisonment conditions can influence post-release behavior points toward prison life having a direct effect on recidivism. The evidence for harsher treatments as a form of deterrence, whether specific or general, is unclear; rather there seems to be consistent evidence that interactions with other prisoners reinforce criminal skills. More modeling consistent with economists' view of recidivism as a process separate from the committed crimes may lead to a better understanding of the quandary that the prison experience presents for policy-setting.

4.6   Alternatives to Prison

In evaluating the cost of imprisonment as "the discounted sum of the earnings forgone and the value placed on the restrictions in consumption and freedom," Gary Becker discusses the difficulties in establishing sufficiently deterrent equivalents that do not implicitly value inmates' time too low. This question gets even more complex if one is to equally factor in the differential effect of incarceration on expected future earnings. Because of all the ways through which prison distorts prospects of rehabilitation beyond the direct effect of the sentence, it is worth investigating alternatives to incarceration, such as electronic monitoring or sentence commutation.

Electronic monitoring (EM) is typically offered to offenders who, first of all, have a home in which to be under home arrest and, in general, have a reason to be under EM as opposed to incarcerated (e.g., in order not to lose a job). Studying inmates who received electronic monitoring, Benaouda, Kensey, and Levy (2010) find more general recidivism rates than for released inmates (around 40 percent reoffended, and 23 percent were subsequently sentenced to prison). These are promising results, but they do account for unobserved heterogeneity of EM recipients.

Di Tella and Schargrodsky (2009) argue that in Argentina, the random assignment of cases to judges being more or less prone to using EM allows for the causal effects to be identified. They find that being confined by EM reduces recidivism rates by half. More studies should be done in that promising direction, since recidivism rates are so low in Argentina, even for those EM recipients who spend some time in prison. Perhaps being sentenced to EM is like receiving a "suspended sentence," with dreadful Argentine prison conditions being a formidable deterrent tool. This Argentine study further suggests the importance of surveillance of ex-prisoners right after their release from prison.

4.7.   Conclusion: Rehabilitating the Rehabilitation Hypothesis

Tossing up their arms in the early 1970s and 1980s in desperation that "nothing works," and thereafter putting more emphasis on the deterrent effects of imprisonment, policy makers had possibly overlooked the fact that miserable prison conditions and interactions with career criminals can reduce chances for a prisoner's rehabilitation after release. The disproportional use of long sentences for small offenses has now reached budgetary limits: the California Supreme Court has mandated that overcrowding in prisons be dealt with before 2013, thus bringing the question of rehabilitation back on the bargaining table. Yet economics of crime has few theoretical, experimental, or quasi-experimental studies on rehabilitation programs,[20] especially compared to the extensive literature on the deterrent effects of sentencing. This review of existing work on re-offending attempts to draw attention to the limits of economic theory on criminal behavior in modeling the dynamics of incarceration on future criminal activity. Thus far the research efforts on particular features of criminal institutions, such as the rehabilitation programs through work or education opportunities, is a first step toward an evidence-based economics contribution to addressing the relationship of incarceration to recidivism.

Notes

I wish to thank the French Department of Prison Administration for providing data for my various research projects on incarceration, and participants of the CESifo conference "Lessons from the Economics of Crime: What Works in Reducing Offending?" for providing helpful comments.

1. 538 US 11 (2003).

2. The final strike came with Ewing's stealing three golf clubs at a value of $399 each.

3. Although this purpose is often thought of as secondary as compared to incapacitation and deterrence, rehabilitation is officially a part of the criminal-justice system's mission in many countries. For example, the American Federal Bureau of Prisons states that "it is [its] mission to protect society by confining offenders in the controlled environments of prisons and community-based facilities that are safe, humane, cost-efficient, and appropriately secure, and that provide work and other self-improvement opportunities to assist offenders in becoming law-abiding citizens." (http://www.bop.gov/about/mission.jsp)

4. For example, in an influential report, Martinson et al. (1974) reviewed more than 200 studies of rehabilitation in prisons, and came to the conclusion that none of the existing rehabilitation programs worked, either because they are not well tailored to inmates' needs, or—as has been kept from Martinson's work—for holistic arguments of crime in society. If, in principle, deterrence and punishment were to override rehabilitation, spending more on rehabilitation would not seem cost-effective.

5. 488 US 361 (1989).

6. See, for example, Hanson and Bussiere (1998) or Gendreau, Little, and Goggin (1996) for notable meta-analyses of causes of recidivism in clinical psychology and criminology.

7. Sampson and Laub (1995) and Laub and Sampson (2003), following through later decades subjects from the study by Glueck and Glueck (1950), offer a unique longitudinal analysis of how such events as marriage, having children, serving in the army, or entering fulfilling careers affect desistance from crime.

8. In the recent past the French Sénat and other government branches have asked for reports on the role that prisons can play in rehabilitation, for example, see Hyest and Cabanel (2000) or Decisier (2006). Both reports (written by independent committees) recommended that the Prison Administration take more seriously rehabilitation to counter recidivism. The adoption, in 2007, of mandatory sentences for recidivists, known as "peines plancher," was intended to take advantage of deterrence effects.

9. Even in that case, the act of recidivism is not necessarily recorded; thus judges can choose not to consider a repeated offense as recidivism, and they frequently do not have access to the defendants' full past criminal history at the time of the trial.

10. Note, however, that in this study the time of analysis is five years versus three in the US study.

11. For example, Lochner (2003) finds that when arrested, or when siblings are arrested, young males tend to revise the probability of being arrested upward, whereas committing crimes without getting caught leads individuals to revise their expectations downward.

12. I would like to thank Philip Cook for letting me know about this paper.

13. Ganong (2011) notes that a simple t-statistics test shows this difference to be significant, contrary to the authors' interpretation.

14. "Juge d'application des peines" is how sentences determined by either a court judge or a jury are to be carried out.

15. Between 1990 and 2003, the reduction was about one week per remaining month, with a maximum sentence reduction of two months. From 2004 to 2006, the reduction was of two weeks per remaining month, with a maximum of four months.

16. There might be additional costs due to the fact that suspension has to be recorded and used by judges.

17. For example, information about prisons comes from films, or from former inmates who choose to reveal details of their prison life.

18. For example, in Jacques Audiard's film *A Prophet*, the main character Malik gets sentenced for assaulting policemen, but because of his encounters with the Corsican mafia, he becomes involved in organized crime and drug dealing.

19. "Maisons d'arrêt"

20. A notable exception to this is MDRC's work on employing offenders, which are still ongoing.

References

Abrams, D. 2010. Building criminal capital vs. specific deterrence: The effect of incarceration length on recidivism. Working paper.

Bayer, P., R. Hjalmarsson, and D. Pozen. 2009. Building criminal capital behind bars: Peer effects in juvenile corrections. *Quarterly Journal of Economics* 124 (1): 105–47.

Becker, G. 1968. Crime and punishment: An economic approach. *Journal of Political Economy* 76 (2): 169–217.

Benaouda, A., A. Kensey, and R. Levy. 2010. La récidive des premiers placés sous surveillance électronique. *Cahiers d'études pénitentiaires et criminologiques* 33: 1–6.

Berecochea, J., D. Jaman, and W. Jones. 1981. Time served in prison and parole outcome: An experimental study. Discussion paper. Research Division, Department of Corrections, State of California, Sacramento.

Chen, M., and J. Shapiro. 2007. Do harsher prison conditions reduce recidivism? A discontinuity-based approach. *American Law and Economics Review* 9 (1): 1.

Decisier, D. 2006. Les conditions de la réinsertion professionnelle des détenus en France. *Journal officiel de la République française, avis et rapports du Conseil économique et social*: 1–331.

Di Tella, R., and E. Schargrodsky. 2009. Criminal recidivism after prison and electronic monitoring. Working paper 15602. NBER, Cambridge, MA.

Drago, F., R. Galbiati, and P. Vertova. 2009. The deterrent effects of prison: Evidence from a natural experiment. *Journal of Political Economy* 117 (2): 257–80.

Drago, F., R. Galbiati, and P. Vertova. 2011. Prison conditions and recidivism. *American Law and Economics Review* 13 (1): 103.

Ehrlich, I. 1973. Participation in illegitimate activities: A theoretical and empirical investigation. *Journal of Political Economy* 81: 521–65.

Ganong, P. 2012. Criminal rehabilitation, incapacitation, and aging. *American Law and Economics Review* 14 (2): 391–424.

Garland, D. 2001. *The Culture of Control: Crime and Social Order in Contemporary Society.* New York: Oxford University Press.

Gendreau, P., T. Little, and C. Goggin. 1996. A meta-analysis of the predictors of adult offender recidivism: What works. *Criminology* 34 (4): 575–608.

Glueck, S., and E. Glueck. 1950. Unraveling juvenile delinquency. *Juvenile Court Judges Journal* 2: 32.

Goffman, E. 1961. *Asylums: Essays on the Social Situations of Mental Patients and Other Inmates.* New York: Anchor Books.

Hanson, R., and M. Bussiere. 1998. Predicting relapse: A metaanalysis of sexual offender recidivism studies. *Journal of Consulting and Clinical Psychology* 66 (2): 348.

Hjalmarsson, R. 2009. Juvenile jails: A path to the straight and narrow or to hardened criminality? *Journal of Law and Economics* 52: 779–809.

Hyest, J., and G. Cabanel. 2000. Prisons: Une humiliation pour la R République. Sénat, rapport.

Kahneman, D., B. Fredrickson, C. Schreiber, and D. Redelmeier. 1993. When more pain is preferred to less. *Psychological Science* 4 (6): 401–405.

Katz, L., S. Levitt, and E. Shustorovich. 2003. Prison conditions, capital punishment, and deterrence. *American Law and Economics Review* 5 (2): 318.

Kensey, A. 2007. *Prison et récidive.* Paris: Armand Colin.

Kensey, A., and A. Benaouda. 2011. Les risques de récidive des sortants de prison. Une nouvelle evaluation. *Cahiers d'études pénitentiaires et criminologiques* 36: 1–8.

Kuziemko, I. 2013. How should inmates be released from prison? An assessment of parole versus fixed-sentence regimes. *Quarterly Journal of Economics* 128 (2): 371–424.

Langan, P., and D. Levin. 2002. Recidivism of prisoners released in 1994. *Federal Sentencing Reporter* 15 (1): 58–65.

Laub, J., and R. Sampson. 2003. *Shared Beginnings, Divergent Lives: Delinquent Boys to Age 70*. Cambridge: Harvard University Press.

Levitt, S., and T. Miles. 2007. Empirical study of criminal punishment. *Handbook of Law and Economics* 1: 455–95

Lochner, L. 2007. Individual perceptions of the criminal justice system. *American Economic Review* 97 (1): 444–60.

Lochner, L. 2004. Education, work, and crime: A human capital approach. *International Economic Review* 45 (3): 811–43.

Martinson, R. 1974. What works? Questions and answers about prison reform. *Public Interest* 35 (1): 22–54.

Maurin, E., and A. Ouss. 2010. Collective sentence reductions and recidivism. Working paper.

Ouss, A. 2011. Prison as a school of crime: Evidence from cell-level interactions. Working paper.

Pager, D. 2007. *Marked: Race, Crime, and Finding Work in an Era of Mass Incarceration*. Chicago: University of Chicago Press.

Pager, D., B. Western, and N. Sugie. 2009. Sequencing disadvantage: Barriers to employment facing young black and white men with criminal records. *Annals of the American Academy of Political and Social Science* 623 (1): 195.

Sampson, R., and J. Laub. 1995. *Crime in the Making: Pathways and Turning Points through Life*. Cambridge: Harvard University Press.

5   The Young Prisoner's Dilemma: Juvenile: Recidivism in Germany

Stefan Pichler and Daniel Römer

5.1   How to Treat Young Offenders?

The optimal punishment of criminal acts represents a trade-off. On the one hand, classic theory (e.g., Becker 1968) suggests that more severe punishments lead to higher general deterrence and thus to less crime. On the other hand, too harsh sentences can reduce future income opportunities and thereby increase the likelihood of re-offending. This view of punishment has gained prominence over the last decade, as modern economic models consider additional incentives beyond basic payoff maximization. Today, in the particular case of incarceration, different channels have been identified that can stimulate recidivism. Psychologists have found long-term imprisonment to increase the taste for violence (Banister et al. 1973), while economic studies have confirmed that inmate peer effects enhance post-release offenses (Bayer et al. 2009; Glaeser et al. 1996). According to Western et al. (2001), also the mere stigma of incarceration reduces future lawful income of the released inmate, thus rendering illegal income opportunities more attractive.

If individuals underestimate the probability of being caught (Fender 1999) or exhibit trenchant criminalities, recidivism deterrence may be more important than general deterrence. Juveniles seem to meet both characteristics. Because of a maturity gap (as suggested by Moffitt 1993), they are conditionally more inclined toward criminal behavior (e.g., Thornberry et al. 2004). Furthermore Lee and McCrary (2009) found evidence that young adults hardly respond to the harsher punishments they face on turning 18. They argue that young offenders misjudge likelihood and severity of the imminent punishments and can thus be characterized as myopic. This view challenges the rational offender hypothesis for the case of juvenile delinquents and is reflected in the empirical evidence: while Levitt (1998) found increased general deterrence when transferring adolescents to adult courts and thus confirmed Becker's hypothesis, other studies have found no general deterrence effect (Singer and McDowall 1988; Steiner et al. 2006) or even increased arrest rates (Jensen and Metsger 1994).

These pieces of evidence help one understand why (in most countries) juveniles are treated with less severe sentences, but with stronger focus on reintegration into society. However, there is still no clear answer to the question, for which age group this preferential treatment should be applied. While in the 1960s and 1970s, there was a strong focus on rehabilitation, this view changed to a "getting tough" movement in the 1980s, driven by the then predominant belief that "nothing has worked." As a consequence, in many US states, juveniles were transferred to criminal courts at younger ages. Most empirical studies taking advantage of these natural experiments found that the earlier transfers rather increased recidivism instead of decreasing it. While we do not question these studies per se, we point out that they only provide insights for a specific legal environment and a specific age group. A generalization to different settings might not be straightforward.

In particular, given the sharp differences in juvenile laws across countries, we look at recent evidence from Germany and try to draw conclusions for the optimal treatment of young offenders. These results add to the current discussion on juvenile legislation across Europe where, in the last decades, an increasing number of serious and highly aggressive acts of juvenile violence have called the current policy into question (see Aebi 2004; Oberwittler and Höfer 2005). Moreover the Committee of Ministers of the Council of Europe is trying to establish European standards of juvenile law. In this context the German juvenile legislation can be seen as exemplary, based on both its flexible mechanism and the general state-based legal framework, which resembles the legal structure of the European Union (Bochmann 2009, p. 122).

The chapter is structured as follows: Section 5.2 compares different legal settings in the Western World. Section 5.3 looks at different empirical studies from the United States, while section 5.4 presents recent evidence from Germany. In section 5.5 we try to reconcile the different results and we conclude with consequences for public policy in section 5.6.

5.2   Juvenile Law in Germany, Europe, and the United States

In Germany, juvenile law is mandatory for all minors, that is, for all persons who have not yet turned 18 at the time the criminal act was committed. For adolescent delinquents, namely those aged between 18 and 21 years when offending, the legislation has left the decision to the courts, that is, whether to apply juvenile or criminal law. More specifically, judges are asked to apply juvenile law whenever the offender acts "equal to a juvenile regarding moral and mental development at the time of the act" (§105 (1) Juvenile Justice Act—*Jugendgerichtsgesetz*). Delinquents of at least 21 years are to be sentenced under criminal law. We compare this fact with the US practice and find no state where the maximum age of application of juvenile law has been extended as far as in Germany. In 2006 the automatic treatment as an adult started at age 18 (37 states), age 17 (10 states), or age 16 (3 states) (see Bishop and Decker 2006, p. 13). Hence German legislation allows for a much wider application of juvenile law than its US counterpart.

The same holds true for many other European countries that use age barriers identical or similar to the German system. In fact ten other European countries have implemented the same age barriers, and roughly 70 percent share the stepwise transition from juvenile to criminal law. That is to say, more than half of the European countries allow the application of juvenile law to offenders aged 18 and above. Table 5.1 summarizes the different thresholds and illustrates the limited transferability of American studies to the European context.[1]

German juvenile law allows for milder sanctions for juvenile offenders, as certain minimum penalties that exist in criminal law (e.g., three years in the case of robbery) do not have to be considered. Moreover most juvenile records get erased after three years, while most criminal records get erased only after five years (§34 Federal Central Criminal Register—*Bundeszentralregister*).[2]

The applied type of law also implies the type of custody in case of incarceration. Section 141 of German Penal Law (*Strafvollzugsgesetz*) states that juveniles and adults must be kept in separate prisons or at least in separate departments of the same prison. Entorf et al. (2008, pp. 139–52) summarize differences between juvenile and criminal prisons in Germany. The authors find that, on average, juvenile prisons have more money at their disposal and thus can offer a more convenient and stimulating environment. Juvenile prisons offer, for instance, more common rooms for eating, sports, and other activities. Also a higher fraction of juvenile delinquents is placed in a single room (83 percent) as compared to adult delinquents (55 percent). While criminal prisons hire fewer than 50 employees for 100 inmates, there are almost 70 employees in juvenile prisons looking after 100 juveniles. This allows

Table 5.1
Juvenile justice across Europe: Application of criminal law

Country	Application of criminal law[a]	Country	Application of criminal law[a]
Belarus	14/16	Greece	15/21
Macedonia	14/16	Denmark	15/18/21
Moldova	14/16	Sweden	15/18/21
Finland	15/18	Portugal	16/21
Turkey	15/18	Scotland	16/21
Poland	15/17/18	Cyprus	16/18/21
Belgium	16/18	Netherlands	16/18/21
Bulgaria	18	North. Ireland	17/18/21
Czech Republic	18	Austria	18/21
England/Wales	18	Croatia	18/21
Estonia	18	Germany	18/21
France	18	Italy	18/21
Hungary	18	Lithuania	18/21
Ireland	18	Montenegro	18/21
Latvia	18	Russia	18/21
Norway	18	Serbia	18/21
Spain	18	Slovakia	18/21
Switzerland	18	Slovenia	18/21
Romania	18/20	Ukraine	18/21

Source: Junger-Tas and Dünkel (2009)
a. The given numbers denote the minimum age at which criminal law is applied, where x indicates a sharp transition at age x; x/y indicates a case-dependent transition with x as lower and y as upper bound; $x/y/z$ indicates a system where criminal law exceptionally can be applied at age x (in very serious cases), can regularly be applied at age y and must be applied at age z.

juvenile prisons to provide schooling opportunities and to offer more seminars, such as on how to deal with drug and alcohol problems. As discussed by Lange (2007), the most notable difference between juvenile and criminal prisons is that criminal prisons have the primary goal of punishment while juvenile prisons are focused on social education, for example, by assignment of personal custodians to delinquents. Furthermore, according to Dölling et al. (2007), juvenile law is generally less stigmatizing than criminal law.

Hence a juvenile prison, as opposed to a criminal prison, can affect recidivism in two ways. On the one hand, being an inmate in a more convivial environment may dampen the deterrence effect and lead to higher recidivism rates. On the other hand, juvenile prisons may decrease the likelihood of recidivism due to the emphasis on education and the less stigmatizing effect of juvenile detention on future job prospects. The relative differences between juvenile and criminal law seem to be close to those in other European countries (O'Mahony and Doak 2009) and in the United States (Taylor et al. 2006). However, the two mentioned effects can be diverse in intensity, especially for different age groups. In this chapter we shed light on the issue of under what conditions one of the two effects dominates.

5.3   Empirical Evidence from the United States

Many empirical studies have been conducted on the effect of criminal law on juvenile recidivism. Before presenting recent evidence from Germany, we briefly summarize the previous literature. The academic work is mostly based on US data. The typical identification strategy in these studies is to focus on state variations of punishment as the natural experiment—even though it is not always clear whether the initial assumption about the natural experiment holds, since policy changes may arise endogenously.

A good example is Fagan (1996), who studied differences in recidivism rates of 15- and 16-year-old juveniles, taking advantage of the fact that in New Jersey young delinquents were sentenced by a juvenile court whereas in New York they appeared before a criminal court. He found significantly lower recidivism rates for those sentenced by juvenile courts, suggesting that the special jurisprudence for juvenile crimes is an effective measure. This finding, however, would suffer from an endogeneity bias if the policy in New York were set up to counteract higher preexisting recidivism rates. In this case, a mere comparison (of ex ante different inmates) would not lead to identification of the treatment effect. To ensure that compared individuals are similar in all respects, except for the type of court they are sent to, Kupchik et al. (2003) refine the estimation model and apply matching techniques. In using this advanced methodology, the authors were able to confirm their original results.

Another line of literature focuses on the application of either juvenile or criminal law based on an individual decision process. In such a framework a selection bias is a serious threat to identification. If the individuals selected for criminal court are more likely to re-offend a priori, observing higher recidivism rates in this sample does not imply that transfer was causal for this observation. Therefore researchers have developed sophisticated strategies to separate the effect of the applied law type from potential selection biases, which represents one of the main challenges in this setting. Bishop et al. (1996), for example, analyzed recidivism in Florida, where transfer depends on the decision of the prosecutor. They found higher recidivism rates for those delinquents transferred to criminal courts. Initially they could not rule out the existence of a selection bias distorting the results. However, in a follow-up study Lanza-Kaduce et al. (2005) still found a positive effect of transfers when using both a richer dataset and matching techniques. In a related paper, Myers (2003) also looked at law assignments based on human decision. He used a two-stage regression model, representing transfer in the first stage and re-arrest in the second stage. He used data from Pennsylvania where the juvenile court decides on the transfer and confirmed that transfer to criminal courts increases the rate of recidivism. Podkopacz and Feld (1995) applied the same approach and obtained similar results.

Summarizing, the evidence suggests that transferring young offenders to criminal courts backfires in the United States and leads to higher recidivism rates.

5.4   Recent Evidence from Germany

Pichler and Römer (2011) provide one of the first analyses of juvenile recidivism based on European data. They combine the earlier identification strategies. Due to the flexible transition from juvenile to criminal law, in Germany there are offenders of the same age but receiving different treatment. The law assignment mechanism, however, allows for the possibility that individuals sentenced under criminal law have a different initial likelihood of recidivism than those sentenced under juvenile law: §105 Juvenile Justice Act asks judges to apply a maturity criterion, which might include unobservables that also determine the inclination to re-offend.[3] Given this selection process, it is very likely that offenders selected for juvenile law differ systematically from those who are not, in particular, in their ex ante likelihood to recidivate. Hence the econometric analysis requires an identification strategy that circumvents this problem. Pichler and Römer (2011) use a bivariate probit model that contains an equation of the selection process. In addition they take advantage of a jump in treatment assignment and apply a regression discontinuity design to identify the treatment effect. In the following sections we discuss in detail the results and the applied methodology.

5.4.1 Data

The data used in Pichler and Römer (2011) stem from a prison survey conducted in 31 German prisons in 2003 and 2004 using 123 questions.[4] The questionnaire was given to 13,340 selected inmates. All questionnaires within a prison were handed out at the same point in time. For the full sample, only 1,771 inmates agreed to participate in the survey, which led to a general response rate of only 13.3 percent. In the final sample used in this study, which consists of 245 inmates younger than 25, the response rate amounts to 18.8 percent. Despite the low response rate, there is no evidence of a selection bias when comparing sample characteristics to those of the average prison population in Germany.[5]

The outcome variable used as a proxy for actual recidivism is based on the following question: Do you believe that after you are released from prison, you might commit another crime and end up in prison?[6] If inmates answered that recidivism was possible or (very) likely, they were categorized as possible recidivists and the binary outcome variable *recidivism* was set to one. Inmates, who replied that recidivism was very unlikely, or were certain not to commit further crimes, are represented by a zero outcome variable.[7]

In addition to *recidivism* and the binary treatment variable *criminal law* that captures the applied law type, the authors also considered information on socioeconomic variables, such as *age*, club membership (*poor social capital*), *nationality*, extent of intimacy with a spouse or partner before the incarceration (*social contact*), and job prospects. Moreover the survey included information on previous convictions of the inmate, convictions of parents or siblings (*criminal family*), the type of crime committed, and details on the current punishment.

5.4.2 Discussing the Choice of the Outcome Variable

Since it is impossible to get a direct measure of recidivism, empirical studies use proxies like administrative data on re-arrests or re-convictions, self-reported recidivism, or intentions to re-offend. The clear advantage of administrative data is that it is fact based. However, the problem with these data is that the inmate in question may recidivate and not be caught. Especially contact with other (career-type) criminals in prison can alter the detection probability of future crimes. Moreover, if researchers use re-arrest or re-convictions, the optimal point in time of the follow-up study may not be clear. If the chosen time interval is very short, recidivism might not have yet occurred, leading to an underestimation of recidivism. Extending the interval, however, increases the bias due to unobservable post-release factors. Self-reported recidivism, on the one hand, might conceal crimes unobserved by the authorities. On the other hand, it leads to underestimates of the prevalence of re-offending (Uggen 2000; Schore et al. 1979).

As described above, Pichler and Römer (2011) use the third option, namely the respondent's report of the likelihood to commit crimes in the future. Despite enjoying less popularity than the other mentioned measures, the use of self-reported likelihoods or intentions is considered "generally a sound and productive strategy with abundant advantages over other methodologies" (Wright et al. 2004, p. 189), and this has been used in other studies as well (e.g., Nagin and Pogarsky 2001; Piquero and Paternoster 1998; Pogarsky 2002). More recently Maxson et al. (2011) provide one of the first studies to use this outcome variable in an adolescent offender sample.

A limitation of this approach is that it might contain an overestimation of the criminal propensity (due to youthful boasting) or an underestimation (to create a good impression). However, we are aware of two studies that verify the connection between stated intentions and real behavior. Corrado et al. (2003) use a measure very similar to that of Pichler and Römer (2011) in an adolescent sample and show how it correlates with observed subsequent behavior. In a related study Green (1989) favorably compares self-reported future drinking-and-driving assessments with data on actual future behavior. Moreover the data in Pichler and Römer (2011) were collected in a way that does not allow one to expect strategic answers, since the questionnaires were returned in a sealed envelope to guarantee anonymity. Finally, an advantage of the "intention to recidivate" variable is that it excludes factors that appear after the release from prison and captures the effect of punishment on the inmate's motivation. Extending this line of thought, one could study other questions of the survey used by Pichler and Römer (2011) that allow assessment of the specific deterrence effect on different prisoner types, which also is of interest for the policy maker. Inmates were asked to rate the following sentences:

• If I had known what it is like in jail, I would not have committed my crime.

• Imprisonment is suitable for the betterment of the imprisoned and preventing the prisoner from committing more offenses.

Entorf (2012), using the same dataset, estimates a linear probability model with self-assessed intention to recidivate, constructed as described above, as dependent variable and finds that inmates who "fully agree" with the statements above show a much lower likelihood of recidivism as compared to those who answered they did not agree at all.

Even though there remain some pitfalls—the most important being a general misperception of inmates in assessing future behavior—a general bias, affecting all individuals in the same way, resulting in a generally too high (or too low) rate of recidivism, would not pose a threat to the validity of the estimated treatment effect of criminal law. However, if the size of the measurement error depends on the treatment, then results might be misleading. Therefore we will shortly discuss the direction of a potential bias.

Pichler and Römer (2011) find that criminal law reduces recidivism. In juvenile prisons there are more schooling possibilities and personal custodians. Along with general education, crime deterrence education might take place, potentially leading to a temporary underestimation of the real rate of recidivism. Yet this bias could go in the opposite direction as well and lead to an underestimation of the treatment effect. Alternatively, stronger peer pressure in juvenile prisons could lead to competition in toughness and an exaggerated report of recidivism. Where such peer effects exist, however, the evidence is that they will also drive real behavior after release (e.g., see Bayer et al. 2009).

5.4.3   Method and Results

Taking advantage of the law assignment mechanism, Pichler and Römer (2011) apply two different identification strategies. First, they look at adolescents aged between 18 and 21 when offending, and model recidivism and treatment selection in a bivariate probit approach. In this way they allow for a correlation between unobservable determinants of both the delinquent's decision to recidivate and the judge's choice of law. This correlation is a factor of the present selection bias. Controlling for the empirical correlation in the sample allows for pure selection effects to be disentangled from treatment effects.

By this method Pichler and Römer (2011) find that contrary to most US studies, the application of criminal law to adolescent offenders leads to lower rates of recidivism. The estimated treatment effect is robust across model specifications and indicates a drop in recidivism of roughly 25 to 30 percent (see table 5.2), in particular when controlling for individual criminal history and the type of crime committed. The estimate for the correlation (*rho*) is positive and mostly significant meaning that higher risk offenders are selected into criminal law.

In an additional robustness check, in which the authors set the correlation to zero, they find that in absence of selection in the model, the estimate for the treatment effect is still be of the same sign, but smaller and not significant (see Pichler and Römer 2011 for more detail). The regression results are in line with German survey data that report actual recidivism rates within four years after unconditional prison sentences. For the group of incarcerated adolescent offenders, Jehle et al. (2003) find that inmates sentenced under juvenile law recidivated in 79.0 percent of the cases, whereas only 43.6 percent of those sentenced under criminal law re-offended. This is further proof that the sample used in this study is representative despite the low response rate of the survey.

Pichler and Römer (2011) corroborate this result using their second identification strategy, a regression discontinuity design. While criminal law becomes mandatory for offenders aged 21 when committing the crime, it is only selectively applied in the discretionary phase between 18 and 21. In the sample, the corresponding treatment assignment function exhibits a jump at 21, from around 35 to 100 percent. Comparing individuals shortly before 21 with peers who have just passed this cutoff allows for the identification of the effect of criminal law on recidivism.[8] Figures 5.1 and 5.2 illustrate the discontinuities in treatment assignment and recidivism, respectively.

A necessary condition for identification in a regression discontinuity design is random selection around the relevant cutoff point. In the given context this requires that offenders do not adjust the point of offense according to treatment assignment. Put differently, the two samples to the left and to the right of the cutoff point should not differ except for the treatment. If this assumption holds, comparing individuals shortly before 21 with peers who have just passed the cutoff point allows for the identification of the treatment effect based on a regression discontinuity design. This assumption is not completely innocuous, since some strategic offenders might commit a crime earlier to get a milder punishment. In their sample, however, Pichler and Römer (2011) do not find an overrepresentation of inmates that committed the crime

Table 5.2
Biprobit estimates

	(1)	(2)	(3)	(4)	(5)
Equation 1	Recidivism	Recidivism	Recidivism	Recidivism	Recidivism
Age	−2.757**	−3.321**	−3.395**	−2.823*	−5.385***
	(0.017)	(0.042)	(0.024)	(0.090)	(0.000)
Age2	0.0643**	0.0774**	0.0790**	0.0659*	0.123***
	(0.022)	(0.038)	(0.021)	(0.086)	(0.000)
Criminal law	−1.183	−1.566**	−1.710***	−1.527***	−1.781***
	(0.131)	(0.034)	(0.001)	(0.006)	(0.004)
Job contact		−0.502***	−0.514***	−0.350***	−0.700***
		(0.000)	(0.000)	(0.000)	(0.000)
Criminal family		0.449***	0.376***	0.381**	1.470***
		(0.002)	(0.000)	(0.040)	(0.008)
Constant	29.02**	35.27**	35.92**	29.41	55.33***
	(0.016)	(0.049)	(0.028)	(0.104)	(0.000)
Equation 2	Criminal law	Criminal law	Criminal law	Criminal law	Criminal law
Age offense	0.921***	0.904***	0.880***	1.125***	1.204***
	(0.000)	(0.000)	(0.000)	(0.000)	(0.000)
Criminal family		−0.0577	−0.312	−0.171	0.129
		(0.891)	(0.422)	(0.507)	(0.826)
Constant	−19.48***	−19.12***	−19.48***	−24.82***	−25.48***
	(0.000)	(0.000)	(0.000)	(0.000)	(0.000)
rho	0.396	0.623	0.699*	1.000***	1.000***
	(0.154)	(0.226)	(0.075)	(0.000)	(0.000)
Socio econ	No	No	Yes	Yes	Yes
Crim hist	No	No	No	Yes	Yes
Crime type	No	No	No	No	Yes
Personal	No	No	No	No	Yes
ATE	−0.290**	−0.340***	−0.354***	−0.320***	−0.267***
	(0.030)	(0.001)	(0.000)	(0.001)	(0.001)
NObs	90	85	85	81	79

Source: Pichler and Römer (2011)
Note: $*p < 0.10$, $**p < 0.05$, $***p < 0.01$; p-values in parentheses; socio econ (socioeconomic variables): social contact, poor social capital; crim hist (criminal history): prison experience, total years in prison, number of previous convictions; crime type: drug dealing, fraud, theft, robbery, vandalism; personal (miscellaneous): German nationality, high school, months in jail, sentence length.

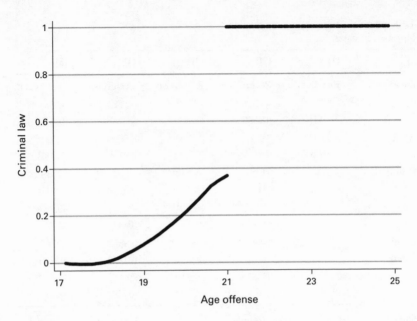

Figure 5.1
Treatment assignment over age at offense Source: Pichler and Römer (2011)

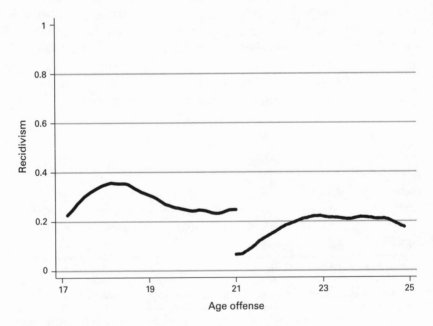

Figure 5.2
Expected recidivism over age at offense Source: Pichler and Römer (2011)

shortly before their 21st birthday. Moreover empirical evidence suggests that young offenders are myopic with respect to their punishment (e.g., see Lee and McCrary 2009; Hjalmarsson 2009a) and highly underestimate the probability of getting caught. Hence it seems very unlikely that the observed data suffer from a problem of self-selection.

The results from the regression discontinuity design show a drop in recidivism ranging from roughly 0.30 to 0.55 (see table 5.3). Therefore the average sentence is a little higher for older offenders. This result suggests that especially for these individuals, juvenile detention is not the right punishment.

The several control estimates used by the authors as robustness checks proved to confirm these earlier results. Also the findings are in line with Entorf (2012) who analyzes German data in a related study. He focuses at the effect of turning 18 and obtains similar estimates in employing a two-equation probit model.

5.5   Reconciling the Different Pieces of Evidence

At first sight, the presented findings on juvenile recidivism may appear contradictory. While most studies relying on US data find that the application of criminal law increases recidivism, German data suggests the opposite effect. However, there is one important difference: the studies using US data look at the effects of application of criminal versus juvenile law in general, whereas the discussed paper exclusively studies incarceration. This alone may immediately explain the apparent difference in results. Moreover Pichler and Römer (2011) sort out three mechanisms that could be behind the difference in the observed results.

A first argument can be made based on a fundamental difference between the law systems in the United States and Germany. As Whitman (2003) writes in the introduction to his book on the difference between the legal systems on the two continents, "criminal punishment in America is harsh and degrading—more so than anywhere else in the liberal West." Accordingly adolescents are generally punished more severely in the US system, especially if they end up in criminal prison, and after release they may find it hard to enter or re-enter lawful employment. In contrast, the German system is rather mild, and incarceration is regarded as the "ultima ratio," especially for juveniles. To capture this difference, Pichler and Römer (2011) introduce the notion of a U-shaped relationship between harsh punishment and recidivism,

Table 5.3
RD estimates (cutoff: age 21)

	(1)	(2)	(3)	(4)	(5)	(6)	(7)	(8)	(9)
	Bdw = 1	Bdw = 2	Bdw = 2.5	Bdw = 2.5	Bdw = 2.5	Bdw = 2.5	Bdw = 2.5	Bdw = 2.5	Bdw = 2.5
Recidivism21–	0.264	0.252	0.245	0.315	0.331	0.330	0.303	0.334	0.329
Recidivism21+	–0.038	0.034	0.048	0.002	–0.002	–0.028	–0.049	0.076	0.079
ΔRecidivism	–0.301*	–0.218	–0.197	–0.313*	–0.333**	–0.358**	–0.351**	–0.258	–0.250*
	(0.051)	(0.126)	(0.135)	(0.086)	(0.071)	(0.026)	(0.027)	(0.117)	(0.080)
Crimlaw21–	0.229	0.350	0.370	0.378	0.393	0.427	0.407	0.458	0.399
Crimlaw21+	1	1	1	1	1	1	1	1	1
ΔCrimlaw	–0.771	–0.650	–0.630	–0.622	–0.607	–0.573	–0.593	–0.542	–0.601
Socio econ1	No	No	No	Yes	Yes	Yes	Yes	Yes	Yes
Socio econ2	No	No	No	No	Yes	No	Yes	No	Yes
Sentence1	No	No	No	No	No	yes	Yes	Yes	Yes
Sentence2	No	No	No	No	No	No	Yes	No	Yes
Crime1	No	No	No	No	No	No	No	Yes	Yes
Crime2	No	No	No	No	No	No	No	No	Yes
ATE	–0.391*	–0.335	–0.313	–0.503**	–0.548**	–0.625**	–0.592**	–0.476	–0.415*
	(0.061)	(0.134)	(0.141)	(0.042)	(0.029)	(0.030)	(0.043)	(0.119)	(0.071)
NObs	55	102	131	129	127	125	113	125	113

Source: Pichler and Römer (2011)
Note: $*p < 0.10$, $**p < 0.05$, $***p < 0.01$; p-values in parentheses; socio econ (socioeconomic variables) 1: age, age2, criminal family; 2: poor social capital, German nationality; sentence (sentence-related variables) 1: sentence length, current months in prison; 2: open prison, job contact, total years in prison; crime (type of crime)1: theft, vandalism; 2: robbery. Group "1" contains those controls significantly different between samples; "bdw" reports the applied bandwidth; "21–" denotes estimates using only data below the cutoff point; "21+" denotes estimates using only data above the cutoff point; "Δ" denotes jumps at the cutoff point.

with German prisons generally more to the left at the minimum and the US counterparts more to the right. Consequently German criminal prisons come closer to the optimum whereas in the United States juvenile prisons tend to be the preferable facility. This view is in agreement with Hjalmarssson (2009b), who shows that incarceration in juvenile facilities can be effective in combating juvenile crime as opposed to mild punishments such as probation or a fine. She argues that in the case of American juvenile prisons, the deterrent effect may outweigh the drawbacks of incarceration, in particular the stigma and potential peer effects. In terms of the U-shaped pattern, that may be assumed to be the optimal level of harsh punishment.

Second, the age group is different. Whereas the authors of American studies look at adolescents under 18, Pichler and Römer (2011) analyze a sample where most of the individuals sent to criminal prisons are older than 20. Hence the optimal legal framework might also take age into consideration.

A third explanation for the competing results can be different levels of peer effects between the countries. As reported by Bayer et al. (2009), incarceration can fuel subsequent criminal behavior, especially where individuals are incarcerated for similar offenses. The difference in results may thus be due to stronger peer effects in German juvenile prisons as compared to the US counterparts. In this sense, the German attitude toward incarceration as the "ultima ratio" could result in a selective population in German juvenile prisons—with a higher proportion of the "toughest guys" as compared to American juvenile prisons.

5.6   Consequences for Public Policy

As this chapter focuses only on incarceration, we cannot derive policy recommendations for the general application of juvenile law. However, we can offer some policy advice concerning incarcerations. Whereas the Council of Europe's recommendation Rec(2008)11 on the "European Rules for Juvenile Offenders Subject to Sanctions and Measures" suggests an extended application of juvenile law, our findings in Pichler and Römer (2011) question this policy. Regarding imprisonment, the data suggest the opposite: it may be beneficial to send more adolescents to criminal prisons instead of juvenile prisons in order to lower their intentions to re-offend.

The empirical analysis we present considers two different ways to deal with self-selection issues. The results from both approaches identify a stronger inclination toward re-offending among adolescent inmates in a juvenile prison as compared to adolescent inmates in a criminal prison. While the exact mechanisms at work remain unknown, we discern a weakness in the German system. In the current setting, inmates in a juvenile prison can stay at this facility until they reach age 24. At this point, the inmates are far beyond the stage for which personal-development studies suggest a preferential juvenile treatment. Of course, our study cannot shed light on the question whether adult incarceration in general is the optimal punishment for inmates at this age. We do see, however, that sending adolescent offenders aged 18 and above to a prison where most other inmates are young and highly selected youths is ineffective in reducing recidivism. At the older age, a regular criminal prison would be the better facility.

Notes

1. See Junger-Tas and Dünkel (2009) for a more detailed description of the different legal systems.

2. The complete regulation is as follows: Juvenile registers are erased after three years if sentence length does not exceed one year and after five years otherwise. Criminal registers are erased after three years if sentence length does not exceed three months and five years otherwise. Sexual offenses are erased after ten years for both juveniles and adults and criminals. For all cases, the sentence length is added to the indicated time period.

3. Furthermore, when faced with a different set of sentence possibilities, judges may think strategically and choose whether to apply criminal or juvenile law (Dünkel 2006).

4. The survey was initiated and carried out by Horst Entorf and a team of researchers from Darmstadt University of Technology.

5. For a more detailed analysis of this issue and the dataset in general, see Entorf (2009).

6. While this question includes both the intention to recidivate and an estimated likelihood of detection, inmates of juvenile and criminal prisons gave very similar estimates for the overall probability of detection pertaining to the various crime types. Only for property crimes do inmates of juvenile facilities report a significantly lower probability of getting caught. However, our results in section 5.4.3 show a higher likelihood of recidivism among inmates in juvenile prisons. And, if anything, this suggests an underestimate of actual fact.

7. This strategy has been suggested and used by Entorf (2009). Pichler and Römer (2011) also tried different ways of bundling the original multinomial variable, which did not change the results.

8. In principle, one could do the same for the cutoff point (age 18); however, the study revealed that judges rarely apply criminal law in cases where the youths have just turned 18.

References

Aebi, M. 2004. Crime trends in Western Europe from 1990 to 2000. *European Journal on Criminal Policy and Research* 10 (2): 163–86.

Banister, P., F. Smith, K. Heskin, and N. Bolton. 1973. Psychological correlates of long-term imprisonment. *British Journal of Criminology* 13 (4): 312–30.

Bayer, P., R. Hjalmarsson, and D. Pozen. 2009. Building criminal capital behind bars: Peer effects in juvenile corrections. *Quarterly Journal of Economics* 122: 105–47.

Becker, G. 1968. Crime and punishment: An economic approach. *Journal of Political Economy* 76 (2): 169–217.

Bishop, D., and S. Decker. 2006. Punishment and control: Juvenile justice reform in the USA. In J. Junger-Tas and S. H. Decker, eds., *International Handbook of Juvenile Justice*. Berlin: Springer, 3–35.

Bishop, D., C. Frazier, L. Lanza-Kaduce, and L. Winner. 1996. The transfer of juveniles to criminal court: Does it make a difference? *Crime and Delinquency* 42 (2): 171–91.

Bochmann, C. 2009. *Entwicklung eines europäischen Jugendstrafrechts*. Baden-Baden: Nomos.

Corrado, R., I. Cohen, W. Glackman, and C. Odgers. 2003. Serious and violent young offenders' decisions to recidivate: An assessment of five sentencing models. *Crime and Delinquency* 49 (2): 179–200.

Dölling, D., P. Bauer, and H. Remschmidt. 2007. Besonderheiten des Jugendstrafrechts. In D. Dölling, P. Bauer, and H. Remschmidt, eds., *Handbuch der Forensischen Psychiatrie*. Stuttgart: Steinkopf, 435–510.

Dünkel, F. 2006. Juvenile justice in Germany: Between welfare and justice. In J. Junger-Tas and S. H. Decker, eds., *International Handbook of Juvenile Justice*. Berlin: Springer, 225–62.

Entorf, H. 2009. Crime and the labour market: Evidence from a survey of inmates. *Journal of Economics and Statistics* 229 (2–3): 254–69.

Entorf, H. 2012. Expected recidivism among young offenders: Comparing specific deterrence under juvenile and adult criminal law. *European Journal of Political Economy* 28: 414–29.

Entorf, H., J. Möbert, and S. Meyer. 2008. Evaluation des Justizvollzugs. *Physica*. Available at: http://www.amazon.com/Evaluation-Justizvollzugs-Ergebnisse-bundesweiten -Feldstudie/dp/3790819956.

Fagan, J. 1996. The comparative advantage of juvenile versus criminal court sanctions on recidivism among adolescent felony offenders. *Law and Policy* 18: 77–114.

Fender, J. 1999. A general equilibrium model of crime and punishment. *Journal of Economic Behavior and Organization* 39 (4): 437–53.

Glaeser, E., B. Sacerdote, and J. A. Scheinkman. 1996. Crime and social interactions. *Quarterly Journal of Economics* 111 (2): 507–48.

Green, D. 1989. Measures of illegal behavior in individual level deterrence research. *Journal of Research in Crime and Delinquency* 26 (3): 253–75.

Hjalmarsson, R. 2009a. Crime and expected punishment: Changes in perceptions at the age of criminal majority. *American Law and Economics Review* 11 (1): 209–48.

Hjalmarsson, R. 2009b. Juvenile jails: A path to the straight and narrow or to hardened criminality? *Journal of Law and Economics* 52: 779–809.

Jehle, J., W. Heinz, and P. Sutterer. 2003. *Legalbewährung nach strafrechtlichen Sanktionen. Eine kommentierte Rückfallstatistik.* Bundesministerium der Justiz, Berlin.

Jensen, E., and L. Metsger. 1994. A test of the deterrent effect of legislative waiver on violent juvenile crime. *Crime and Delinquency* 40 (1): 96–104.

Junger-Tas, J., and F. Dünkel. 2009. Reforming Juvenile Justice: European Perspectives. In J. Junger-Tas and F. Dünkel, eds., *Reforming Juvenile Justice.* Berlin: Springer, 215–33.

Kupchik, A., J. Fagan, and A. Liberman. 2003. Punishment, proportionality, and jurisdictional transfer of adolescent offenders: A test of the leniency gap hypothesis. *Stanford Law and Policy Review* 14: 57–83.

Lange, N. 2007. *Resozialisierung im Gefängnis.* Munich: Grin.

Lanza-Kaduce, L., J. Lane, D. Bishop, and C. Frazier. 2005. Juvenile offenders and adult felony recidivism: The impact of transfer. *Journal of Criminal Justice* 28 (1): 59–77.

Lee, D., and J. McCrary. 2009. The deterrence effect of prison: Dynamic theory and evidence. Working paper 550. Industrial Relations Section, Princeton University.

Levitt, S. 1998. Juvenile crime and punishment. *Journal of Political Economy* 106 (6): 1156–85.

Maxson, C., K. Matsuda, and K. Hennigan. 2011. "Deterrability" among gang and nongang juvenile offenders: Are gang members more (or less) deterrable than other juvenile offenders? *Crime and Delinquency* 57 (4): 516–43.

Moffitt, T. 1993. Adolescence-limited and life-course-persistent antisocial behavior: A developmental taxonomy. *Psychological Review* 100: 674–701.

Myers, D. 2003. The recidivism of violent youths in juvenile and adult court: A consideration of selection bias. *Youth Violence and Juvenile Justice* 1 (1): 79–101.

Nagin, D., and G. Pogarsky. 2001. Integrating celerity, impulsivity, and extralegal sanction threats into a model of general deterrence: Theory and evidence. *Criminology* 39: 865–91.

Oberwittler, D., and S. Höfer. 2005. Crime and justice in Germany: An analysis of recent trends and research. *European Journal of Criminology* 2 (4): 465–508.

O'Mahony, D., and J. Doak. 2009. Restorative justice and youth justice: Bringingtheory and practice closer together in Europe. In J. Junger-Tas and F. Dünkel, eds., *Reforming Juvenile Justice.* Berlin: Springer, 165–82.

Pichler, S., and D. Römer. 2011. Juvenile law and recidivism in Germany—New evidence from the old continent. Discussion paper series 519. University of Heidelberg.

Piquero, A., and R. Paternoster. 1998. An application of Stafford and Warr's reconceptualization of deterrence to drinking and driving. *Journal of Research in Crime and Delinquency* 35: 3–39.

Podkopacz, M., and B. Feld. 1995. End of the line: An empirical study of judicial waiver. *Journal of Criminal Law and Criminology* 86: 449–42.

Pogarsky, G. 2002. Identifying "deterrable" offenders: Implications for research on deterrence. *Justice Quarterly* 19: 431–52.

Schore, J., R. Maynard, and I. Piliavin. 1979. *The Accuracy of Self-Reported Arrest Data*. Princeton: Mathematica Policy Research.

Singer, S., and D. McDowall. 1988. Criminalizing delinquency: The deterrent effects of the New York juvenile offender law. *Law and Society Review* 22: 521–35.

Steiner, B., C. Hemmens, and V. Bell. 2006. Legislative waiver reconsidered: General deterrent effects of statutory exclusion laws enacted post-1979. *Justice Quarterly* 23 (1): 34–59.

Taylor, R., E. Fritsch, and T. Caeti. 2006. *Juvenile justice: Policies, programs, and practices*. New York: McGraw-Hill.

Thornberry, T., D. Huizinga, and R. Loeber. 2004. The causes and correlates studies: Findings and policy implications. *Juvenile Justice* 9 (1): 3–19.

Uggen, C. 2000. Work as a turning point in the life course of criminals: A duration model of age, employment, and recidivism. *American Sociological Review* 65 (4): 529–46.

Western, B., J. Kling, and D. Weiman. 2001. The labor market consequences of incarceration. *Crime and Delinquency* 47 (3): 410–27.

Whitman, J. 2003. *Harsh Justice: Criminal Punishment and the Widening Divide between America and Europe*. New York: Oxford University Press.

Wright, B., A. Caspi, T. Moffitt, and R. Paternoster. 2004. Does the perceived risk of punishment deter criminally prone individuals? Rational choice, self-control, and crime. *Journal of Research in Crime and Delinquency* 41: 180–213.

6   What Works in Reducing Hooliganism?

Mikael Priks

6.1   Introduction

Sports fan violence has plagued many countries throughout history. An early incident occurred in the amphitheater in Pompeii, 19 years before the volcano. Citizens of Pompeii and the neighboring city Nuceria were cheering different gladiators as hooligan violence broke out. As a result "many families from Nuceria lost a father or a son" (Tacitus, *Annals*, AD 14–68, bk 24, p. 109). In Constantinople in 532, team cheering at chariot races escalated from insults to mob riots, which finally led to some 30,000 deaths and laid the town in ruins. Much later, in 1314, soccer was banned in London for the fear of tumult and disorder surrounding the games (Armstrong 1998).[1]

Hooligan violence continued to afflict countries around the world during the last century. A general pattern is that hooliganism escalated during the 1980s, in particular in England. An infamous example is the violence in Heysel stadium in Belgium in 1985, which resulted in chaos and the death of 39 persons. In the Hillsborough disaster in 1989, 96 Liverpool fans died in a stampede. Also the Netherlands were plagued by violence. Van der Brug (1994, p. 177) writes ". . . the period after 1980 shows an enormous increase in violence outside the stadia. Supporters often raise hell in the inner cities and sometimes the residents are not spared. Shops are looted, passers-by are robbed." This type of violence is still highly prevalent in many countries in Europe and Latin America with numerous recent severe incidents in, for example, Italy, the Netherlands, and France.

Hooliganism is particularly undesirable as it generates large costs due to negative externalities. Specifically, potential spectators avoid attending games in fear of violence. A recent Swedish survey, for example, indicates that 25 percent of those interested in football do not attend games due to hooligan violence (Novus 2011). The policing costs are also vast. In Italy, the annual policing cost related to the soccer championship amounted to 40 million euro (De Biasi 1997). In the Premier Leauge, the costs amount to more than 9 million euro (*The Independent*, August 13, 2008).

These observations raise the questions: Can police reduce hooliganism and, if so, which form of policing is more efficient? While England experienced large problems in the 1980s, the situation has now improved substantially. The authorities have since then changed strategy from a relatively indiscriminate form of policing to more discriminative policing. This means that they employ intelligence units with spotters and try to identify exactly which hooligan is behaving unlawfully. Other countries, such as Sweden and Denmark, have followed the English example. However, countries in southern Europe and Latin America still tend to use indiscriminate forms of policing, such as water cannons or tear gas to scatter groups of hooligans.

The question how police could deter hooliganism has attracted much interest in the media. Hooliganism has also been extensively studied in the social sciences, namely sociology, psychology, anthropology, and criminology. While this work has generated many insights, the impact of policing on hooliganism has not yet been studied, neither empirically or theoretically as the research approaches are different from those used in economics. It is, for example, often suggested that the English practice of discriminative policing has been effective. But since the society responds to crime by employing more police it is very difficult to isolate this effect.

In this chapter, I report on my recent work with Panu Poutvaara on this topic. In the first part, I discuss a theoretical model of utility-maximizing hooligans that has implications for which form of policing is efficient. In the second part, I report findings from an empirical study using two natural experiments to learn if intelligence police units reduce hooliganism. The first part is based on Poutvaara and Priks (2009a) and the second part is based on Poutvaara and Priks (2009b).

I here briefly report our main findings. In line with Becker (1968), more discriminative police will, for a given size of the violent fan clubs, tend to reduce the incentives to engage in violence. However, we also consider another, more subtle, mechanism. When indiscriminate policing is intensified, this affects all fan club members. So club members who are least inclined toward violence are punished relatively harshly. They may consider dropping out of the clubs. In response to this, the leaders may strategically decide to limit the size of the club to a small but very brutal group. This can increase the overall level of violence. Such a possible outcome suggests the need for policy makers to carefully study the group dynamics of fan clubs before making policy decisions.

Whether policing works in reducing hooliganism is ultimately an empirical question. But empirical work would be plagued by possible reversed causality between hooliganism and policing. We use two exogenous shocks to police to address this problem: the first due to the 9/11 terrorist attack and the second due to the Asian Tsunami disaster in 2004. Subsequent to both catastrophic events the Stockholm police intelligence unit monitoring hooligans was reallocated. Using self-reported Swedish data on hooligan violence, we show that Stockholm-related violence went up dramatically each time the unit was shut down. Various robustness analyses show that the hooligan violence was not due to a societal trend. We do not address empirically how indiscriminate policing affects hooliganism. This should be an interesting area for future research.

In a nutshell, hooligan violence is costly both from the damage of violence and from the resources expended to prevent it. Our analyses take the question of how policing can prevent hooligans, consider the different effects of different policing strategies, and show empirically that discriminative policing is effective. We hope that our suggestions can be used by policy makers to reduce hooliganism.

The outline is the following: Section 6.2 describes some characteristics of hooligan groups. The effect of police on hooliganism is analyzed in section 6.3. Section 6.4 provides some concluding remarks.

6.2   The Hooligan Scene

Hooligan groups are characterized by leaders and members. Young members have to prove themselves by taking part in fights. One, perhaps obvious, reason for why individuals take part in such groups is a taste for violence. Another reason is that some individuals look for social identity (e.g., see the work by psychologist Marsh 1978 and sociologists Dunning, Murphy, and Waddington 2002). As a Swedish former hooligan states, "We asked for violence and we appreciated the fights, but this was not the main reason for why we were there. It was a combination of obsession for the club, the fights surrounding it, and most of all the fellowship with each other we found there" (Höglund 2005, p. 183, own translation).

The groups are characterized by strong leaders who organize fights with each other so as to test their fighting strengths. While the different leaders of clubs build hostilities toward other clubs, they also adhere to rules that govern the fights. In Sweden, for instance, club members are not allowed to bring weapons or kick on anyone on the ground. In Turkey, the hooligan groups have codes of conduct that state that the intention must be to injure rather than to kill. Any stabbing must be below the waist.

Unlike other types of gangs, hooligan groups by and large do not engage in economic crimes, which means that there are no payments from members to leaders. Another hooligan group characteristic is that members are not recruited between groups. If there is more than one such group in a city, participation is typically by geographic location or social classes. In Rome, for example, the club AC Roma is regarded as a team of the urban working class whereas Lazio is known to draw its members from the wealthy suburbs (Telegraph.co.uk, "Roman football's cause for divide," November 7, 2007). Similar patterns are found in other cities.

6.3   Policing and Hooliganism

6.3.1   What Are the Different Policing Strategies?

As we noted at the start of the chapter, there are, roughly speaking, two different ways of policing hooligans. Discriminative policing is when, early on, police make the effort of finding out who did what. One example is the use of spotters, who try to identify unlawful behavior as it occurs. Such intelligence units are also often used to gather information before violent incidents can take place. Another example is the use of surveillance cameras. Apart from deterring crime, they can obviously be used to sort out the details after a hooligan incident has occurred. Special cars are even sometimes used to target specific violent hooligans so as to separate them.

The alternative, indiscriminate method of policing basically affects hooligans as well as others standing close to the hooligans, regardless of which individual was actually unruly. Grouping many hooligans together and ousting them out of an arena, or jailing them over night, is a type of indiscriminate policing. Yet other such policing involves the use of tear gas, baton charges, rubber bullets, or water cannons to scatter hooligan crowds.

6.3.2 Which Policing Type Is Efficient?

In this section, I report our findings from a micro-founded model of hooliganism that focuses on inherent violence as due to group dynamics.

The Model

To analyze the empirical evidence, we set up a model for the case where, in order to stay in the club, members are required to engage in fights with other clubs. The individual club has a monopoly position relative to an exogenous given number of potential hooligans. Members value the social identity they get in being associated with the club, but they differ in their attitudes toward violence. Some members enjoy fighting more than other members. However, leaders cannot observe the preferences of individual members.

Results

The effect of discriminative policing is standard; more police presence increases the marginal cost of violence and therefore reduces violence. However, the indiscriminate type of policing may not reduce violence. Because leaders do not observe which members are more prone to fight, more violent members have the possibility to mimic those who prefer less violence. The leaders therefore face a trade-off. One possibility is to opt for a small but very violent organization. Another possibility is to go for a larger organization with less violence per member. This trade-off may produce a backfiring effect. The cost of membership when indiscriminate policing is used reduces more than proportionally the amount of violence that can be required from those members not valuing violence highly. Even if the leaders before the change in policy had opted for a low level of violence to keep all members in the club, they may change strategy and embrace a level of brutality among members, absent those willing to fight less. In general, we find that parameter changes that increase the difference between the maximum level of violence—where more violent and less violent types are willing to commit—tend to increase the parameter range in which the adverse effect of policing backfiring can occur.

In other words, the backfiring effect arises because the group size may change in response to police intervention. If a group size does not change, more indiscriminate policing will deter violence. The main goal of this analysis is to identify the group dynamics that sustain and encourage hooliganism.

Discussion

Scholars in social sciences, namely sociologists and psychologists, have for long been arguing that more policing can incite hooligan violence (e.g., see Cohen 1971; Buford 1991; Kerr 1994; Adang and Stott 2004). The belief here is that hooligans get agitated when confronted by harsh police opposition. Sometimes they even start fights with police as a result. In a press release psychologists Adang and Stott advised Dutch police in their preparations for the European Championship in 2004 that: "Indiscriminate, heavy-handed policing can create rather than reduce conflict. Police should instead be concentrated on those that actually misbehave. This may obviously be more expensive, but our analysis indicates that it may still be worth it." (Adang and Stott 2004)

In the differences between discriminative and indiscriminate policing, it is ultimately an empirical question of which form of policing is most efficient. I next discuss some recent evidence on the effect of discriminate policing using intelligence units.

6.3.3   The Effect of Police Intelligence on Hooliganism

The effect of police intelligence units on hooligan violence has not been studied until recently. One explanation is that data are lacking; another is that research traditions in other social sciences such as sociology and psychology have focused on other methods. Yet a third explanation is that it is hard to evaluate the effect of policing on crime in general. There is normally a positive correlation between police and hooligan violence, which does not, of course, imply that more police presence leads to more violence. In order to break the causality, it is necessary to have a source of exogenous variation for police.

We recently used such variation to study how police affect hooliganism. We were able to do a difference-in-difference analysis using a change that took place in Stockholm when after the 9/11 terrorist attack and the Asian Tsunami in December 2004, the intelligence unit that works on Stockholm hooligans was shut down. There exists a recent literature that approaches the causality problem with similar methods. A seminal work by Levitt (1997) used gubernatorial elections as an instrument for policing and found that more policing tends to reduce crime. Using terrorist attacks as sources of exogenous variation in police, a number of works have shown that police presence reduces auto theft (Di Tella and Schargrodsky 2004 and Klick and Tabarrok 2005) as well as violence, theft, and sexual offenses (Draca et al. 2010). Additionally Machin and Marie (2011) study policy initiatives when particular police forces were given more resources to combat crime. The strength of our analysis here is that the exogenous shocks to police took place outside Sweden's boarders. I next present the data we used.

Data
There are three intelligence units monitoring hooligans in Sweden. One works in Stockholm, the other in Gothenburg, and the third in the south province of Skåne. There are six officers in the Stockholm unit who keep track of potentially violent supporters attached to the three Stockholm clubs AIK, Djurgårdens IF, and Hammarby IF. Each officer is specialized in following hooligans of a certain team. Hooligans recognize the officer who is attached to monitor them, which is supposed to have a calming effect. According to police, hooligans realize very quickly when officers in the unit are not present. The officers in the intelligence unit follow the supporters to away games and provide police units in other parts of the country with intelligence information. When the police officer has information indicating that a fight is coming up, he contacts the commander-in-chief at the game who commands the requested number of officers. If violence is initiated, it is filmed and later analyzed so that the hooligans responsible can be prosecuted. The officer may also serve as a witness in a trial.

Following the 9/11 terrorist attack, the Sport Intelligence and Tactical Unit in Stockholm was reallocated for a 16-day period to guard a Stockholm mosque. Following the Tsunami in December 2004, the unit was reallocated to the Stockholm airport to be safeguard incoming goods from Swedish victims. We use these exogenous sources of variation in policing to identify the effect of the supporter policing on hooligan violence. The reallocation due to the terrorist attack took place during the soccer season and the reallocation due to the Tsunami took place during the ice hockey season. We therefore treat the two experiments separately. Because the reallocations only affected the Stockholm police, we use incidents when Stockholm teams were involved as the treatment group and other incidents as the control group.

Consider first the reallocation due to the Tsunami. Following this catastrophe, the Stockholm Intelligence Unit was reallocated from

January 3, 2005, until April 3, 2005. We therefore collapsed the ice hockey season data into two periods per year; the fall season and the spring season. This generated 30 periods.

After the terrorist attack in September 2001, the intelligence unit was reallocated from October 8 until October 30. There was not much time until the season ended. We therefore collapse the data during the soccer season into thirteen 16-day periods per year.

The data are collected by the largest hooligan group in Sweden, Firman Boys. They support one of the three large Stockholm clubs, AIK, and claim to have recorded "all major incidents in connection to soccer and ice hockey when Swedish hooligans have been involved" since 1990. According to the head of the intelligence police unit, the data are very well structure, well written and of high quality. Supporters have in many cases been wounded and sometimes suffered from life-threatening injuries during hooligan fights. We constructed two different dependent variables. The first one takes on the value 1 if Firman Boys reports any type of violence and 0 otherwise. The second variable, which has not been reported before, is a violence index we created. It goes from 0 to 3 where no violence is denoted by 0.

There were 41 violent incidents in the ice hockey seasons reported from the fall season 1992 until the end of the spring season 2007. While the fans of the Stockholm teams are the most frequent participators, fans of other teams participate in 35 instances. Figure 6.1 shows the differences between Stockholm-related violence and violence not

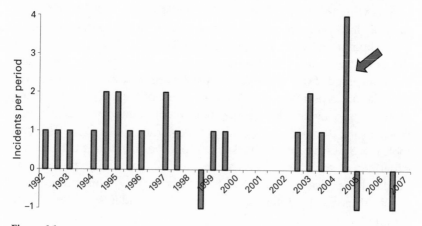

Figure 6.1
Difference between violence related and not related to Stockholm clubs during the ice hockey season

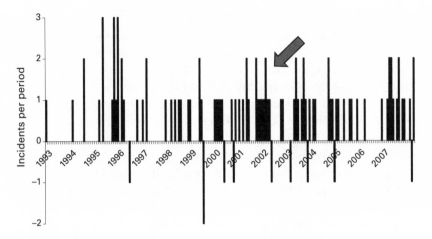

Figure 6.2
Difference between violence related and not related to Stockholm clubs during the soccer season

related to the Stockholm teams during the ice hockey season. The reallocation period is noticeable because while non-Stockholm fans sometimes fight each other, in the reallocation period they did not. In the reallocation period, marked with an arrow, there were four Stockholm-related incidents. This should be compared to the average number of Stockholm-related incidents in other periods, which is 0.96.

Violence is more common during the soccer season. There were 152 incidents in the time period we considered. The fans of the Stockholm teams and the teams IFK Göteborg and Helsingborgs IF are highly over represented. However, other teams participated on 63 occasions.

Figure 6.2 shows the difference between Stockholm-related violence and other violence during the soccer season. Also here we observe an increase in the period when the intelligence unit was shut down, although the effect is smaller in this time period. There were two Stockholm-related incidents and no other incidents in this period. While this is not a large number, it is large compared to the average of Stockholm-related incidents in other periods: 0.55.

Empirical Strategy

To isolate the causal effect of police on hooliganism, we ran the following regression:

$$Violence_{it} = \alpha + \beta\, Stockholm_i + \gamma\, Tsunami_t + \delta(Stockholm_i \times Tsunami_t) + \theta_t + e_{it}.$$

The dependent variable $Violence_{it}$ first denotes the number of violent incidents in group i in period t. We then used the index of violence, which goes from 0 to 3. The group is either Stockholm-related violence (the treatment group) or not Stockholm-related violence (the control group). $Stockholm_i$ is a dummy variable that takes on 1 if there was Stockholm-related violence and zero otherwise. The parameter β measures the difference in Stockholm-related violence compared to other violence. $Tsunami_t$ is a dummy variable that takes on one in the spring season of 2005 when the supporter police was reallocated. The parameter γ measures the general effect during the Tsunami period.

In the second part of the analysis, we studied the effect of reallocations during the terrorist attack. We then used the variable "attack" instead, which denotes the time period during which the police were reallocated due to the 9/11 terrorist attack.

The coefficient of largest interest is δ. It measures the effect on Stockholm-related violence in the period when the supporter police units were reallocated. θ_t denotes time-specific effects for every period and e_{it} is the error term.

Results

Consider first the effect during the Tsunami period in the ice hockey season. The results are reported in table 6.1. In the first column, the results without time-fixed effects are reported. The Stockholm clubs are involved in much more violence than other clubs, which also the raw data showed. There were approximately 0.6 more Stockholm-related incidents than other incidents per period and this result is highly significant. There was no general change in violence in Sweden during the Tsunami period as the second row shows. More important, there was during the reallocation period a dramatic increase in relative terms in Stockholm-related violence. The estimated effect of the reallocation is 3.42, which should be compared to the average 1.03. The result is significant at the 1 percent level. There was in other words a more than 300 percent increase in Stockholm-related violence in this period. Column 2 reports the results when period-fixed effects are included in the regression. This increases the precision of the difference-in-difference estimate.

One concern with this analysis is that the type of incidents in the reallocation period could be mild. In this case, while many incidents were reported, the overall level of violence would not have been particularly high. Table 6.2 reports the results when the dependent variable

Table 6.1
Effect of policing on violent incidents related to ice hockey

Dependent variable: Number of violent incidents

Sample	(1)	(2)
Stockholm	0.586***	0.586***
	(0.212)	(0.153)
Tsunami	−0.345	−0.207
	(0.820)	(0.718)
Stockholm *Tsunami	3.414***	3.414***
	(1.160)	(0.839)
Period fixed effects	No	Yes
Adjusted R^2	0.28	0.62
Observations	60	60

Note: Standard errors are in parentheses below coefficients. *** indicates significance at the 1 percent level, ** at 5 percent, and * at 10 percent.

Table 6.2
Effect of policing on total violence related to ice hockey

Dependent variable: Violence (0–3)

Sample	(1)	(2)
Stockholm	1.448***	1.448***
	(0.383)	(0.411)
Tsunami	−0.345	−0.276
	(1.485)	(1.923)
Stockholm *Tsunami	6.552***	6.552***
	(2.010)	(2.251)
Period fixed effects	No	Yes
Adjusted R^2	0.37	0.27
Observations	60	60

Note: Standard errors are in parentheses below coefficients. *** indicates significance at the 1 percent level, ** at 5 percent, and * at 10 percent.

is the index of total violence. Again, the difference-in-difference estimate is highly significant at the 1 percent level. The result is not affected by adding different time-period fixed effects. The increase in the index, 6.55, should be compared to the Stockholm average 2.17. The increase is almost exactly the same as before, approximately 300 percent. In other words, it was not the case that the incidents that took place during the reallocation period were particularly mild.

In sum, our results show that ice hockey related violence was significantly increased during the time when the Sport Intelligence and Tactical Unit for exogenous reasons was not monitoring hooligans.

Consider next the results from the regressions that focused on the period during the soccer season when the Stockholm intelligence unit was reallocated due to the 9/11 terrorist attack. Column 1 in table 6.3 shows that there, again, was much more Stockholm-related violence than in the control group (0.4 more incidents in a 16-day period). There was no change in hooliganism in Sweden at large during the reallocation period. However, there was a strong significant effect on Stockholm-related violence in this period. Compared to the average number of Stockholm related incidents, 0.61, there was an increase by 1.58 incidents in the reallocation period. While this is a small number in absolute terms, the relative increase is as much as 260 percent. Controlling for 195 period-fixed effects increases the precision of the estimate somewhat. It is now significant at the 5 percent level.

Table 6.3
Effect of policing on violent incidents related to soccer

Dependent variable: Number of violent incidents		
Sample	(1)	(2)
Stockholm	0.423***	0.423***
	(0.058)	(0.055)
Attack	−0.175	−0.289
	(0.812)	(0.664)
Stockholm *9/11 attack	1.577*	1.577**
	(0.812)	(0.768)
Period fixed effects	No	Yes
Adjusted R^2	0.13	0.22
Observations	390	390

Note: Standard errors are in parentheses below coefficients. *** indicates significance at the 1 percent level, ** at 5 percent, and * at 10 percent.

Table 6.4
Effect of policing on total violence related to soccer

Dependent variable: Violence (0–3)

Sample	(1)	(2)
Stockholm	0.861***	0.861***
	(0.116)	(0.113)
Attack	–0.258	–0.570
	(1.147)	(1.366)
Stockholm *9/11 attack	3.139***	3.139***
	(1.622)	(1.560)
Period fixed effects	No	Yes
Adjusted R^2	0.37	0.18
Observations	60	60

Note: Standard errors are in parentheses below coefficients. *** indicates significance at the 1 percent level, ** at 5 percent, and * at 10 percent.

Table 6.4 reports the results when the index of total violence is used as the dependent variable. The increase in the index is given by 3.14, which should be compared to the Stockholm-related average 1.13. The increase amounts to 240 percent, which is just below the estimated change in the regression with the number of incidents as the dependent variable. Our estimate is statistically significant at the 5 percent level when controlling for the period-fixed effects. This again indicates that the incidents in the reallocation period were not soft.

A concern with this type of analysis is that the increase in violence might have occurred before the reallocation periods. To address this possibility, we ran dummy treatments in the periods surrounding the true allocation periods. We did not find any significant changes neither before nor after these periods. Using data from the Swedish National Police Force, we also did not find any evidence for significant changes in violence or theft in Sweden during the reallocation time periods.

A question that arises is whether the games that have a high risk of violence are equally distributed between the periods. Because the fan clubs of the four teams AIK, Djurgårdens IF, Hammarby IF, and IFK Göteborg are much more violent than other clubs, the fact that these teams meet relatively often within a specific period could explain much of the variation between periods. We addressed this by counting the number of times any combination of these four teams meet within each 16-day period. There were, on average, 0.63 high-risk games each

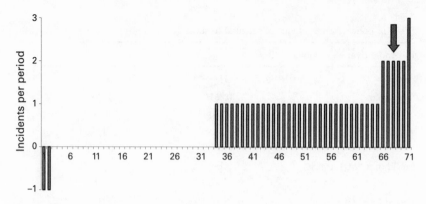

Figure 6.3
Difference between violence related and not related to Stockholm clubs during the soccer season when there was one high-risk game

period. The maximum number of times the high-risk teams met was three. The number of high-risk games in the reallocation period was one.

In figure 6.3 we report the difference between Stockholm-related violence and violence not related to Stockholm teams for the periods that had exactly one high-risk game. To illustrate the distribution of violence, we order these periods from the lowest to the highest number of violent incidents in a period. Out of 71 observations, only one has more violence than the reallocation period and four periods have the same level of violence. Since most of the other high-violence periods have more than one high-risk game, our regression result was in fact strengthened when controlling for the number of high-risk games.

Discussion

A natural question is if the benefits of police dominate the costs. The police has informed us that the annual costs for the six officers in the intelligence unit amounts to approximately 380,000 euro. We know that there were ten Stockholm-related incidents per year in the time period 1993 to 2007. Based on the estimated effect 300 percent, we would expect an increase by 30 incidents each year if the intelligence unit was shut down. In other words, 380,000 euro reduces the number of incidents by 30. The cost of avoiding one hooligan incident is therefore approximately 12,700 euro.

What are the costs of hooliganism? This question is difficult to answer. It includes loss in consumer surplus, destroyed property, medical bills, and human suffering. As mentioned above, many individuals do not dear to go to soccer games and the loss in consumer surplus can therefore be massive. The hooligans regularly destroy bars, subway trains, and so on, which is costly for both the private owners and the public in terms of government revenue. The medical bills are probably smaller compared to the human suffering and the other costs. There is also a possibility that violence feeds violence. Youths without much prospect in life may take part in hooliganism the more of it that exists. At the end of the day, it is up to policy makers to decide if preventing one significant incident is worth 12,700 euro.

6.4 Concluding Remarks

Our research has addressed the question how hooligans respond to policing. Our first method was to develop a micro-founded model of hooliganism where different types of policing could be introduced. We found that harsh, indiscriminate policing, which is sometimes still used in southern Europe can potentially backfire and incite violence. Discriminative policing, in contrast, is not risky to use even though it can be expensive. We then tested if discriminative policing is effective by exploring two unique Swedish natural experiments where the sports game police was reallocated for other reasons than changes in the extent of previous violence. The result for this type of policing proved to be strong and suggests it to be highly efficient. From a methodological standpoint, the main benefit of the analysis is that the reasons for the change in policy was due to two exogenous events, the 9/11 terrorist attack and the Tsunami in 2004, which took place outside Sweden's borders. Since we used a difference-in-difference approach with Stockholm-related violence as treatment group, it is unlikely that the exogenous shocks would affect the Stockholm hooligans only.

The overall conclusion, then, is that discriminate policing works but that using indiscriminate policing could be hazardous. Having said this, I should be careful when giving policy recommendations. A problem with our empirical analysis was that we had few observations, and we only analyzed the case of Sweden. The effects of indiscriminate policing are theoretical and we have no information on the empirical effects of this type of policing. More solid empirical work addressing the causal effect of different types of police on hooliganism would certainly help policy makers in their fight against supporter violence.

I wish to thank panu poutvaara for allowing me to use our joint work. I also thank Alberto Alesina, Larry Blume, Matz Dahlberg, Stefano Della Vigna, Edward Glaeser, Henrik Hordahl, Ethan Kaplan, Katarina Keller, Hans löfdahl, John Matsusaka, Torsten Persson, Per Pettersson-Lidbom, Andrei Shleifer, David Strömberg, Daniel Sturm, Jakob Svensson, Jenny Säve-Söderbergh, Alex Tabarrok, and many seminar participants for comments on the underlying work.

1. For other historical incidents, see, for example, Carnibella et al. (1996).

References

Adang, Otto, and Stott Cliff. 2004. Disorderly conduct: Social psychology and the control of football hooliganism at Euro2004. *Psychologist* 17: 318–19.

Armstrong, Gary. 1998. *Football Hooligans—Knowing the Score*. New York: Berg.

Becker Gary, S. 1968. Crime and punishment: An economic approach. *Journal of Political Economy* 76: 169–217.

van der Brug, Hans H. 1994. Football hooliganism in the Netherlands. In Guilianotti Richard, Bonney Norman, and Hepworth Mike, eds., *Football Violence and Social Identity*. London: Routledge. 174–95.

Buford, Bill. 1991. *Among the Thugs*. London: Seker and Warburg.

Cohen, Stanley. 1971. *Folk Devils and Moral Panics*. London: Paladin.

De Biasi, Rocco. 1997. The policing of mass demonstrations in contemporary democracies: The policy of hooliganism in Italy. Working paper 97/10. European University Institute, Florence.

Di Tella, Rafael, and Ernesto Schargrodsky. 2004. Do police reduce crime? Estimates using the allocation of police forces after a terrorist attack. *American Economic Review* 94: 115–33.

Draca, Mirco, Stephen Machin, and Robert Witt. 2010. Panic on the streets of London: Police, crime and the July 2005 terror attacks. *American Economic Review* 101: 2157–81.

Dunning, Eric, Murphy Patrick, and Waddington Ian. 2002. Towards a sociological understanding of football hooliganism as a world phenomenon. In Eric Dunning, Patrick Murphy, Ian Waddington, and Antonios E. Astrinakis, eds., *Fighting Fans: Football Hooliganism*. Dublin: University College Dublin Press, 1–23.

Höglund, Johan. 2005. *En av grabbarna*. Stockholm: MMG Books AB.

Independent, The. 2008. Premier league content with current policing costs. August 13.

Kerr, John H. 1994. *Understanding Soccer Hooliganism*. Bristol, PA: Open University Press.

Klick, Jonathan, and Alexander Tabarrok. 2005. Using terror alert levels to estimate the effect of police on crime. *Journal of Law and Economics* 68: 267–79.

Levitt, Steven. 1997. Using electoral cycles in police hiring to estimate the effect of police on crime. *American Economic Review* 87: 270–90.

Machin, Steven, and Olivier Marie. 2011. Crime and police resources: The street crime initivative. *Journal of the European Economic Association* 9: 678–701.

Marsh, Peter. 1978. *Aggro: The Illusion of Violence.* London: Dent.

Novus 2011. Rapport—Allmänheten om fotbollsvåld. Report for Novus.

Poutvaara, Panu, and Mikael Priks. 2009a. Hooliganism and police tactics. *Journal of Public Economic Theory* 11: 441–53.

Pouvaara, Panu, and Mikael Priks. 2009b. The effect of police intelligence on group violence: Evidence from reassignments in Sweden. *Journal of Public Economics* 93: 403–11.

Tacitus. [AD 109] 1937. *The Annals* (Jackson, John, trans.). Cambridge: Harvard University Press.

Telegraph.co.uk. 2007. Roman football's cause for divide, November 7.

7   Crime and Immigration: What Do We Know?

Brian Bell and Stephen Machin

7.1   Introduction

It is commonplace, in many countries, to hear some politicians, media commentators, and members of the general public assert that immigrants harm the labor market prospects of natives. Indeed there is a very large, sometimes controversial, academic literature that investigates whether one can marshal evidence to support this assertion (e.g., see Borjas 1999; Card 2005, 2009). Similarly a view often expressed is that immigrants cause crime when they locate in foreign countries. Yet this key question has received far less attention than the labor market work. This seems surprising given that the economic and social costs of crime are usually estimated to be large.[1] It turns out that evidence on crime and immigration is much less common, and there is currently only a very sparse academic literature studying the subject.

The link between crime and immigration therefore forms the subject matter of this chapter. We review the small (though growing) literature that exists and try to draw some general conclusions. To do so, we begin by considering how we can think about possible crime–immigration links in the orthodox Becker (1968) and Ehrlich (1973) economic model of crime. This model tends to emphasize the different economic incentives and sanctions faced by different individuals, so we frame our discussion in terms of how these may vary for immigrants versus natives and for different immigrant groups.

We next turn to the empirical evidence on crime and immigration. There are several different methodological approaches that have been taken in the literature. These very clearly deliver evidence that varies in quality of data, in research design and in empirical implementation. We thus critically appraise the findings from the various approaches, with the intention of trying to produce some insight into the key findings that emerge from the empirical work studying crime and immigration. The chapter ends with a summary of these conclusions and with a discussion of directions for future research.

7.2   The Economic Model of Crime and the Crime–Immigrant Relation

7.2.1   The Orthodox Economic Model of Crime

The "orthodox" economic model of crime participation was first introduced by Becker (1968) and further developed by Ehrlich (1973) and others (see Freeman 1999 for a review). In this model, individuals rationally choose between crime and legal labor market work depending on the potential returns each sector offers. The "returns" from crime are calculated relative to the probability of getting caught and the expected sanction if caught, and this is then compared to the labor market earnings from employment. If the former outweighs the latter, then an individual will engage in crime.

More formally, individuals choose between criminal and legal activity by comparing the expected utility from each. If E denotes legal earnings and E_c denotes earnings from crime, we can define the utility from working at a legal wage as $U(E)$ and the utility from a successful (i.e., not caught) crime as $U(E_c)$. If p denotes the probability of being caught and S represents the monetary equivalent of the expected sanction if caught, then an individual decides to engage in criminal activity if:

$$(1 - p)U(E_c) - pU(S) > U(E). \tag{7.1}$$

This model can be manipulated so as to form a crime participation equation

$$C = C(E_c, E, p, S) \tag{7.2}$$

in which $\partial C / \partial E_c > 0$, $\partial C / \partial E < 0$, $\partial C / \partial p < 0$, and $\partial C / \partial S < 0$.

Thus this basic model yields simple, testable predictions on crime participation, which can be thought of as incentive effects (on the labor market side) and deterrence effects (on the criminal-justice side). From the labor market side, the key prediction of the model is that relative labor market opportunities matter. People without a job ($E = 0$) are more likely to participate in crime.[2] So are those where the formal wage E is low relative to the crime wage E_c. From the criminal-justice side, a higher probability of being caught p or a higher sanction S are predicted to have a crime reducing deterrence effect.

There is extensive evidence showing that relative labor market opportunities do have an effect on criminal activity. For example, Gould, Weinberg, and Mustard (2002) show that there are strong links between local labor market conditions (measured both by the unemployment rate and the local wage) and crime rates in the United States. Similarly Machin and Meghir (2004) demonstrate that areas that experienced lower wage growth at the lower end of the wage distribution (i.e., a relative deterioration of the area-specific low wage labor market) during the 1980s and 1990s in England and Wales were more likely to see rising property crime rates.

Individual characteristics have also been shown to be correlated with criminal activity. There are numerous ways to think how these characteristics affect such behavior, but two occur naturally within the model above. First, labor market opportunities (both the wage and the probability of finding employment) are correlated with individual characteristics. For example, higher educational attainment is associated with higher wages and lower unemployment. Thus we would expect, all else equal, for educational attainment to be negatively correlated with crime participation.[3] Second, individual characteristics may directly affect the utility function. For example, education may increase an individual's civic engagement and reduce the utility from criminal participation (see Dee 2004) or may affect the discount rate used in the utility comparisons.[4]

With regard to the criminal-justice side, the model predicts that the probability of being caught and the expected sanction if caught are also important determinants of the criminal participation decision. Note that the individual participation decision depends on the individual's estimate of these parameters rather than the actual probabilities and sanctions. Again, there is substantial evidence that these factors do matter, although this evidence tends to suggest that it is the probability of being caught and sanctioned, rather than the size of the penalty, which is the strongest determinant. Lochner (2007) shows that individual perceptions of the probability of arrest are strongly correlated with individual criminal activity and that such perceptions adjust with experience of criminal behavior and arrests. Similarly Langan and Farrington (1998), building on a large body of cross-national studies, find substantial negative correlations between the likelihood of conviction and crime rates.

7.2.2   Possible Crime–Immigration Links

How can we use this model to help frame our thinking about immigration and crime? For our purposes, it is evident that a crime–immigration link can exist in this economics of crime framework if immigrant groups have different demographic characteristics to natives and if the perceptions associated with the criminal-justice system and its functioning differ. Stated another way, differences in the values of the various parameters in (7.1) will generate different criminal participation decisions. To the extent that natives and immigrants differ in these parameters, the model would predict different criminal participation rates. However, the cultural and motivational differences between natives and immigrant communities may also alter propensity to crime participation.

To illustrate this, in tables 7.1 and 7.2 we provide some summary statistics on various characteristics and perceptions of male natives and immigrants in the United Kingdom. In table 7.1 we compare natives and immigrants in terms of labor-market relevant characteristics as derived from the Labour Force Survey (LFS). In table 7.2 we provide descriptive evidence on the perceptions of natives and immigrants to the probability of apprehension as a result of criminal activity and

Table 7.1

Characteristics of male natives and immigrants

| | Natives | Immigrants | Immigrant cohort | | |
			1970–1999	2000–2009	A8 wave
Age	39.8	37.3	40.6	32.2	30.9
% White	95.7	45.6	40.8	46.4	95.8
% Married	46.0	54.5	59.7	49.3	43.3
% Degree	21.5	27.7	31.0	26.3	7.9
Years of schooling	12.7	14.7	14.5	15.3	14.7
% English first language	98.6	48.5	57.0	33.7	7.8
Participation rate	82.9	82.7	84.1	83.4	94.4
Unemployment rate	8.8	8.9	8.9	8.5	4.9
% Managers/professionals	43.3	40.5	45.0	36.0	9.7
Mean hourly wage (£)	14.00	13.41	15.37	11.95	8.56
Median hourly wage (£)	11.62	10.33	12.70	9.00	7.50
Sample size	113,609	23,881	5,988	7,727	1,541

Source: UK Labour Force Survey 2010
Notes: Figures for men aged 16 to 64.

consequent sanction, based on data from the British Crime Survey (BCS) and the Offending, Crime and Justice Survey (OCJS).[5]

Let us, first, consider the LFS-based comparisons of natives and immigrants in table 7.1. The table reports differences in mean characteristics for all male natives and immigrants in 2010, and also breaks down the immigrant stock into those who arrived before 2000 and those after and those who arrived from A8 accession countries post-2004 (referred to as the A8 wave).

Note that, on average, immigrants to the United Kingdom are more educated than natives, with an average of two extra years of schooling. The participation and unemployment rates are identical between natives and immigrants, suggesting that at least for working-age males we would expect broadly similar legal labor market attachment. Immigrants do on average earn less than natives, though the mean hourly wage is only 4 percent lower.

The table also makes it very clear that there is considerable heterogeneity in the different immigrant groups.[6] The post-2000 immigrant cohort and the A8 wave, in particular, have stronger labor market attachment than the 1970 to 1999 cohort, although noticeably their wages and occupational standings are lower.

Table 7.2
Natives and immigrant perceptions of apprehensions and sanctions

	Natives	Immigrants
British Crime Survey		
Expected sentence for rape (months)	58.5	67.3
% Effective police	60.7	68.9
% Effective prosecutions	46.0	63.4
% Effective sentences	21.2	43.2
Sample size	39,997	4,641
Offending, Crime and Justice Survey		
% Pr (Assault arrest)	24.6	23.2
% Pr(Car theft arrest)	23.1	22.6
% Pr(Burglary arrest)	21.6	19.2
% Pr(Prison, 3 Strikes assault)	23.6	33.2
% Pr(Prison, 3 Strikes car theft)	42.7	59.4
% Pr(Prison, 3 Strikes burglary)	51.9	63.6
Sample size	8,070	2,157

Sources: GB British Crime Survey 2009/10 and Offending, Crime and Justice Survey 2003

Turning to table 7.2, we also see differences in the perceptions of natives and immigrants to the probability of apprehension as a result of criminal activity and consequent sanction. The 2003 Offending, Crime and Justice Survey (OCJS) asked respondents to predict how many times out of 100 crimes the police would make an arrest. For a variety of crimes the probability was assessed to be around 25 percent, and there is no obvious difference between natives and immigrants in this assessment.[7]

Alternatively, the British Crime Survey (BCS) asked respondents how effective they thought the local police were in catching criminals. Interestingly this produced a much higher percentage and some evidence that immigrants thought the police were more effective than natives did. Certainly, these data suggest that immigrants are unlikely to attach a lower detection probability in (7.1) than natives.

Interestingly, when we turn to perceptions of sanctions, we see a strongly different picture between natives and immigrants. Immigrants attach much higher probabilities to repeat offenders being sent to prison than do natives.[8] In addition, for those that are sent to prison, immigrants expect longer sentences to be handed down. Two obvious explanations arise to account for these differences. First, natives or immigrants may have more experience of the criminal-justice system and therefore more informed views on sanctions. Second, immigrants may simply have more faith in the system. This latter explanation receives some support from the BCS data, which show that immigrants have much higher confidence in the state prosecuting authority effectively prosecuting offenders and in the courts issuing effective sentences. All of this suggests that we would expect both S and p in (7.1) to be higher for immigrants than natives that, ceteris paribus, reduces the likelihood of immigrant crime participation.

This discussion serves to show the potential value of the economic model of crime as a framework to think about the relative propensities of natives and immigrants to engage in criminal activity. It should be noted that while the model is silent on the type of crime committed, it seems intuitive that property crime is best understood with this model. A small literature (e.g., Grogger 2000) does apply the Becker/Ehrlich model to violent crime through violence being complementary to drug crimes, but we suspect that, in general, the model is less useful in this context. In particular, relative labor market opportunities seem unlikely to act as a strong or significant determinant of violent crime.

It is also possible that immigrants can affect crime through spillover effects. Even if immigrants have the same criminal propensity as observationally equivalent natives, immigration could cause an increase in crime if it reduces natives' labor market opportunities, inducing them to substitute toward criminal activity. Such effects will be felt most by those natives who are closest substitutes in the labor market for the newly arriving immigrants. For example, Borjas, Grogger, and Hanson (2010) suggest that such a mechanism may have operated against low-skilled black Americans, who are thought to be close labor market substitutes to the immigrants who arrived in the United States in the 1980s and 1990s. The incarceration rate of such low-skilled black Americans has risen substantially in recent years.

7.3   Empirical Evidence on Crime and Immigration

There are several relevant areas of empirical work that we can consider. These are as follows: panel data models of the crime–immigration relationship, models of individual crime experiences (typically based on self-report data), imprisonment and immigration, crime and migrant legalization, crime victimization and immigration, and immigrant neighborhood effects and crime. In this section we consider each of these in turn.

7.3.1   Panel Data Models of the Crime–Immigration Relationship

To date, this approach probably produces the most convincing evidence we have on the empirical connections between crime and immigration. There are strong similarities between the approach taken with the sizable literature on immigration and the labor market, especially the spatial approach favored by Card (2005, 2009) in his studies of the impact of immigration on wages and employment.

These studies use panel data tracking crime rates in the same areas over time, typically relating them to immigrant stocks in an equation specified for area i in year t as:

$$C_{it} = \alpha_i + \beta_1 M_{it} + \beta_2 X_{it} + T_t + \varepsilon_{it}, \tag{7.3}$$

where C is the crime rate, M the immigrant stock, X denotes area control variables, T denotes a set of time dummies, and ε is an error term. An area fixed effect, α, is included and this controls for time-invariant area-specific effects.

This equation is often first differenced (where Δ denotes a first differencing operator) to express the model in changes (i.e., transforming out the spatial fixed effects):

$$\Delta C_{it} = \beta_1 \Delta M_{it} + \beta_2 \Delta X_{it} + \Delta T_t + \Delta \varepsilon_{it}. \tag{7.4}$$

Thus in (7.4) the coefficient β_1 measures the empirical connection between changes in immigrant stocks and changes in crime across areas through time.

Several papers in the literature report estimates based on spatial data through time in either the within-groups panel data setting of equation (7.3) or the first-differenced panel data setting of equation (7.4). However, one concern remains in that these equations treat the immigration variable as exogenous. In the real world, this seems fairly implausible and is likely to bias estimates of the coefficient of interest, β_1. Suppose that immigrants chose locations based on their crime outcomes. Moreover suppose that immigrants chose areas with low crime outcomes (we would, of course, expect natives to do the same but immigrants have arguably freer choice over location when they first arrive in a new country—in particular, for more skilled immigrants). Then we might observe a negative estimate of β_1. However, this would not demonstrate the causal effect of immigrants on crime, but rather the selection effect of immigrants based on crime. To deal with this problem requires an instrumental variable strategy. One needs a variable that is correlated with immigrant location, but not with crime (other than through immigration).

The recent literature on the broader economic impact of immigration on receiving countries has generally addressed this identification issue either by devising suitable instruments (Altonji and Card 1991; Card 2001) or by exploiting some natural experiment where immigrants are forcibly allocated to areas they had not chosen (Damm 2009; Edin et al. 2003; Gould et al. 2004; Glitz 2012). These kinds of approaches are also taken in the work focused on crime and immigration.

Table 7.3 summarizes the findings from the five papers of which we aware that report causal instrumental variable (IV) estimates using spatial panel data. Bell, Fasani, and Machin (2013) (hereafter BFM) estimate versions of (7.4) for England and Wales over the period 2002 to 2009. They examine the impact on violent and property crime of two large immigrant flows that occurred over the period. The first was associated with a large increase in asylum seekers as a result of dislocations in many countries during the late 1990s and early 2000s (e.g., Iraq,

Table 7.3
Causal estimates of the crime–immigration relationship from longitudinal data

Study	Data	Approach	Findings
Bell, Fasani, and Machin (2013)	England and Wales, Local Authorities, 2002–2009	IV estimates using spatial dispersal policy for asylum wave and prior-settlement patterns for A8 wave	Positive effect of asylum wave on property crime; negative effect of A8 wave on property crime; no effect of violent crime
Bianchi, Buonnano, and Pinotti (2012)	Italian provinces, 1990–2003	IV estimates using prior-settlement patterns	No causal effect of immigration stocks on total crime, nor on subset of property crimes
Spenkuch (2011)	US counties in Census years 1980, 1990, 2000	IV estimates using prior-settlement patterns	Positive effects on property crime, no effect on violent crime; only positive for Mexican migrants
Alonso, Garoupa, Perera, and Vasquez (2008)	Spanish provinces, 1999–2006	IV estimates using lagged values and the service share of GDP	Positive relationship (but not good instruments)
Butcher and Piehl (1998a)	43 US cities, 1981–1990	IV estimates using initial share of immigrants in a city (in 1979)	No effect of immigration (IV estimate < 0 and insignificant)

Afghanistan, Somalia, and former Yugoslavia). The second flow resulted from the expansion of the European Union in 2004 to include Poland, Hungary, Czech Republic, Slovakia, Slovenia, Estonia, Latvia, and Lithuania—the so-called A8. The United Kingdom decided to grant citizens from these countries immediate and unrestricted access to the UK labor market. BFM argue that tighter identification of the impact of immigration on crime can be achieved by focusing on specific and large immigrant flows.

Least squares estimates of (7.4) show that neither asylum seekers nor A8 immigrants had much effect on violent crime. The point estimates in BFM are never anywhere near statistically significant. In contrast, property crime models suggest positive effects of asylum seekers (i.e., rising property crime in areas with rising asylum immigrant stocks) and significantly negative effects for A8 immigrants. That is, the influx of poorer asylum seekers up to the early 2000s appeared to be correlated with a rise in property crime, but the influx of eastern Europeans after 2004 appears to correlate with reductions in property crime.

BFM pay close attention to the importance of instrumenting the immigrant stocks to control for endogenous location choice. For the asylum wave, they make use of the dispersal policy adopted by the National Asylum Support Service (NASS) in 2001. From that date, individuals seeking asylum were dispersed to locations around the United Kingdom while their claims were being decided. The choice of locations was determined by the NASS with no reference to the wishes of the individual applicant. Thus the dispersal policy itself can be used as an instrument to explain the locations of asylum seekers, assuming locations were not chosen by NASS administrators as a result of correlation with crime shocks. Note that this identification strategy does not require there to be no correlation between location and the *level* of crime, since the fixed-effect controls for this.

For the A8 wave, location choice is entirely up to the individual. However, an extensive literature has established that the prior settlement pattern of immigrants from the same national/ethnic group has a strong predictive effect on location choice of future immigrants. Assuming that prior settlement patterns have no correlation with *changes* in current crime rates allows us to use the prior settlement pattern of A8 immigrants across areas combined with aggregate A8 flow data to produce predicted A8 stocks for each area each year. This instrument is shown to be strongly correlated with actual immigrant stocks (with a clustered F-statistic = 12.8).

The IV estimates in BFM show that the detrimental effect of asylum seekers on property crime rises and becomes substantially more significant than the OLS estimates. In contrast, the effect of the A8 wave on property becomes more beneficial and again more significant. The estimates imply that a 1 percent point increase in the share of asylum seekers in the local population is associated with a rise on 1.09 percent in property crimes, while a similar rise in A8 immigrants reduces property crime by 0.39 percent.

They interpret these results within the economic model of crime. The A8 immigrants had strong attachment to the labor market—indeed that was the reason for their migration. Asylum seekers were, in general, prevented from seeking legal employment in the United Kingdom and the benefits paid to them were substantially less than the out-of-work benefits paid to natives. It is thus not surprising that there were different effects on property crime rates from the two waves. Yet in neither case were the effects quantitatively substantial, so most of the decline in property crime witnessed in the United Kingdom over the last decade was not related to immigration.

A second study by Bianchi, Buonanno, and Pinotti (2012) examines the crime–immigration link across Italian provinces over the period 1990 to 2003. Fixed-effect estimates show that a 1 percent increase in the total number of immigrants is associated with a 0.1 percent increase in total crime. When the authors disaggregate across crime categories, they find the effect is strongest for property crimes and, in particular, for robberies and thefts. To account for endogenous location choice, the authors use a variant of the prior-settlement pattern instrument used by BFM for the A8 immigrants. Again, the first-stage regression suggests that this is a strong predictor of immigrant stocks across localities. In contrast to the OLS results, the IV results show no significant effect of immigrant stocks on total crime, nor on the subset of property crimes. Thus the causal effect of total immigration on crime is not significantly different from zero.

A third paper considered in table 7.3, by Spenkuch (2011), uses panel data on US counties across the three census years 1980, 1990, and 2000. As with BFM and Bianchi et al., Spenkuch also reports IV estimates using prior-settlement patterns to identify the crime–immigration relation. He finds generally positive and significant effects from immigrant stocks on property crime rates but no such effect for violent crime. The estimated elasticity implies that a 10 percent increase in the share of immigrants would lead to an increase in the property crime rate of 1.2 percent. The IV estimates are broadly similar in magnitude but are much less precisely estimated.

Spenkuch breaks the immigrant stock into Mexican and non-Mexican. He argues that this allows him to explore whether the economic model of crime provides a useful guide to examining the impact of immigration on crime. We know that Mexicans tend to have significantly worse labor market outcomes relative to other immigrant groups in the United States and we might therefore expect a more substantial positive coefficient on Mexican immigrants in the property crime regression than for non-Mexican immigrants. This indeed turns out to be the case, with the coefficient being significantly positive for Mexican immigrants while negative and insignificant for all other immigrants. Such a result complements the arguments of BFM that it makes sense to focus on particular immigrants groups in addition to estimating the overall impact of immigration on crime.

Alonso et al. (2008) follow a similar approach for Spain. They have annual data on reported crime and convictions at the province level between 1999 and 2006. In addition to immigrant share in the population, they also include age, education and unemployment rates and the lagged crime rate as additional controls. Though they report IV estimates, their instruments (lagged values of the covariates and measures of the service share of GDP in a province) are not very convincing in dealing with the endogeneity of immigrant location choice. The authors find a significant, positive relationship between immigrant share and crime rates, even after controlling for socioeconomic and demographic characteristics of the province.

Finally, Butcher and Piehl (1998a) present evidence on the crime–immigration link across 43 cities in the United States over the period 1981 to 1990. Again they estimate (7.3) using a fixed-effect panel and various demographic and socioeconomic controls. Whether they focus on overall crime rates or the violent crime rate, the authors find no significant correlation between immigrant stocks in a city and crime. They also estimate an IV model using the initial share of immigrants in a city in 1979 to predict the decadal change in immigrant share that they then regress on the decadal change in crime. This is somewhat similar to the IV strategy of BFM, though they do not use nationality-based settlement patterns that provide arguably stronger identification than aggregate immigrant shares. In addition Butcher and Piehl have only 35 observations in this specification so it is difficult to provide convincing estimates. With these caveats in mind, the IV results also show no effect of immigrant stocks on crime rates—the coefficient is negative but not significant.

7.3.2   Individual-Level Crime Experiences

An alternative strategy is to directly estimate the probability of committing a crime across a large sample of individuals and examine whether the propensity differs between natives and immigrants, controlling for as many other observable characteristics as possible. In an ideal world this approach would use data on actual criminal behavior (or at least some criminal-justice outcome such as arrest or conviction). In practice, such data rarely exist (and even more rarely do such data also provide extensive personal characteristics), so most research in this area tends to use self-reported criminal activity. Unsurprisingly, the evidence suggests that such data tend to substantially underreport criminal behavior.

A standard empirical model for such an approach based on cross-sectional data for individual i is

$$\Pr(\text{Criminal behavior}) = \gamma_0 + \gamma_1 \text{Immigrant}_i + \lambda X_i + u_i, \qquad (7.5)$$

where the dependent variable is a Yes/No report of criminal behavior, X denotes other characteristics, and u is an error term. Because of the discrete $0 - 1$ nature of the dependent variable (7.5) can be estimated by standard probit or logit estimation.

There are two problems with this approach. First, it requires that for the coefficient on the immigrant indicator to measure the true differential of immigrant-native criminal propensity, the model is controlling for all other individual characteristics that are correlated with both immigrant status and criminal propensity. Second, it is assumed that natives and immigrants have the same probability of truthfully revealing criminal behavior. If immigrants are less likely to admit to criminal behavior, we would mechanically find a lower propensity to commit crime, which would tell us nothing about the true effect.

Table 7.4 summarizes three studies in the economic literature that try to estimate the crime–immigration relation using self-report data. Papadopoulos (2011) examines the relationship between immigration

Table 7.4
Estimates of crime–immigration relationship from self-report crime data

Study	Data	Approach	Findings
Papadopoulos (2011)	Offending Crime and Justice Survey, England and Wales	Self-report crime model that tries to correct for underreporting and controls for age, gender, region, ethnicity (but not labour market variables)	Immigrants less likely to report involvement in property crime than natives
Butcher and Piehl (1998a)	US National Longitudinal Survey of Youth	Probit of self-report of being involved in criminal activity or having had contact with the criminal-justice system controlling for individual, family and area variables	Immigrants significantly less likely to report crime or contact with criminal-justice system
Nunziata (2011)	European Social Survey, 17 West European countries	Probability of being crime victim conditioning on individual characteristics and the share of immigrants in the local area	No significant relationship

and property crime offending in England and Wales using the OCJS. He recognizes the problem of nonrandom underreporting of criminal behavior and proposes a parametric model to account for this. The extent to which such models can successfully overcome this problem relies on the exclusion restrictions imposed, and we are doubtful that truly satisfying restrictions exist.

Turning to his empirical results, the range of explanatory variables used in the probability models is somewhat limited. Controls for age, gender, region, and ethnicity are included. Regrettably, because of problems with sample size, no individual measures of labor market activity are included. This is unfortunate since the objective here is essentially to estimate the empirical counterpart of the crime participation equation (7.2). Since this depends crucially on relative labor market opportunities, the exclusion raises doubts as to the robustness of the conclusions regarding immigrant-native crime propensities. He finds that immigrants are less likely to report involvement in property crime than natives. The difference is however generally not statistically significant.

The second paper in the table, by Butcher and Piehl (1998a), also estimates probit models of individual criminal activity using the US National Longitudinal Survey of Youth. Controlling for a range of individual characteristics of the individual, family and area, they find that immigrants are significantly less likely to report having been involved in criminal activity or having had contact with the criminal-justice system (stopped, arrested, charged, or convicted).

The other paper summarized in table 7.4 is by Nunziata (2011) who examines individual-level self-reported data on crime victimization across a sample of 17 western European countries using the European Social Survey. He then models the probability of being a victim of crime on a set of individual characteristics and the share of immigrants in the local area.[9] The data cover repeated cross sections, and this allows for the identification of regional fixed-effects in the probability model to control for unobserved regional heterogeneity in crime. Nunziata also reports specifications that use prior-settlement patterns as an instrument for regional immigration stocks. The empirical results suggest that immigration does not have any significant impact on criminality in destination regions once unobserved regional characteristics are controlled for.

One difficulty with this study is that the number of observations in a region/year cell is small (there are 115 regions and 100,000 observations across all years). The fixed-effect model achieves identification of the impact of immigration on crime victimization by exploiting changes within a region across years. Small cell sizes are likely to generate spurious changes in victimization rates and lead to an attenuation bias toward zero in the coefficient on immigrant stocks.

7.3.3 Imprisonment Rates between Natives and Immigrants

Comparing imprisonment rates of natives and immigrants is of obvious policy interest and can be done relatively easily for many countries.[10] However, it should be recognized that such analysis is investigating a fundamentally different concept of the crime–immigration link than the approaches considered above. Since prison is the outcome of the combined effect of criminal behavior, detection probability and judicial sanction, there is no tight link between immigrant propensity to commit crime and imprisonment. So, for example, if the police are more effective at catching immigrants (or perhaps just allocate more resources to crimes that are thought to be committed by immigrants) or the courts impose more severe penalties on immigrants, we would find higher immigrant imprisonment rates than natives, even if their criminal propensities were identical.

Figure 7.1 shows the share of foreigners in the total population and in the prison population for a set of advanced economies in 2005.[11] For most countries, foreigners appear overrepresented in the prison population. At the extreme, 71 percent of the prison population in Switzerland is foreigners, even though they account for only 23 percent of the total population. Only the United States appears to imprison foreigners at a lower rate than their share of the population, while the ratio for the United Kingdom is toward the lower end of the spectrum.[12] We know of no systematic analysis of why there are such large differences across countries, which may be due to sentencing policy, policing strategies, differences in immigrant types, and so on.

Indeed such aggregate measures can be misleading. Since we know that the prison population tends to be disproportionately male, young, and poorly educated, if immigrants are overrepresented in such at-risk populations, they will have higher imprisonment rates even if individual probabilities of imprisonment are the same.[13] This underscores the need to control for individual characteristics in the prison population. In a series of papers, Butcher and Piehl (1998b, 2005) have examined US census data to evaluate the relative incarceration rates of natives and immigrants. One difficulty with this analysis is that only

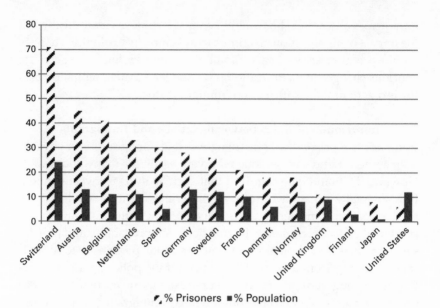

r, % Prisoners ■ % Population

Figure 7.1
Foreign population in prison. Note the percent Prisoners shows the percentage of prisoners who are foreigners, while percent Population shows the percentage of the population who are foreigners. If imprisonment rates were identical between foreigners and natives, the bars would be the same height within a country. Source: OECD (2007)

the 1980 census allows for an exact identification of imprisonment. Both the 1990 and 2000 censuses only identify individuals in institutionalized group quarters—this includes prison, mental hospitals, long-term care homes, and so on. To mitigate the effect, Butcher and Piehl only focus on males aged 18 to 40. In the 1980 census, 70 percent of this group that was institutionalized was in prison.

They find that immigrants were less likely than natives to be institutionalized. In 1990, 2.1 percent of the male population aged 18 to 40 were institutionalized. Among natives, the percentage was 2.2 percent while it was only 1.5 percent for immigrants. Furthermore immigrants were much less likely to be institutionalized than native-born men with similar demographic characteristics. Nevertheless, earlier immigrants were more likely to be institutionalized than more recent cohorts, suggesting an unfortunate assimilation effect as immigrants with longer time in the country approach the higher native incarceration rates.

The fact that recent immigrant cohorts into the United States have lower incarceration rates than comparable natives is particularly surprising since the literature on immigrant earnings suggests that recent immigrants have worse permanent labor market characteristics than earlier immigrants. Butcher and Piehl (2005) suggest that immigrant self-selection may explain why, despite poor labor market outcomes, immigrants may have better incarceration outcomes. For example, those immigrants who have high illegal earnings in the source country may decide to remain there rather than take the risk of developing their capacities in a new legal environment. Alternatively, migration costs may be correlated with success in multiple social dimensions (including criminality). Such hypotheses are hard to test in practice.

BFM also report data on the relative imprisonment rates of immigrants and natives in the United Kingdom. Their data come directly from official prison statistics on inmates. One difficulty, however, is that the data relate to nationality rather than country of birth or immigrant status. This means that it is not possible to examine successive cohorts of immigrants to see whether changes in cohort composition or quality led to different imprisonment rates. The data show that foreign nationals on average have marginally higher imprisonment rates than natives. Furthermore imprisonment rates vary strongly across nationalities. It would be interesting to understand whether the different imprisonment rates could be explained by the personal characteristics of the individuals, their labor market opportunities, the type of crime, or whether a true country-of-origin effect exists.[14]

7.3.4   The Impact of Migrant Legalization on Crime

The economics of crime model highlights the importance of the relative returns to legal and illegal activities. One important determinant of such returns for immigrants relates to their legal status in their adopted country. Illegal immigrants have much more limited opportunity to obtain legal employment and are rarely entitled to public assistance if they are unemployed. While this suggests that we would expect, ceteris paribus, higher criminal propensities among illegal immigrants, it is difficult to evaluate this empirically since we cannot in general observe illegal immigrants. However, two recent papers have made progress on this question by examining the effect of policy changes on the legal status of immigrants to assess the impact on crime.

Mastrobuoni and Pinotti (2011) examine the combined impact of a clemency granted to prisoners in Italy in 2006 and the expansion of the EU. Clemencies are a common feature of the Italian system and generally eliminate around two to three years of a sentence, with all inmates whose residual sentence is below such length being immediately released. The 2006 clemency led to 22,000 inmates being immediately released (more than one-third of the entire prison population). At the start of 2007, Romania and Bulgaria acceded into the European Union and were immediately able to legally seek employment in a number of sectors in Italy. Prior to this date, they would have been illegal. In contrast, foreigners from candidate EU members would be illegal both before and after 2007. Thus the authors propose examining the recidivism rate between Romanians and Bulgarians (the treatment group) and candidate EU foreigners (the control group) released as part of the clemency but from January 2007 subject to different legal status. A difference-in-difference estimator allows a comparison between relative outcomes pre- and post-legalization.

They find a strong and statistically significant reduction in the recidivism rate of Romanians and Bulgarians after the 2007 legalization relative to the control group. During 2007 the hazard rate for the control group does not change but it decreases from 5.8 to 2.3 percent for the treatment group. Breaking down by type of crime for which the individuals were originally incarcerated shows that the effect of legalization on recidivism is only significant for economically motivated offenders and not for violent offenders. Furthermore the effects are strongest in those areas that provide relatively better labor market opportunities to legal immigrants. While these results are consistent with the economics of crime model, it should be noted that the sample sizes of the study are quite small. In addition the authors need to use propensity score matching to adjust for different characteristics between the treatment and control group. This raises the question as to whether the identification of the difference-in-difference estimator is legitimate since unobserved differences between treatment and control group could account for the results.

Baker (2011) considers the impact of the 1986 Immigration Reform and Control Act (IRCA) in the United States. The Act was introduced in response to the rapid rise in illegal immigration during the late 1970s. The legislation imposed harsh penalties on employers who hired illegal immigrants, increased border security, and provided a near-universal amnesty for illegal immigrants currently in the United States. Almost 3 million immigrants were legalized across the United States.

Evidence from surveys of legalized immigrants suggests strong effects of legalization on labor market outcomes. Seventy-five percent of respondents reported that having legal status made it "somewhat" or "much" easier to find work, and 60 percent reported it helped them advance in their current job. Furthermore wages appear to be 30 to 40 percent higher for those who successfully obtained legal status following the passage of IRCA. This all suggests that there may be strong effects on crime patterns following the legalization.

To estimate the effect on crime, Baker collects data on both reported arrests and reported crime at the county level each year. This is matched to administrative data on the annual number of IRCA applicants in each county. In a fixed-effect model he finds that a one percentage point increase in the number of legalized IRCA applicants per capita is associated with a fall in overall crime of 1.6 percent. Both violent and property crime fall as a result of legalization, though the effect is larger for property crime. An extensive set of robustness checks confirms the key result that legalization led to reductions in crime.

7.3.5   Immigrants and Crime Victimization

Thus far we have reviewed evidence on the impact of immigration on reported crime, arrests, and imprisonment. However, there is also the alternative channel through which crime and immigration may be linked, namely that immigrants may be disproportionately victims of crime. Perhaps any positive correlations between crime and immigration rates in an area actually signal increased crime *against* immigrants rather than *by* immigrants. Most research in this area uses self-reported rates of victimization or victim reports from the police. Again, a key difficulty is that if immigrants have different reporting rates than natives, perhaps because they are more cautious in having contact with the authorities, it will be difficult to identify the true differential in victimization between natives and immigrants from the reported differential.

BFM use UK data from the BCS and the New Deal Evaluation to estimate probit models of self-reported crime victimization. Controlling for an extensive range of individual covariates, they find that immigrants are less likely to report being victims of crime than natives. This is true for all immigrants and for the two waves of immigrant inflows, asylum seekers and A8 that were the focus of their paper. This raises an interesting question as to why immigrants appear to be less exposed to crime. One possibility is that immigrants have moved into neighborhood clusters that provide a natural protection against crime, assuming immigrant-on-immigrant crime is less socially acceptable.

Krueger and Pischke (1997) collected data from German newspapers on reports of the number and nature of violent crimes against foreigners at the county level. In total they collect data on 1,056 such incidents, of which 651 are defined as serious (arson and murder). They find significant differences in the patterns of violence in the east and west of the country. The incidence of anti-foreigner crime is higher in the East and rises with distance from the former West German border. Interestingly, economic variables such as unemployment and wages do not affect the level of violent crime once location is accounted for. This is consistent with our observation that the economic model of crime is most appropriate for property crime rather than violent crime. Eckert (2002) provides further evidence on violent victimization of immigrants in Germany. He finds that most perpetrators already had a criminal record. He argues that the local communities, particularly in the East, often implicitly approved of attacks on asylum centers and that this encouraged violent youths who for the first time received recognition for their violence beyond their peer group.

Martens (1997) explores the experience of immigrants in Sweden. The evidence suggests that immigrants are more exposed to violence and threats of violence than are native Swedes. Interestingly, second-generation immigrants appear to be most exposed. Controlling for individual characteristics, second-generation immigrants are 30 percent more likely to experience violence than indigenous Swedes. The gap is a result of higher levels of violence in the street and other public places and for women, higher rates of domestic violence. In contrast, Killias (1997) reports that immigrants have broadly similar victimization rates compared to natives in Switzerland. He hypothesizes that this may be a result of the lower concentration of immigrants in poor neighborhoods than in some other countries.

There appears to be no consistent pattern of immigrant victimization across countries. It seems that violence against immigrants is more likely in poor areas in which immigrants have rapidly become a substantial and visible minority in previously homogeneous communities. The neighborhood seems to be important in this context, but more research is clearly needed on this aspect of the crime–immigration relationship.

7.3.6 Immigrant Neighborhood Effects and Crime

There is an extensive literature on neighborhood effects and crime. Examples include Kling, Ludwig, and Katz (2005), who examine the causal effect on youth criminal activity of relocating to lower poverty areas using a randomized housing voucher experiment, and Glaeser, Sacerdote, and Scheinkman (1996) who model the social interactions that occur between individuals, which lead to cross-neighborhood variances in crime rates. In an extensive review, Sampson, Morenoff, and Grannon-Rowley (2002) argue that neighborhood effects appear to be strongest for crime and other problem behaviors. Again, however, there has been very little work examining immigrant neighborhoods and crime. In the sociology literature there has been some work that has examined whether neighborhoods that are more ethnically heterogeneous have higher crime rates (as suggested by social disorganization theory[15]), but immigration effects are rarely separately identified.

To help fill this gap, Bell and Machin (2013) examine the link between immigrant concentration in a neighborhood and both crime victimization and recorded crime rates using data on over 30,000 neighborhoods in England and Wales. Controlling for a rich set of individual and neighborhood characteristics, they find that immigrant enclaves (i.e., neighborhoods with more than a 30 percent immigrant share of the local population) have significantly lower rates of nonviolent crime than similar areas with lower immigrant concentrations. This beneficial effect on crime is reported both by natives and immigrants, and appears to arise primarily from lower rates of less serious offenses such as motor vehicle crime and vandalism, rather than burglary and robbery. This perhaps suggests that immigrant enclaves are better able to control the antisocial behavior that is often associated with such low level crime.

7.4 Conclusions

This chapter has considered economic research that studies the connection between immigration and crime. Unlike the huge body of work on immigration and the labor market, this area is still in its infancy and, perhaps surprisingly given the importance of the issue, only a small literature exists on this subject.

Our critical appraisal of this literature concludes that, while it proves hard to find evidence of an impact of total immigration on crime, the series of papers that identifies a causal impact of immigration tends to emphasize the labor market attachment and opportunities of different immigrant groups. Where attachment is low (e.g., asylum seekers in the United Kingdom) or labor market opportunities are poor (e.g., low-wage migrants in the United States), an impact on property crime can be detected. It is hard to find evidence of any connection with violent crime. Moreover crime victimization seems to be, if anything, lower for immigrants.

More research is certainly needed in this area. Promising avenues for future research attention include more in-depth explorations on the causal impact of migration on crime outcomes, with perhaps more emphasis on distinguishing between different groups of migrants; a clearer understanding of the potential spillover effects from migrants to native crime activity, to focus on possible differences in the way that migrants are treated at different stages of the criminal-justice system (e.g., on types of crime activity, whether arrested or convicted, and on sentencing); and the time it takes for immigrants to start to look more like natives in terms of crime (i.e., a parallel question of investigation to the economic assimilation literature).

Notes

We would like to thank participants at the CESifo Summer Institute conference in July 2011 for a number of helpful comments. Finance was partly provided by the Economic and Social Research Council at the Centre for Economic Performance and by the Home Office.

1. See Cohen and Bowles (2010).

2. Of course, there are out-of-work benefits that offset this—though the replacement rate is less than 100 percent.

3. Indeed there is evidence showing a causal crime reducing impact of education (for the United States, see Lochner and Moretti 2004, and for England and Wales, see Machin, Marie, and Vujić 2011, 2012).

4. Other demographic characteristics display connections with crime participation. Examples include age (e.g., see Farrington 1986; Gottfredson and Hirschi 1983); marriage (e.g., see Sampson, Laub, and Wimer 2006); and gender (e.g., see Heimer 2000).

5. The LFS is a quarterly household survey currently covering around 120,000 individuals per quarter in the United Kingdom. The BCS is an annual household survey currently covering around 45,000 individuals per year in Britain. The OCJS was a cross-sectional survey conducted in 2003 and covered around 11,000 individuals, with an oversample of young people and ethnic minorities.

6. For another illustration of this based on US data, see Cortes (2004).

7. Unfortunately, immigrants cannot be directly identified in the OCJS since neither country of birth nor nationality is reported. However, respondents are asked how long they have been resident in the United Kingdom. We define natives as those who respond all their lives and all others as immigrants. This potentially mis-identifies those who come in and out of the United Kingdom but summary statistics on the characteristics of

the two groups are consistent with other surveys that directly identify immigrants. In contrast, the BCS asks country of birth for all respondents.

8. The same differences emerge if we focus on first-time and youth offenders.

9. Note that this paper is using the crime victimization data purely as an alternative measure to reported crime. This is different from the victimization work discussed below, which explicitly seeks to understand whether immigrants are more or less likely to be *victims* of crime than natives.

10. It is important in such comparisons to exclude imprisonment for immigration offenses, which obviously distorts the relative magnitudes.

11. We select countries where the shares of foreign-born and foreign-nationals in the total population are broadly similar as it is unclear in all cases which definition is used in the prison statistics (OECD 2007).

12. The most recent data (mid-2009) show that 13.7 percent of the prison population in England and Wales were foreign nationals (Offender Management Caseload Statistics, Ministry of Justice). The Annual Population Survey estimates that 7.4 percent of the population was foreign nationals.

13. A further difficulty is that drug offenses often dominate the effect, and it is unclear whether the foreigners in prison for such offenses actually lived in the country or were arrested in transit. Therefore, for example, in England and Wales in 2009, foreign nationals accounted for 10.6 percent of the male prison population with a custodial sentence. However, they accounted for 18.8 percent of prisoners with drug offenses compared to only 8.3 percent for violence and 3.8 percent for burglary.

14. Such an effect could occur, for example, if immigrants from failing countries with weak law enforcement had been more heavily involved in criminal activity in the source country and had developed human capital in crime.

15. See Shaw and McKay (1969) or Sampson and Groves (1989).

References

Alonso, C., N. Garupa, M. Perera, and P. Vazquez. 2008. Immigration and crime in Spain, 1999–2006. Documento de Trabajo 2008–43. Fundación de Estudios de Economía Aplicada, Madrid.

Altonji, J., and D. Card. 1991. The effects of immigration on the labor market outcomes of less-skilled natives. In J. Abowd and R. Freeman, eds., *Immigration, Trade and the Labor Market*. Chicago: University of Chicago Press, 201–34.

Baker, S. 2011. Effects of the 1986 Immigration Reform and Control Act on crime. Mimeo. Stanford University.

Becker, G. 1968. Crime and punishment: An economic approach. *Journal of Political Economy* 76: 175–209.

Bell, B., F. Fasani, and S. Machin. 2013. Crime and immigration: Evidence from large immigrant waves. *Review of Economics and Statistics*, forthcoming.

Bell, B., and S. Machin. 2013. Immigrant enclaves and crime. *Journal of Regional Science* 53 (1): 118–41.

Bianchi, M., P. Buonanno, and P. Pinotti. 2012. Do immigrants cause crime? *Journal of the European Economic Association* 10 (6): 1318–47.

Borjas, G. 1999. The economic analysis of immigration. In O. Ashenfelter and D. Card, eds., *Handbook of Labor Economics*, vol. 3. Amsterdam: North Holland Press, 1697–1760.

Borjas, G., J. Grogger, and G. Hanson. 2010. Immigration and the economic status of African-American men. *Economica* 77: 255–82.

Butcher, K., and A. Piehl. 1998a. Cross-city evidence on the relationship between immigration and crime. *Journal of Policy Analysis and Management* 17: 457–93.

Butcher, K., and A. Piehl. 1998b. Recent immigrants: Unexpected implications for crime and incarceration. *Industrial and Labor Relations Review* 51: 654–79.

Butcher, K., and Piehl, A. 2005. Why are immigrants' incarceration rates so low? Evidence on selective immigration, deterrence, and deportation. Working paper 2005-19. Federal Reserve Bank of Chicago.

Card, D. 2001. Immigrant inflows, native outflows, and the local market impacts of higher immigration. *Journal of Labor Economics* 19: 22–64.

Card, D. 2005. Is the new immigration really so bad? *Economic Journal* 115: F300–23.

Card, D. 2009. Immigration and inequality. *American Economic Review* 99: 1–21.

Cohen, M., and R. Bowles. 2010. Estimating costs of crime. In A. Piquero and D. Weisburd, eds., *Handbook of Quantitative Criminology*. New York: Springer, 143–62.

Cortes, K. 2004. Are refugees different from economic immigrants? Some empirical evidence on the heterogeneity of immigrant groups in the United States. *Review of Economics and Statistics* 86: 465–80.

Damm, A. 2009. Ethnic enclaves and immigrant labor market outcomes: Quasi-experimental evidence. *Journal of Labor Economics* 27: 281–314.

Dee, T. S. 2004. Are there civic returns to education? *Journal of Public Economics* 88 (9–10): 1697–1720.

Eckert, R. 2002. Hostility and violence against immigrants in Germany since 1992. In J. Freilich, G. Newman, S. Shoham, and M. Addad, eds., *Migration, Culture Conflict and Crime*. Aldershot: Ashgate Publishing, 211–22.

Edin, P.-A., P. Fredriksson, and O. Aslund. 2003. Ethnic enclaves and the economic success of immigrants: Evidence from a natural experiment. *Quarterly Journal of Economics* 118: 329–57.

Ehrlich, I. 1973. Participation in illegitimate activities: A theoretical and empirical investigation. *Journal of Political Economy* 81: 521–63.

Farrington, D. 1986. Age and crime. *Crime and Justice* 7: 189–250.

Freeman, R. 1999. The economics of crime. In O. Ashenfelter and D. Card, eds., *Handbook of Labor Economics*, vol. 3. Amsterdam: North Holland, 3529–71.

Glaeser, E. L., B. Sacerdote, and J. A. Scheinkman. 1996. Crime and social interactions. *Quarterly Journal of Economics* 109: 507–48.

Glitz, A. 2012. The labour market impact of immigration: A quasi-experiment exploiting immigrant location rules in Germany. *Journal of Labor Economics* 30: 175–213.

Gottfredson, M., and T. Hirschi. 1983. Age and the explanation of crime. *American Journal of Sociology* 89: 552–84.

Gould, D., B. Weinberg, and D. Mustard. 2002. Crime rates and local labor market opportunities in the United States: 1979–1997. *Review of Economics and Statistics* 84: 45–61.

Gould, E., V. Lavy, and D. Paserman. 2004. Immigrating to opportunity: Estimating the effect of school quality using a natural experiment on Ethiopians in Israel. *Quarterly Journal of Economics* 119: 489–526.

Grogger, J. 2000. An economic model of recent trends in violence. In A. Blumstein and J. Wallman, eds., *The Crime Drop in America*. Cambridge, UK: Cambridge University Press, 266–87.

Heimer, K. 2000. Changes in the gender gap in crime and women's economic marginalization. In *Criminal Justice 2000. Vol. 1: The Nature of Crime: Continuity and Change*. Washington, DC: National Institute of Justice.

Killias, M. 1997. Immigrants, crime, and criminal justice in Switzerland. *Crime and Justice* 21: 375–405.

Kling, J. R., J. Ludwig, and L. F. Katz. 2005. Neighborhood effects on crime for female and male youth: Evidence from a randomized housing voucher experiment. *Quarterly Journal of Economics* 120: 87–130.

Krueger, A., and J.-S. Pischke. 1997. A statistical analysis of crime against foreigners in unified Germany. *Journal of Human Resources* 32: 182–209.

Langan, P. A., and D. P. Farrington. 1998. *Crime and Justice in the United States and England and Wales, 1981–96*. Washington, DC: Bureau of Justice Statistics.

Lochner, L. 2007. Individual perceptions of the criminal justice system. *American Economic Review* 97 (1): 444–60.

Lochner, L., and E. Moretti. 2004. The effect of education on crime: Evidence from prison inmates, arrests and self-reports. *American Economic Review* 94 (1): 155–89.

Machin, S., O. Marie, and S. Vujić. 2011. The crime reducing effect of education. *Economic Journal* 121 (552): 463–84.

Machin, S., O. Marie, and S. Vujić. 2012. Youth crime and education expansion. *German Economic Review* 13 (4): 366–84.

Machin, S., and C. Meghir. 2004. Crime and economic incentives. *Journal of Human Resources* 39: 958–79.

Martens, P. 1997. Immigrants, crime, and criminal justice in Sweden. *Crime and Justice* 21: 183–255.

Mastrobuoni, G., and P. Pinotti. 2011. Migration restrictions and criminal behaviour: Evidence from a natural experiment. Mattei 53.2011. Fondazione Eni Enrico, Milan.

Nunziata, L. 2011. Crime perception and victimization in Europe: Does immigration matter? Mimeo. Centro Studi Economici Antonveneta, Padova.

OECD. 2007. *Society at a Glance: OECD Social Indicators—2006 Edition*. Paris: OECD.

Papadopoulos, G. 2011. Criminal behaviour and immigration: An application of some estimators for under-reported outcomes using the Offending, Crime and Justice Survey. Mimeo. University of Essex.

Sampson, R., and W. Groves. 1989. Community structure and crime: Testing social-disorganization theory. *American Journal of Sociology* 94 (4): 774–802.

Sampson, R., J. Laub, and C. Wimer. 2006. Does marriage reduce crime? A counterfactual approach to within-individual causal effects. *Criminology* 44 (3): 465–508.

Sampson, R., J. Morenoff, and T. Gannon-Rowley. 2002. Assessing "neighborhood effects": Social processes and new directions in research. *Annual Review of Sociology* 28: 443–78.

Shaw, C., and H. McKay. 1969. *Juvenile Delinquency and Urban Areas.* Chicago: University of Chicago Press.

Spenkuch, J. 2011. Understanding the impact of immigration on crime. Mimeo. University of Chicago.

8 Organized Crime, Violence, and the Quality of Politicians: Evidence from Southern Italy

Paolo Pinotti

8.1 Introduction

The presence of criminal organizations represents one of the main obstacles to the economic growth and development of several regions and countries around the world. Besides the immediate costs imposed by violence and predatory activities, such organizations may take advantage of their economic and military power to influence the political decision-making process.

For instance, criminals may want to attract public investments toward their geographic areas of influence, as public works and procurement contracts traditionally represent important profit opportunities for mafia-type organizations. Indeed mafia rackets often force firms to purchase overpriced inputs or hire individuals that are close to the organization. Such practices levitate production costs and are therefore easier to impose on firms that may offload such costs or are somehow shielded from market competition (Schelling 1971); contractors for public works fit perfectly into these categories. Alternatively, firms connected with the mafia may adjudicate directly public contracts by threatening the other potential bidders in procurement auctions. According to the Italian anti-mafia judge Giovanni Falcone, who was killed by the organization in 1992, "more than one-fifth of Mafia profits come from public investment" (Falcone 1991).

Another important reason for interfering with political decisions may be to obtain amnesties and other leniency acts in favor of the organization. In a recent paper on the relationship between politics and paramilitary organizations in Colombia, Acemoglu et al. (2010) show that members of parliament connected with the paramilitaries, among whom the former President Uribe, voted laws deemed to be "pro-paramilitary" by international legal analysts and human rights NGOs.

When trying to influence politics, criminals may resort to corruption and violence: in practice, most of the times they will combine both of them. Dal Bò et al. (2006) provide a formal principal–agent model in which criminal organizations adopt an optimal mix of rewards and punishments (*plata o plomo*, silver or bullet) to induce cooperation by politicians. The main prediction of the model is that the availability of threats implies that politicians would be negatively selected in terms of ability, because the personal risks to which they are exposed in the areas most pervaded by criminal organizations would discourage individuals with better outside opportunities from entering a political career.

In this chapter, I empirically examine the relationship between organized crime, violence, and the quality of the political class in Italy. In particular, I first show that electoral periods (i.e., one to two years before an election) are characterized, on average, by increases of the homicide rate in mafia-affected regions. I then examine the relationship between the intensity of violence during the electoral period and the individual characteristics of the politicians appointed in each election. It appears that politicians appointed during more violent elections exhibit on average a higher probability of being subsequently involved in scandals and lower human capital, the latter effect being particularly strong. The results are qualitatively similar when I consider all mafia-affected regions and when I restrict to two regions, Apulia and Basilicata, which experienced a marked discontinuity in the presence of criminal organizations during the late 1970s.

Focusing on the same two regions in a parallel study (Pinotti 2012), I estimated that the expansion of organized crime lowered GDP per capita by 16 percent over a thirty-year period, relative to a control group of regions less affected by mafia presence. The decrease was caused primarily by a contraction of private investment, which was progressively replaced by (less productive) public capital. While in principle a greater presence of the state could cushion the social and economic consequences of the withdrawal of private investors, additional evidence on labor market outcomes suggests that higher public investment was not accompanied by a parallel increase in (public) employment opportunities. The present chapter provides evidence consistent with the view that greater public investment in mafia-affected regions was due to the capture of politicians on the part of criminal organizations.

The next section briefly describes the main characteristics of Italian mafias. Section 8.3 provides regression-based evidence on the increase in violence around electoral periods, and section 8.4 focuses on the specific case of Apulia and Basilicata. Section 8.5 concludes.

8.2   Organized Crime and Political Violence in Italy

The most important criminal organizations operating in southern Italy, namely the Mafia in Sicily, the Camorra in Campania, and the 'Ndrangheta in Calabria, are active (at least) since the Unification of the Italian state (1861). They survived different stages of economic and social development, expanding during the postwar period toward other southern regions (primarily Apulia and Basilicata) as well as toward the center-north.

The original business of private protection, which characterized mafia-type organizations at the dawn of the Italian state (Gambetta 1996; Bandiera 2003), naturally evolved into a capillary control of the territory, which allows in turn shady natives to enter complex criminal businesses such as large-scale extortion of shopkeepers and firms, tobacco smuggling, and drug-trafficking. In addition the monopoly of violence exerted in some areas of the country allows such organizations to threaten politicians and public officials.

From its very beginning, the chronicles of the Sicilian mafia provide a great deal of anecdotal evidence in this respect. Already in 1893 Emanuele Notarbortolo, a former mayor of Palermo, was assassinated on behalf of a fellow parliamentary member colluded with the mafia. Another famous case occurred one century later, as Piersanti Mattarella, the governor of the region leading a political renewal of his own party, the Christian Democrats, was killed in 1980.

Similar episodes abound also in the history of other criminal organizations in Italy. After a major earthquake hit Campania in 1980, the Camorra started a terrorist campaign aimed at conditioning the allocation of the procurement contracts for the re-construction. Indeed, less than a month after the disaster, the mayor of a town in Campania was killed for refusing to award the contract for clearing the detritus to a company connected with the Camorra.

In the next section I examine whether in mafia-affected regions such episodes intensify systematically in the years before an election and their effects on the selection of the political class.

8.3   Regression Analysis

8.3.1.   Elections and Violence

Figure 8.1 plots the homicide rate during the period 1956 to 2007 in
Italian regions with an historical presence of criminal organizations
(Sicily, Campania, and Calabria), regions with a more recent presence
(Apulia and Basilicata) and all other regions; the shaded areas correspond to pre-electoral years. The graph shows that such years include
(at least) three main peaks of violence in mafia-affected regions: 1975,
1982, and 1991. Interestingly, the three subsequent elections were characterized by a significant uncertainty. Both in 1976 and 1983, leftist
parties in fact eroded a significant share of the electoral advantage of
the Christian Democrats, though they eventually failed to overcome
the center coalition; as to the 1992 elections, they landmarked the collapse of the traditional parties amid widespread corruption scandals
and the transition from the First to the Second Republic.

To assess the statistical significance of these visual insights, I regress
the yearly homicide rate in each region on indicator variables for the
electoral years (*ELECTIONS*$_t$) and the years immediately before (*ELEC-*

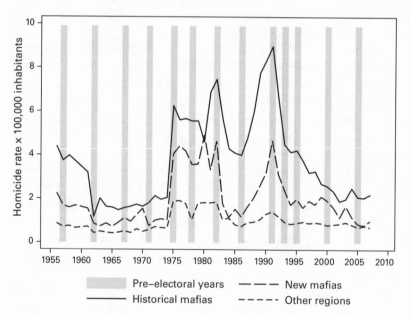

Figure 8.1
Homicide rate before elections across different areas of the country, 1956 to 2007. The
shaded areas of the graph correspond to the two years before each election.

$TIONS_{t+1}$, $ELECTIONS_{t+2}$); the results are presented in table 8.1. The top, middle, and bottom panels report the estimates obtained across all Italian regions, the five regions with a significant presence of criminal organizations and the three regions with an historical mafia presence, respectively. It turns out that in general, the years immediately before an election are characterized by significant upturns in homicides. As an average across all regions, the average increase ranges between 0.14 and 0.25 homicides more every 100,000 inhabitants (columns 2–3), but it decreases below 0.10 and is no longer statistically significant after an autoregressive term is included (column 4).

Still the effect remains strongly significant in the regions most affected by mafia organizations; see the middle and bottom panels of table 8.1. In particular, after controlling for the autoregressive term, we see that such regions exhibit on average 0.5 homicides more every 100,000 inhabitants in the years immediately before an election; the effect two years before the election is also positive but very imprecisely estimated.

8.3.2   Violence and the Quality of the Political Class

Figure 8.1 and table 8.1 document the existence of abnormal upswings in the level of violence observed in mafia-affected regions during electoral periods. One question is whether such changes in criminal activity reflect an attempt, on the part of mafia organizations, to influence political candidates. To empirically investigate this issue, I next exploit variation in the characteristics of politicians appointed and the intensity of violence across different elections. Specifically, I regress the probability of being subsequently involved in scandals and the average human capital level of the politicians appointed in each election on the homicide rate in the two years before the election.

Table 8.2 shows the relationship between the change in murders before the election and the probability that the newly appointed politicians are subsequently involved in scandals. It turns out that there exists a positive, statistically significant relationship only in the regions most affected by criminal organizations. After controlling for the (log) GDP per capita across regions and years, the 0.5 increase in the murder rate observed on average in such regions before the elections raises the probability of future political scandals by 1.3 percentage points (column 4), corresponding to about 10 percent standard deviations of the same variable; the estimate is slightly higher when restricting to the three regions traditionally affected by mafia organizations.

Table 8.1
Murders and elections, 1956 to 2007

	(1)	(2)	(3)	(4)
All regions				
ELECTIONS$_t$	−0.005	0.025	0.141	0.017
	(0.085)	(0.091)	(0.097)	(0.058)
ELECTIONS$_{t+1}$		0.136	0.247**	0.075
		(0.091)	(0.100)	(0.070)
ELECTIONS$_{t+2}$			0.253***	0.035
			(0.095)	(0.058)
Constant	1.578***	1.549***	1.438***	1.511***
	(0.042)	(0.053)	(0.067)	(0.030)
AR(1) term	No	No	No	Yes
Observations	1,040	1,020	1,000	980
R^2	0.000	0.002	0.010	0.001
Number of regions	20	20	20	20
All mafia-affected regions				
ELECTIONS$_t$	−0.028	0.142	0.478	0.166
	(0.326)	(0.350)	(0.370)	(0.184)
ELECTIONS$_{t+1}$		0.618*	0.927**	0.493**
		(0.350)	(0.383)	(0.225)
ELECTIONS$_{t+2}$			0.705*	0.200
			(0.365)	(0.185)
Constant	3.567***	3.402***	3.098***	3.123***
	(0.165)	(0.209)	(0.262)	(0.094)
AR(1) term	No	No	No	Yes
Observations	222	217	212	207
R^2	0.000	0.015	0.033	0.027
Number of regions	5	5	5	5

Table 8.1
(continued)

	Historically mafia-affected regions			
ELECTIONS$_t$	0.045	0.203	0.592	0.288
	(0.439)	(0.469)	(0.497)	(0.231)
ELECTIONS$_{t+1}$		0.601	0.967*	0.546*
		(0.469)	(0.514)	(0.279)
ELECTIONS$_{t+2}$			0.833*	0.278
			(0.488)	(0.232)
Constant	4.130***	3.972***	3.606***	3.674***
	(0.220)	(0.274)	(0.347)	(0.118)
AR(1) term	No	No	No	Yes
Observations	156	153	150	147
R^2	0.000	0.011	0.032	0.027
Number of regions	3	3	3	3

Notes: OLS estimates give the empirical relationship between elections and violence across different groups of Italian regions. The units of analysis are region-year observations over the period 1956 to 2007. The dependent variable is the homicide rate per 100,000 inhabitants in each regions-year. The explanatory variables are dummy indicators for electoral years (ELECTIONS$_t$) as well as 1 and 2 years before an election (ELECTIONS$_{t+1}$ and ELECTIONS$_{t+2}$, respectively). The top, middle, and bottom panels report the estimates across all Italian regions, all regions with a strong presence of mafia organizations, and the regions with an historical presence, respectively. Robust standard errors are reported in parenthesis; *, **, and *** denote coefficients significantly different from zero at the 90, 95, and 99 percent confidence levels, respectively.

Table 8.3 shows the results along the other dimension of politicians' quality considered in this chapter, namely their schooling level. In this case the estimated effect of the increase in violence is extremely uniform across regions; in particular, one additional homicide every 100,000 inhabitants would lower the fraction of politicians with a college degree by 1.3 percentage points.

8.4   Evidence from a Case Study

The findings in presented so far are consistent with the hypothesis that the risks associated with the presence of criminal organizations drive "good" candidates away from the electoral competition. Yet any causal interpretation of such results clashes with the fact that the level of violence might be determined endogenously with political outcomes and the selection of politicians. For instance, more corrupt and less able

Table 8.2
Murders and politicians' involvement in scandals, 1956 to 2007

	(1)	(2)	(3)	(4)	(5)	(6)
	All regions		All mafia-affected		Historically affected	
Murder rate during the electoral period	0.012	0.014	0.016*	0.026***	0.016*	0.029***
	(0.009)	(0.010)	(0.008)	(0.009)	(0.008)	(0.009)
Log GDP per capita		−0.028		−0.181**		−0.222**
		(0.044)		(0.076)		(0.079)
Constant	0.173***	0.416	0.144***	1.669**	0.129**	1.981***
Observations	180	180	37	37	27	27
R^2	0.133	0.137	0.440	0.520	0.430	0.594

Notes: OLS estimates are of the empirical relationship between the level of violence during the electoral period and the quality of politicians appointed in each election. The units of analysis are region-election observations over the period 1956 to 1994. The dependent variable is the fraction of politicians appointed in each region-election that were subsequently involved in a political scandal. The explanatory variables are the homicide rate in the region during the two years before an election and the log of GDP per capita in each region-election. Columns 1–2, 3–4, and 5–6 report the estimates across all Italian regions, all regions with a strong presence of mafia organizations, and the regions with an historical presence, respectively. Robust standard errors are reported in parenthesis; *, **, and *** denote coefficients significantly different from zero at the 90, 95, and 99 percent confidence levels, respectively.

Table 8.3
Murders and politicians' schooling, 1956 to 2007

	(1)	(2)	(3)	(4)	(5)	(6)
	All regions		All mafia-affected		Historically affected	
Murder rate during the electoral period	-0.014***	-0.013***	-0.015**	-0.012***	-0.019***	-0.013**
	(0.005)	(0.004)	(0.006)	(0.004)	(0.006)	(0.005)
Log GDP per capita		-0.170***		0.016		-0.055
		(0.029)		(0.147)		(0.199)
Constant	0.835***	2.338***	0.891***	0.970	0.932***	1.508
	(0.014)	(0.236)	(0.029)	(1.106)	(0.031)	(1.494)
Observations	240	162	52	32	36	24
R^2	0.229	0.634	0.235	0.737	0.282	0.663

Notes: OLS estimates are of the empirical relationship between the level of violence during the electoral period and the quality of politicians appointed in each election. The units of analysis are region-election observations over the period 1956 to 2007. The dependent variable is the fraction of politicians appointed in each region-election that holds a college degree. The explanatory variables are the homicide rate in the region during the two years before an election and the log of GDP per capita in each region-election. Columns 1–2, 3–4, and 5–6 report the estimates across all Italian regions, all regions with a strong presence of mafia organizations, and the regions with an historical presence, respectively. Robust standard errors are reported in parenthesis; *, **, and *** denote coefficients significantly different from zero at the 90, 95, and 99 percent.

politicians may be themselves the cause of the increase in murders observed before the elections (rather than the effect of violence by criminal organizations).

To address this issue, I focus on the specific experience of two southeastern regions, namely Apulia and Basilicata, which were exposed only in recent decades to the presence of criminal organizations. As I discuss at length in Pinotti (2012), the sudden expansion of mafia in such regions was mainly determined by three important events occurring during the postwar period. The first such event (and probably the most important one) was the growing importance of smuggling during the 1970s. After the closure of the free port of Tangier in 1960 and the consequent transfer of tobacco companies' depots in eastern European countries, the Italian crime syndicates most involved in smuggling abandoned the "Tirrenian route" (from Morocco to Marseilles through Sicily and Naples) in favor the "Adriatic route" (from Albania and former Yugoslavia toward Cyprus and Turkey), searching for new bases on the Adriatic coasts of Apulia and using Basilicata as a corridor between the Tirrenian and Adriatic coasts.

Another important event was the major earthquake that stroke Basilicata on November 1980, destroying an area of 10,000 square miles at the border with Campania and Apulia. In the wake of the disaster, the massive amounts of relief money and public investments attracted the interest of criminal organizations. In particular, the absence of a sound legislative and administrative framework for crisis management left local public administrations with a great deal of discretion, which encouraged widespread mafia infiltrations in procurement contracts.

Finally, during the 1960s and 1970s Apulia and Basilicata received from other regions many suspected mafia members in *confino*, a measure imposed on individuals that had been either convicted for mafia or were strongly suspected of belonging to the organization. In the intention of its proponents, the policy was aimed at breaking the links between criminals and the surrounding environment; in practice, its main (unintended) consequence was to favor the transplantation of mafia into other regions, particularly Apulia and Basilicata (as recognized in several occasions by the Antimafia Commission).

Figure 8.2 shows indeed that the years in which these events occurred (between the late 1970s and the early 1980s) coincide with a sudden increase in homicides in Apulia and Basilicata. Mafia whistleblowers do also confirm that this is the period in which historical criminal organizations (Mafia, Camorra, and 'Ndrangheta) expanded in the two

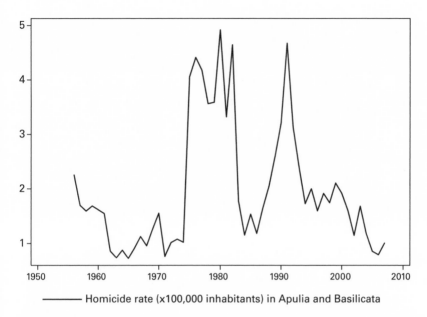

— Homicide rate (x100,000 inhabitants) in Apulia and Basilicata

Figure 8.2
Homicides and other mafia related crimes in Apulia and Basilicata, 1956 to 2007.

regions (Sciarrone 1998). Over the following years, the homicide rate exhibits a "boom and bust" dynamics that is typical of mafia-affected regions, in which periods of *pax mafiosa* alternate with explosions of violence as the equilibria between different factions (or between criminals and the state) break down.

We may thus exploit the change in mafia presence around the mid-1970s to estimate the consequence of criminal organizations for politicians' quality. In practice, I compare the average quality of national members of parliament elected in Apulia and Basilicata with those elected in a control group of other Italian regions less affected by mafia presence, before and after the advent of mafia in Apulia and Basilicata. To reduce the scope for omitted variable bias, I apply the *synthetic control method* devised by Abadie and Gardeazabal (2003) and Abadie et al. (2010), weighting units in the control group to construct a counterfactual that replicates the regions of interest in terms of initial socio-economic conditions before exposure to mafia presence. This data-driven method delivers positive weights for three southern regions that are actually very similar to Apulia and Basilicata, namely Abruzzo, Molise, and Sardinia: the detailed procedure is described at length in Pinotti (2012).

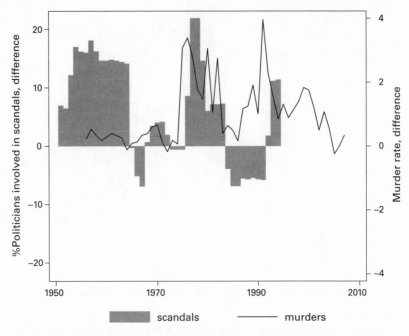

Figure 8.3
Organized crime and politicians' involvement in scandals, 1956 to 1994. Note the probability that national members of parliament appointed in each region are subsequently involved in scandals.

Figure 8.3 plots the difference between the fraction of national politicians elected in Apulia and Basilicata that are subsequently involved in scandals (as measured by the requests of prosecutors to proceed with criminal investigation) and the same fraction for those elected in the control regions. While there is some increase in corruption cases immediately after the upswing in homicides, the evidence is quite mixed for the following decades. However, underreporting of corruption is severe and may grow even more as criminal organizations increase their influence on the public administration. The evidence is more compelling for the other measure of the quality of the political class, namely the schooling level of politicians.

Figure 8.4 shows that until the beginning of the 1970s, the treated regions exhibits about the same percentage of politicians with a university degree as the other regions in the control group. The situation changes dramatically with the elections of 1976, amid the upsurge in murders and violence by mafia organizations. On this occasion

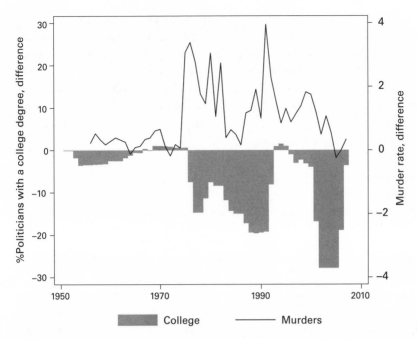

Figure 8.4
Organized crime and schooling level of politicians, 1956 to 2007. Note the fraction of national members of parliament appointed in each region holding a college degree.

Apulia and Basilicata bring into the national parliament a group of individuals with a lower level of education, on average, than the politicians appointed in the control regions; the same occurs in all the following national elections with the exception of those held in 1994 and 1996.

8.5 Conclusions

This chapter documents the existence of abnormal upswings in the homicide rate in mafia-affected regions during electoral periods and shows that the extent of such increases is inversely correlated with the quality of politicians appointed in each election. In particular, individuals elected in more violent periods are characterized by a higher probability of being involved in scandals and a lower schooling level. The same results hold true when I focus on the particular case of two regions that experienced a significant presence of the mafia only since the late 1970s.

Of course, if such findings are really driven by a selection effect, they should show up also for candidate members of parliament that are not elected, as well as for politicians competing in local-level elections. Unfortunately, information on schooling for these categories of individuals is not publicly available. Given that local politicians are more exposed to the threats brought by regional mafias, however, the results for the national members of parliament may provide a lower bound to the effect on local politicians.

References

Abadie, A., A. Diamond, and J. Hainmueller. 2010. Synthetic control methods for comparative case studies: Estimating the effect of California's tobacco control program. *Journal of the American Statistical Association* 105 (490): 493–505.

Abadie, A., and J. Gardeazabal. 2003. The economic costs of conflict: A case study of the basque country. *American Economic Review* 93 (1): 113–32.

Bandiera, O. 2003. Land reform, the market for protection, and the origins of the Sicilian mafia: Theory and evidence. *Journal of Law, Economics and Organization* 19(1): 218–44.

Dal Bò, E., P. Dal Bò, and R. Di Tella. 2006. *Plata o plomo*: Bribe and punishment in a theory of political influence. *American Political Science Review* 100 (1): 41–53.

Falcone, G. 1991. *Cose di Cosa Nostra*. New York: Biblioteca Universale Rizzoli.

Gambetta, D. 1996. *The Sicilian Mafia: The Business of Private Protection*. Cambridge: Harvard University Press.

Pinotti, P. 2012. The economic costs of organized crime: Evidence from southern Italy. Working paper 054. Dondena Centre for Research on Social Dynamics, Bocconi University, Milan.

Sciarrone, R. 1998. *Mafie vecchie, mafie nuove. Radicamento ed espansione*. Rome: Donzelli Editore.

Schelling, T. C. 1971. What is the business of organized crime? *Journal of Public Law* 20: 71–84.

9 Centralized versus Decentralized Police Hiring in Italy and the United States

Paolo Buonanno and Giovanni Mastrobuoni

9.1 Introduction and Motivation

Crime and crime-preventing strategies impose relevant costs on society and are often in the political debate. Crime influences individual welfare, even of non-victims (Cornaglia and Leigh 2011; Dustmann and Fasani 2011) and expected economic returns through investment choices. The social and economic costs related to criminal activities should increase policy makers' awareness of how to achieve a significant reduction in crime rates through adequate policy interventions. In particular, provision of public safety is one the primary policy objectives of both central and local government. Police forces are responsible for public safety, representing one of the main instruments policy makers have to contrast crime in a timely manner. Indeed one of the most common strategies to tackle crime is to increase or redeploy police forces. In this chapter we first document substantial differences in hiring procedures between Italy and the United States. In particular, Italian police officers are hired nationally through a centralized public contest, while in the United States police department are organized at the city level with the police forces hired locally. Later we provide evidence on the effect of police hiring with regard to crime reduction.

Our analysis might seem excessively critical of the Italian system, but there are advantages to using a centralized system. Most obvious is that a centralized system can take negative spillovers in police deployment, sometimes called displacement (Di Tella and Schargrodsky 2004), into account, whereas a decentralized system cannot, which may lead to excessive hiring. Evidence against this possibility is that in 1991 Italy had among all European countries the largest number of officers per capita (one every 286 citizens), whereas the United States had one officer every 459 citizens (Wolff et al. 1992).[1] A centralized hiring system also may be less prone to nepotism and corruption. While all these issues are clearly important and should be studied, we are going to focus on how a centralized system can be used to learn something about the average productivity of police officers.

The literature in the economics of crime has largely concentrated on the effect of police forces on crime rate, providing compelling evidence on the deterrent effect of police from a theoretical point of view. Despite these unambiguous predictions it is hard to empirically demonstrate the causal relationship between police enforcement and crime, because of the reverse causality issue that may affect it. Indeed we may expect a positive relationship between police and crime since policy makers tend to increase police enforcement where crime rates are higher.

Many previous and more recent contributions try to distinguish between correlation and causation in this relationship. Fisher and Nagin (1978)'s critique of the existing literature and the availability of richer data led to the use of more sophisticated econometric techniques to break the simultaneity between crime and police. Marvell and Moody (1996) use twenty years of US state and city data to show that more police Granger causes crime rates to fall.[2] Levitt (1997) uses gubernatorial elections in 59 major US cities to instrument changes in police enforcement and finds that an increase of 10 percent in police forces implied a reduction 3 to 10 percent in crime rates.[3] More recently Evans and Owens (2007) use centralized federal hiring grants to increase the number of police officers, and such changes in the size of a police force are unrelated to past and (presumably) future changes in the crime rate. Their estimates are similar to those found in Levitt (1997, 2002).

Our analysis also concentrates on a centralized policy intervention, as in Evans and Owens (2007), but we exploit documented delays between the time the hiring procedures started and the time the newly recruited police officer become operational, as in Corman and Mocan (2000). Italian recruiting procedures have some advantages over the one based on the COPS program analyzed in Evans and Owens (2007): (1) local police offices do not need to apply to hire more officers; (2) several years may pass between the centralized financial decision to increase the number of police forces and the actual hiring, making it less likely that the number hired will depend on expected changes in crime rates; (3) the relative changes in police forces that are driven by the centralized hiring system tend to be larger.[4]

In section 9.4 we discuss the existing links between hiring and firing decisions of police officers and crime rates. The main implication is that the number of police depends on the optimal level of police work and that such changes introduce hiring and firing costs, both immediately and in expectations for the future. We use data on police and crime for Italian regions over the period 1983 to 1997 and for the 59 large US cities from 1970 to 1992. As we widely discuss in the next section, Italy displays very interesting features for the purpose of our analysis. In those years every police officer was hired through a centralized public contest (*concorso pubblico*). The parliament would sign a law establishing the total number of allowed hirings, over the following two to three years. In section 9.3 we prove that it would take at least three years before the hirings are implemented. The United States presents very different characteristics since police officer are hired locally. Our empirical analysis helps us understanding how crime rates are related to hiring procedures. We find that Italy presents some similarities but also striking differences with respect to the United States. The raw elasticity between police and crime is only slightly lower than in the United States (50 versus 75 percent), but once we control for year and region fixed-effects the similarities end. In particular, for Italy the police–crime elasticity turns out to be negative, while for the US cities the elasticity decreases in magnitude but remains positive. The yearly changes in crime rates lead to larger and more immediate adjustments in police enforcement sizes in the United States than they do in Italy.

9.2   Previous Research on Police and Crime

In recent years economists and criminologists have attempted to estimate the causal effect of police force on crime rates by looking more and more into police hiring practices. The usual approach is to find policy instruments that don't depend on past crime rates that change the number of police forces. This allows one to properly identify crime–police elasticities. As briefly we noted above, US police forces are mostlyhired at the local level. Levitt (1997) emphasizes the link between elections and the timing of change in the size of city police forces. He argues that given the political relevance of crime, incumbents that try to be reelected may have incentives to increase police to show their willingness to fight crime. This is especially the case in mayoral elections, since police departments are organized at city level and represent an ideal target for political manipulation. Governors may get involved in city police politics indirectly. That is, state government provides significant aid to large cities, and intergovernmental programs provide substantial grants to state and local law enforcement agencies. For instance, in 1994 the US congress passed the Violent Crime Control and Law Enforcement Act (VCCA) that authorized over $30 billion for local law enforcement and crime prevention program.

Evans and Owens (2007) exploit the Community Oriented Policing Services (COPS) program included in the VCCA, to study its effect on crime. The COPS program authorized the US Department of Justice to provide grants for the sizable amount of $8.8 billion from 1994 to 2000 to local police agencies for crime prevention programs. In particular, centralized federal grants covered up to 75 percent of the cost for new police officers. As a result over 64,000 new police officers were hired at local level. The VCCA is an example of a centralized intervention that has favored a substantial increase of police forces locally.

Both Levitt (1997) and Evans and Owens (2007) explore, in different ways, changes in the hiring of local police officers and deal with endogeneity issues in the relationship between number of police and number of crimes committed; they find negative elasticities that are usually smaller for violent than for nonviolent crimes. But a relevant issue in the police hiring practices is the effective deployment of officers in the streets. As emphasized by Purdum (1990) "even if Mayor David N. Dinkins agrees next week, as expected, to hire thousands of new police officers for New York City, the process of recruiting and training them is so complex that the last of them would probably not ready for duty on the streets for the two years, with luck." Corman and Mocan (2000) take advantage of the fact that new police officers are required to attend a six-month course at the Police Academy before their effective deployment, which would eliminate the simultaneity issue of police hiring and incidence of crimes.

Another set of papers has tried to solve the reverse causality problem between crime and police by way of small-scale experiments or quasi-experiments. Following a quasi-randomized experiment for different districts in Kansas City that received different levels of patrolling, Kelling (1974) finds little evidence of the deterrent effect of police on crime rates. Di Tella and Schargrodsky (2004) show instead that after terrorists' attacks, reinforced police deployment around mosques and temples in Buenos Aires generated sudden reductions in crime. Similarly Draca et al. (2011) consider the large and unanticipated redeployment of police officers to central London after the terrorist attacks that hit central London in July 2005, and they show an elasticity of crime with respect to police of approximately –30 percent. While these papers certainly use clever identifying variations, the external validity of their results might be limited.

9.3   Mass Hiring in Italy

Our analysis highlights the striking differences between the United States and the Italian hiring procedures of police officers. As we noted in section 9.2, US police departments are organized at the city level, and the grand majority of police forces are hired at the local level. The federal and state police departments are quite small compared to city police departments. In Italy, however, public safety and police forces are organized at the national level.[5] Law enforcement in Italy is provided by five national police forces: *Polizia di Stato*, *Carabinieri*,[6] *Guardia di Finanza*, *Polizia Penitenziaria*, and *Corpo Forestale dello Stato*. *Polizia di Stato* and *Carabinieri* are responsible for maintaining public security and keeping public order, while *Guardia di Finanza*, as the name suggests, fights financial or white-collar crimes, frauds, and smugglings. The *Polizia Penitenziaria* is responsible for security and surveillance in Italian prisons, while *Corpo Forestale dello Stato* officers are a park ranger force responsible for protecting Italy's natural resources, the environment, countryside, and ecosystems, especially national parks and national forests. We focus on the role of the *Polizia di Stato* and *Carabinieri* since these police forces are responsible for law enforcement.

The existence of two police forces that have identical duties and follow the same practices may seem extravagant. But it is an historical accident. The crucial difference between *Polizia di Stato* and *Arma dei Carabinieri* is that the first is a civil national police under the authority of the Minister of Interior, whereas the latter is a military police force (gendarmerie) that depends on the Minister of Defense. The *Carabinieri* were created during the Kingdom of Sardinia and became the national police force after Italian reunification in 1861; the *Polizia di Stato*, originally established in 1852 and subsequently merged to the *Carabinieri* in 1922, was founded again in 1925 by the Fascist regime. It is commonly believed that after World War II policy makers decided to keep the two forces to make *Coup d'etats* more difficult. Whether having two forces that compete more than collaborate with each other is good for society is another interesting research question.

Crucially for our identification purposes, both types of police officers are hired nationally through centralized public contests set by parliamentary law.[7] Indeed the discussion and approval of the hiring law, as with any other Italian law, requires, on average, around one year. Once approved, the law needs to be published in the *Gazzetta Ufficiale*, and then the potential candidate can apply for the position within one month. Police candidates have to undertake an oral and a written exam, and successful candidates must complete a one-year training course before becoming active police officers. The deployment of new police officers takes place, on average, three years after the approval of the law. This lengthy hiring procedure allows for sizable time lags between the time the law gets approved and the time the newly recruited police officers become operational, and so controverts the presumed relationship between police hiring and crime.

Finally, given the centralized organization of the police forces, new police officers will be allocated to regional police offices. The mechanism governing the effective allocation is not fully transparent. Police officers may express preferences for their geographical destination. However, the Minister of Interior may choose to allocate police officers without regard to these preferences, following a detailed manning schedule (or *pianta organica*) that determines the number of police officers each province and city should have.

9.4   Causal Links between Police Hiring Procedure and Crime

The relationship between police and crime is prone to reverses. Policy makers should redeploy or increase the number of police officers in those areas characterized by high crime rates. And if there is a reduction in the crime rates in subsequent periods, it is likely to be a direct consequence of police redeployment.

In this section we discuss the mechanism that we believe describes the way hiring and firing decisions depend on crime rates. This discussion is intended to elucidate the rationale behind Italian hiring practices. As was described at the end of section 9.3, in Italy a very detailed manning schedule (or *pianta organica*) implicitly defines what should be the optimal distribution and size of police forces. Under the assumption that the government has the objective to minimize both the expected cost of crime and the cost of police, using the police in the most efficient way, any departure from this optimal level of police would generate some losses. More specifically, as the literature shows, the optimal level of police depends on its optimal level in a frictionless economy and on how changes in police introduce hiring or firing costs, both immediately, and in expectation for the future (see Buonanno and Mastrobuoni 2011). On the one hand, if the optimal size of police changes because there has been a sudden large change in crime that is believed to persist, law enforcement is going to adjust the size of the police forces. On the other hand, whenever those changes and the implied long-term losses are not large enough to compensate the hiring or firing costs, police forces are not going to be adjusted from one period to the next. Larger discount rates and larger costs are thus going to increase the "attrition" of police forces. Moreover, if hiring costs are extremely large compared to firing costs, as in the Italian case, adjustments when crime increases are less likely than when crime decreases.

Relative to the Italy, in the decentralized US system hiring and firing are often much smaller, enabling more immediate reactions to changes in crime rates. Additionally, in the United States, local policy makers are typically held accountable for concurrent changes in crime rates and so might exhibit lower discount rates than Italian crimes. Given that the level of crime is one of the main issues in the political debate, it is very likely that incumbents seeking to be reelected will undertake adequate policies (i.e., increasing the number of police officers) aimed at reducing the actual crime rate. In the United States even small losses caused by changes in crime may lead to law enforcement adjustments.

9.5   Data Description

In our empirical analysis for Italy we use a regional, yearly, balanced panel over the period data that go from 1983 to 1997 and for the United States a panel of data for large cities from 1970 to 1992. Before describing the two datasets, it is important to stress that Italian and US crime rates differ in many ways. Indeed crime categories are not perfectly comparable due to significant differences in the Italian and US judicial system. Moreover, after comparing Italian data over the above-mentioned period with the 1995 Uniform Crime Reports—comparing the data to the sample of large cities would bias the results because crimes tend to be concentrated in those cities—we find that both property crimes and violent crimes seem less frequent in Italy (respectively 1,880 versus 4,590 and 96 versus 684). When we turn to consider crimes that because of their specific nature allow a better comparison, like

Table 9.1
Summary statistics for the Italian dataset

Variable	Obs.	Mean	Std.dev.	Min	Max
Police officers	285	359.67	132.82	86.87	750.40
Population (in thousand)	285	3,014	2,211	330	8,974
Fraction population aged 15–35	285	0.325	0.019	0.28	0.36
Percentage of population with high school diploma	285	0.17	0.04	0.08	0.27
Percentage of population with university degrees	285	0.04	0.01	0.02	0.08
Gross domestic product	285	14.13	3.68	7.49	21.97
Unemployment rate	285	9.22	3.98	3.19	23.48
Total crimes per 100,000 inhabitants	285	3,099	1,319	1,032	7,710

murders and motor vehicle thefts, these differences remain: Italy had on average 1.87 murders per 100,000 inhabitants, the United States 8.2. The differences are lower for motor vehicle thefts: 324 per 100,000 inhabitants in Italy versus 560 in the United States.

Our panel dataset for Italy comprises annual observations for the 20 Italian regions (NUTS2) over the period 1983 to 1997. Table 9.1 presents the summary statistics of the variables used in our analysis. Our main explanatory variable is the total number of *Carabinieri* and *Polizia di Stato* force, in short the "police force."[8] Total crime is based on the official crime statistics as recorded by the police and published yearly by the Italian Statistics Institute (ISTAT). Total crime is normalized by the resident population in each region and each year; population is taken from ISTAT. We completed our dataset by adding a set of socioeconomic and demographic controls usually included in crime regressions. We include the percentage of men aged 15 to 35, since young men are said to be more prone to engage in criminal activities than the rest of the population (Freeman 1991; Grogger 1998). For the socioeconomic variables, we include the (log of) real GDP per capita and the unemployment rate, which measure the legitimate and illegitimate earning opportunities (Ehrlich 1973; Gould et al. 2002; Raphael and Winter-Ember 2001). We complete our dataset by including educational measures: the percentage of population with high school diplomas, and the percentage of population with university degrees.[9]

The data for the US analysis consist of a panel of 59 US cities over the period 1970 to 1992 (see table 9.2). The 59 cities selected have a

Table 9.2
Summary statistics for the US panel dataset

Variable	Obs.	Mean	Std. dev.	Min	Max
Police officers	1,342	237	99	70	781
Population (in thousand)	1,353	718	1,039	85	7,896
Fraction population aged 15–29	2,360	0.15	0.13	0	0.36
Fraction blacks	1,357	23.08	17.97	0.1	78.22
Education spending per capita	1,357	765.23	122.94	445.92	1,193.44
Public welfare spending per capita	1,357	255.16	126.02	33.49	847.74
Gross domestic product	1,155	12.05	1.80	7.43	19.14
Unemployment rate	1,414	0.06	0.02	0.02	0.15
Total crimes per 100,000 inhabitants	1,353	8,840	2,681	0	20,690

population larger than 250,000 inhabitants and direct mayoral elections. Crime data are taken from the Uniform Crime Report. As for the Italian analysis, a set of demographic and economic variables is included. In particular, we consider the percentage of population between the ages of 15 and 29, real income per capita and unemployment rate at state level, share of blacks at city level, and finally public welfare and education spending per capita.[10]

Since in both cases, our list of control variables is likely to be incomplete, in order to control for unobserved factors, we take the panel structure of our data and either difference the data over time or include region or city-specific fixed effects. We also include year dummies in order to adjust for exogenous shocks in crime rates that are common to all regions or cities.

From the comparison of the summary statistics we find that, on average, Italian regions have 50 percent more police officers per 100,000 inhabitants than the 59 large US cities. To put these data into an EU perspective, we should mention that the number of active police officers in Italy is the highest number in the European Union both overall and per capita, twice the number of agents in the United Kingdom, as is comparable in terms of population. Yet the total crime rate is considerably lower in Italy than in the United States. Over the period 1983 to 1997 there were, on a yearly basis, an average of close to 3,000 crimes per 100,000 inhabitants, while in the considered sample of 59 US cities the total crime rate over the period 1970 to 1992 was around 9,000 per 100,000 inhabitants.

9.6   Evidence on Police–Crime Relationship in the United States and Italy

In this section we present some explorative evidence on the police–crime relationship. Substantial differences in the police hiring procedure between Italy and the United States offer the possibility to test to what extent crime rates are responsive to policy interventions. We should note that we are considering simple correlations and do not make claims of causality. Though, given that the endogeneity of police hiring would bias the estimates toward finding a positive effect, an negative effect can presumably be interpreted as a lower bound of the causal effect of police on crime. Moreover, in light of what we discussed in section 9.4, we were able to isolate some channels through which this occurs.

We start by considering the US case, where police forces are reputedly hired locally (see Levitt 2002; McCrary 2002). In the first column of table 9.3 we simply regress the logarithm of total crime rates on the logarithm of the number of police forces per 100,000 inhabitants. The elasticity is clearly positive, significant, and large (75 percent). This is simply showing that in a cross section the distribution of police force tracks the distribution of crime across space. Controlling for year fixed effects reduces the elasticity by one-half, but the elasticity keeps on being positive and significant. This means that controlling for the average presence of crime and police the endogeneity bias becomes less pronounced, but doesn't disappear. It means that in US cities even when crime rates deviate from their average levels police departments react by changing their staffing accordingly. Columns 3 and 4 show that even controlling for potential confounders does not eliminate the endogeneity of police, while columns 5 and 6 shows that first-differencing the data does not prevent the elasticity from being positive and significant. What this means is that for US cities the evidence is that local police hiring depends on local year-to-year changes in crime rates. Fixed-effects panel data estimates would thus be unable to identify the effect of police on crime, requiring the use of alternative strategies, for example instrumental variables (Levitt 2002), or regression discontinuities (Di Tella and Schargrodsky 2004; Klick and Tabarrok 2005).

Next we show that the picture drastically changes in Italy, where police forces are hired nationally through a centralized public contest. In table 9.4 we show that Italy presents some similarities but also striking differences with respect to the United States. Column 1 shows that

Table 9.3
Police and crime in the United States

	(1)	(2)	(3)	(4)	(5)	(6)
	log Total crime				Δlog Total crime	
	OLS	OLS	OLS	OLS	OLS	OLS
log or Δlog Police officers	0.749***	0.368***	0.168	0.183*	0.167***	0.131***
	(0.139)	(0.104)	(0.105)	(0.103)	(0.052)	(0.048)
log or Δlog SMSA % pop 25–29			-0.093	0.778		0.839
			(0.224)	(0.599)		(0.537)
log or Δlog State Real income per capita			1.044***	0.118		-0.119
			(0.143)	(0.366)		(0.183)
log or Δlog % City pop black (interpolated)			0.083	-0.005		0.022
			(0.088)	(0.090)		(0.056)
log or Δlog State unemployment rate			0.251***	0.175**		0.084***
			(0.030)	(0.068)		(0.021)
log or Δlog Real state+local education spending per capita			0.210**	0.375***		-0.005
			(0.101)	(0.136)		(0.053)
log or Δlog Real state+local public welfare spending per capita			-0.053	-0.058		0.015
			(0.066)	(0.085)		(0.042)
Year effects	No	Yes	No	Yes	Yes	Yes
Observed	285	285	285	285	266	266
R^2	0.704	0.947	0.922	0.952	0.549	0.553

Notes: In columns 1 to 4, regressors are in log, and in columns 5 and 6, regressors are expressed in log changes. Regressions are estimated using ordinary least squares. Clustered (by city) standard errors in parentheses: ***$p < 0.01$, **$p < 0.05$, *$p < 0.1$.

Table 9.4
Police and crime in Italy

	(1)	(2)	(3)	(4)	(5)	(6)
	log Total crime				Δlog Total crime	
	OLS	OLS	OLS	OLS	OLS	OLS
log or Δlog Police officers	0.501**	−0.238***	−0.100*	−0.244***	−0.109***	−0.105***
	(0.229)	(0.049)	(0.050)	(0.044)	(0.037)	(0.034)
log or Δlog % Population aged 15–35			4.388***	0.411		−0.843
			(0.907)	(1.555)		(2.053)
log or Δlog GDP			2.191***	1.188***		0.032
			(0.393)	(0.382)		(0.228)
log or Δlog % Population with high school diploma			0.043	−0.107		0.023
			(0.117)	(0.065)		(0.037)
log or Δlog % Population with university degree			0.060	0.116		−0.048
			(0.116)	(0.116)		(0.094)
Unemployment rate			−0.056	0.008		−0.085
			(0.083)	(0.069)		(0.060)
Year effects	No	Yes	No	Yes	Yes	Yes
Observed	285	285	285	285	266	266
R^2	0.704	0.947	0.922	0.952	0.549	0.553

Notes: In columns 1 to 4, regressors are in log, and in columns 5 and 6, regressors are expressed in log changes. Regressions are estimated using ordinary least squares. Clustered (by city) standard errors in parentheses: ***$p < 0.01$, **$p < 0.05$, *$p < 0.1$.

the raw elasticity between police and crime is only slightly lower than in the United States (50 versus 75 percent), which is evidence of endogeneity across space.

When controlled for year and region fixed effects, the similarities end. Column 2 shows that adding the fixed effects the elasticity goes from positive 0.50 to negative 0.24 percent. Recall that for the US cities, after controlling for the same fixed effects, the elasticity was smaller but still positive. Column 4 shows that controlling for additional confounders does not alter this result; while columns 5 and 6 show that first differencing the data lowers the elasticity from −22.6 to −12.5 percent. This difference might be due to measurement error in the number of police officers.[11]

In order to be conservative we can benchmark our results to the −12.5 percent figure. It is also worth noting that after first differencing the data all the other independent variables stop being significant, while police forces don't.

Our preliminary findings demonstrate how different hiring procedures in police officers are related to crime rate. In particular, it emerges that in the United States, where police officers are hired locally, government reacts more rapidly to changes in the crime rate, whereas in Italy, the centralized and lengthy hiring procedures determine a potential inefficiency in the response of police forces to changes in the crime rate. Empirically, this translates into a positive correlation between police forces and crime rate for the United States, while in Italy the endogeneity between police forces and crime rate vanishes because of the sizable delays between the hiring decisions and the effective police officers deployment.

9.7 Conclusions

In this chapter we document striking differences in the police hiring procedures between Italy and the United States. Italian police hiring is characterized by a centralized and lengthy procedure that generates substantial delays in the effective deployment of new police officers. Instead, US police departments are organized at the city level, including their decisions to hire additional officers.

We exploit these differences between the Italian and US police hiring system to present evidence about heterogeneity in the endogeneity within the police-crime relationship. Our empirical findings show that the raw elasticity between police and crime is only slightly lower in

Italy than in the United States, but controlling for year and region fixed effects the police–crime elasticity in Italy turns to be negative, while it remains positive for the US cities, despite being lower in magnitude. Our interpretation of these patterns is that yearly changes in crime lead to larger and more immediate adjustments in police enforcement in the United States than they do in Italy because of the different police hiring procedures.

Despite the apparent inefficiencies in the allocation of Italian police forces, evidence shows that the estimated elasticities of crimes with respect to regular police officers, which might still contain some endogeneity bias and thus be even smaller, are only slightly larger than in the United States.

We should further mention that centralized hiring systems can have other advantages (internalization of crime displacement and less nepotism) that we didn't attempt to measure. Future research may develop what we learned about the optimal investment in police and about where the endogeneity between crime and police resides to provide new estimates about the causal effect of police on crime.

Notes

1. The counterfactual might not be exact here, as with a decentralized system Italy could in fact have an even larger police force.

2. A variable "Granger causes" another when changes in the first variable precede changes in the second.

3. In response to McCrary (2002) who challenged these results due to some coding errors, Levitt (2002) uses the number of firefighters and other municipal workers as instruments for the number of police officers and finds evidence of large deterrence effects.

4. Only 1 to 2 percent of police officers receives a COPS grant.

5. Law n.121 of 1981 rules the present organization of Italy's public safety and police forces.

6. *Carabinieri* is the shortened (and common) name for the *Arma dei Carabinieri*.

7. In particular, hiring procedures were set in 1981 (Law n.121) and later modified in 1982 (Decree Law n.335) and in 2000 (Decree Law n.234).

8. These data were used by Marselli and Vannini (1997) and provided to us by the authors.

9. Education may have a sort of "civilization" effect reducing crime over and above its effect through labor market opportunities (Buonanno and Leonida 2009; Fajnzylber et al. 2002; Lochner and Moretti 2004).

10. The dataset is the one used by Levitt (1997) to which we refer for a more complete and detailed description of the data.

11. See Buonanno and Mastrobuoni (2011) for a way to assess the importance of measurement error.

References

Buonanno, Paolo, and Leone Leonida. 2009. Non-market effects of education on crime: Evidence from Italian regions. *Economics of Education Review* 28 (1): 11–17.

Buonanno, Paolo, and Giovanni Mastrobuoni. 2011. Police and crime: Evidence from dictated delays in centralized police hiring. Mimeo. Collegio Carlo Alberto, Turin.

Corman, Hope, and H. Naci Mocan. 2000. A time-series analysis of crime, deterrence, and drug abuse in New York City. *American Economic Review* 90 (3): 584–604.

Cornaglia, Francesca, and Andrew Leigh. 2011. Crime and mental wellbeing. Discussion paper 1049. Centre for Economic Performance, LSE.

Di Tella, Rafael, and Ernesto Schargrodsky. 2004. Do police reduce crime? Estimates using the allocation of police forces after a terrorist attack. *American Economic Review* 94 (1): 115–33.

Draca, Mirko, Stephen Machin, and Robert Witt. 2011. Panic on the streets of London: Police, crime and the July 2005 terror attacks. *American Economic Review* 101 (5): 2157–81.

Dustmann, Christian, and Francesco Fasani. 2011. Crime and mental wellbeing in the UK. Mimeo. University College London.

Ehrlich, Isaac. 1973. Participation in illegitimate activities: A theoretical and empirical investigation. *Journal of Political Economy* 81 (3): 521–65.

Evans, William N., and Emily G. Owens. 2007. COPS and Crime. *Journal of Public Economics* 91 (1–2): 181–201.

Fajnzylber, Pablo, Daniel Lederman, and Norman Loayza. 2002. What causes violent crime? *European Economic Review* 46 (7): 1323–57.

Fisher, Franklin M., and Daniel Nagin. 1978. On the feasibility of identifying the crime function in a simultaneous model of crime rates and sanction levels. In A. Blumstein, J. Cohen, and D. Nagin, eds., *Deterrence and Incapacitation: Estimating the Effects of Criminal Sanctions on Crime Rates*, Washington, DC: National Academy Press, 361–99.

Freeman, Richard B. 1991. Crime and the employment of disadvantaged youths. Working paper 3875. NBER, Cambridge, MA.

Gould, Eric D., Bruce A. Weinberg, and David B. Mustard. 2002. Crime rates and local labor market opportunities in the United States: 1979–1997. *Review of Economics and Statistics* 84 (1): 45–61.

Grogger, Jeff. 1998. Market wages and youth crime. *Journal of Labor Economics* 16 (4): 756–91.

Kelling, George L. 1974. *The Kansas City Preventive Patrol Experiment: A Summary Report*. Washington, DC: Police Foundation.

Klick, Jonathan, and Alexander Tabarrok. 2005. Using terror alert levels to estimate the effect of police on crime. *Journal of Law and Economics* 48 (1): 267–79.

Levitt, Steven D. 1997. Using electoral cycles in police hiring to estimate the effect of police on crime. *American Economic Review* 87 (3): 270–90.

Levitt, Steven D. 2002. Reply: Using electoral cycles in police hiring to estimate the effects of police on crime. *American Economic Review* 92 (4): 1244–50.

Lochner, Lance, and Enrico Moretti. 2004. The effect of education on crime: Evidence from prison inmates, arrests, and self-reports. *American Economic Review* 94 (1): 155–89.

Marselli, Riccardo, and Marco Vannini. 1997. Estimating a crime equation in the presence of organized crime: Evidence from Italy. *International Review of Law and Economics* 17 (1): 89–113.

Marvell, Thomas B., and Carlisle E. Moody. 1996. Specification problems, police levels, and crime rates. *Criminology* 34 (4): 609–46.

McCrary, Justin. 2002. Comment: Using electoral cycles in police hiring to estimate the effect of police on crime. *American Economic Review* 92 (4): 1236–43.

Purdum, Todd S. 1990. More police, eventually. *New York Times*, September 29.

Raphael, Steven, and Rudolf Winter-Ember. 2001. Identifying the effect of unemployment on crime. *Journal of Law and Economics* 44 (1): 259–83.

Wolff, Michael, Peter Rutten, and Albert F. Bayers, III. 1992. *Where We Stand: Can America Make It in the Global Race for Wealth, Health, and Happiness?* New York: Bantam/Dell.

10 The "Program of Integration and Management in Public Safety" in Minas Gerais, Brazil: A Descriptive Analysis

Rodrigo R. Soares and Igor Viveiros

10.1 Introduction

The main police forces in Brazil are organized at the state level, centered at two independent institutions. The Military Police is a militarized uniformed police force responsible for ostensive patrolling, urban traffic control, immediate responses to crime, and so on. The Civil Police is a judiciary police force, responsible for investigations and general assistance to the judiciary power. Besides having different responsibilities, these police forces have different geographic jurisdictions, hierarchical structures, and state agencies they report to.

In Brazil, the lack of coordination between these two law enforcement bodies and constant jurisdictional conflicts have recurrently been identified as major obstacles in the fight against crime. The existence of multiple commands coupled with lack of communication and coordination has also been considered a barrier to the effectiveness and democratization of police action, both in Brazil and elsewhere (see Bayley 1999; Beato 1999; Chesnais 1999; Bicudo 2000).

In the Brazilian state of Minas Gerais—the second most populous state in the country—such concerns have led to an unprecedented effort to integrate the two state level police forces, in the wake of statewide increases in crime starting in the late 1990s. The effort to improve the effectiveness of police action was aimed at rationalizing the use of resources and allocation of police officers and also optimizing the use of information. These goals form the basis of the Program of Integration and Management in Public Safety (Programa Integração da Gestão em Segurança Pública, or IGESP). The IGESP had three main components: (1) integration and coordination of actions across the Civil and Military Police forces, turning the two independent bodies into a single decision-making unit; (2) implementation of a system of information consolidating up-to-date data into a single database accessible to the different agents; and (3) implementation of a management model of decentralized decision-making and accountability. The IGESP, in effect, draws heavily on COMPSTAT methodology but combined with a necessary reorganization of the two existing law enforcement agencies. The pilot program was implemented in the state capital in 2005, and then it was progressively expanded to the rest of the state, covering more than 50 municipalities by 2008.

This chapter describes the implementation of IGESP in the state of Minas Gerais and provides a preliminary assessment of its effect based on crime rates. A full evaluation of the IGESP can be found in Soares and Viveiros (2010). The focus here is on the institutional aspects of the program and on some of the main operational challenges it faced as well as on its specific design.

We start in section 10.2 with a brief description of the structure of Brazilian police, and then follow (section 10.3) with a discussion of the crime and violence in the state of Minas Gerais at the moment IGESP was implemented. In section 10.4 we explain the geographic rearrangement of the Civil and Military Police forces that was a necessary step before the program's implementation, and in section 10.5 we describe the managerial changes instituted by the IGESP. Finally, in section 10.6 we present our preliminary findings on the IGESP's impact on crime rates, and in section 10.7 we add some concluding remarks.

10.2   A Brief Description of the Brazilian Police System

The Brazilian police system is decentralized at the state level and established within each state as two main police forces: the Military Police and the Civil Police.[1] The Military Police is a uniformed force responsible for the policing and maintenance of public order. It is typically involved in day-to-day patrolling of neighborhoods, immediate response to crimes, urban traffic control, crowd management in public events, and riots control, among other things. The Civil Police is a judiciary police force, responsible for investigations, forensic work, judiciary assistance, civil identification of individuals and criminals, temporary custody of prisoners, and enforcement of laws and property rights.

Most of the states' Military Police forces had their origins in the colonial period, and were derived from paramilitary organizations that were subject to control by the Portuguese Ministries of War and Justice

(Muniz 2001). Throughout most of Brazilian history they played a role closer to that of providers of internal stability and national defense than actual police forces. After independence, these duties were enhanced as the Military Police started to be used as an auxiliary force to the army—be it in external wars or in the suppression of internal conflicts and popular rebellions—or, in the first republican period, to oppose the army and navy in states seeking a level of independence from the federation. The usual deployment was for state defense rather than protection of society and maintenance of order. The organizational structure of the Military Police forces reflects this purpose in being almost identical to that of the army. Only with the end of the military dictatorship in 1985 the Military Police forces started to be recognized as providers of service to the civil population (Bicudo 2000; Muniz 2001). The Civil Police likewise had its origins in the colonial period, as a department within the local administration of cities performing duties similar to those of investigative police forces with some judicial power.

In accord with this history Brazilian state polices today are still formally under the control of the national army. De facto, they are subordinate to the state and answer to the governors' executive power. Traditionally the Military Police is under the control of a state level public security agency (or secretariat), whereas the Civil Police is subject to control by the state secretariats of justice, mirroring the military past of the former and the legalist tradition of the latter. In addition to answering to different agencies, the Military and Civil Police forces typically have different, nonoverlapping, geographic territories. Finally, compounding the lack of coordination between the two bodies are the jurisdictional conflicts related to where ostensive policing stops and investigative policing starts (Beato 1999; Bicudo 2000).

In the context of rising crime rates in Brazil since the 1990s, there have been renewed discussions about public security, and the inefficiencies of this dual system have been a recurrent object of debate and policy proposals (e.g., see Beato 1999; Chesnais 1999; Bicudo 2000; Muniz 2001; Brasil and Abreu 2002). The literature has identified problems associated with lack of trust, absence of coordination, differences in training and work methods, increased costs, and excessive militarism, all deemed to be in some measure associated with the lack of integration of the two police forces.

Among the initiatives studied were a pilot program implemented in the capital of the state of Ceará in the late 1990s and a project of constitutional amendment submitted to the Brazilian National Congress in

1992 (Brasil and Abreu 2002; Bicudo 2000). Early assessments of the experience of Ceará indicate that the pilot program did facilitate a coordination of activities between the two police forces. As for the attempt at a constitutional amendment, after positive initial assessments it was blocked by a lobby of groups associated with the army and with some segments of the police forces. A few subsequent legislative initiatives with the same objectives met a similar fate (Bicudo 2000). Brazil would have to undergo one more decade of continual increases in crime rates before seeing a serious and overreaching initiative of integration and coordination of Civil and Military Police forces.

10.3   Crime in Minas Gerais and the Context of IGESP Implementation

Starting in the mid-1990s, the state of Minas Gerais experienced an accelerating growth in crimes rates. As figure 10.1 shows, property crimes, personal crimes, and homicides persisted at an alarming upswing until 2003, when a new government was elected. Property crime rates, for example, increased by 479 percent between 1995 and 2003 while personal crimes rose by 303 percent and homicides by 95 percent. Much of this increase was driven by the negative performance of the state capital, Belo Horizonte, a city with a population of over 2.2 million inhabitants. Still, even excluding the capital, there was a rising trend in other cities in the state as well (see figure 10.1).

The new government took office in early 2003. The recently elected governor identified public safety as a priority area, setting among its main goals the preservation of public order and law enforcement, the reduction in crime rates, and the improvement in the sense of security of the population.

In order to rationalize the actions taken in the prevention and repression of crime, particularly violent crime, an institutional change was introduced with the creation of State Secretariat of Social Defense (Secretaria de Estado de Defesa Social). The new Secretariat consolidated previously distinct agencies from the state public defense system, becoming organizationally responsible for the Civil and Military Police forces, the prison administration, the public defensory, the fire department, and the division handling minors in conflict with the law.

From the perspective of crime-fighting policies, the main change was to modify the standing of the two law enforcement agencies. The Military and Civil Police forces became operationally subordinate to

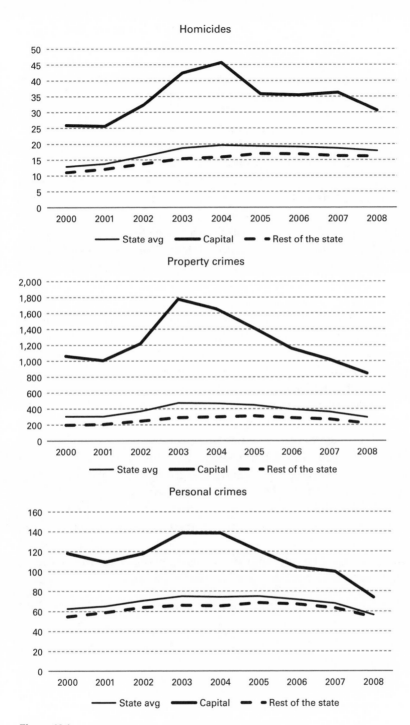

Figure 10.1
Crime rates, state of Minas Gerais, Brazil, 2000 to 2008

the SEDS. Public policy in the area of social defense was from then on
to be driven by a single government unit, in order to avoid dispersed
efforts and fragmented actions. Within this reorganization there was
also the goal of bringing the "Police for Results" principle to all institutions that constituted the public safety system.

Within the process of consolidation of law enforcement agencies in
the Secretariat of Social Defense, a single unified information system
was created. This system was constructed as a service for sharing and
pooling data produced by different parties, including interfaces with
the public prosecution and the judiciary, in an effort to embrace all the
main actors in the criminal-justice system. The system—called Integrated System of Social Defense (Sistema Integrado de Defesa Social)—
was made official in early 2004 (State Decree 43.778, April 12, 2004) and
declared to have as its motivation the integration of criminal intelligence and operational planning. The system would also manage information from the Secretariat of Social Defense related to police and fire
department activities, investigations, prosecutions, and enforcement of
court orders, while respecting the legal powers and independence of
the different organizations.

The redesign of the public safety system had as its main purpose the
alignment of Civil and Military Police operations. A series of measures
were undertaken to bring the two independent bodies of police into a
single planning and decision-making unit. This effectively required a
geographical restructuring to allow the integration between the two
organizations. We review this effort in the next section.

The first big step in integrating the activities of the two police forces
was a geographical restructuring of their areas of action to bring
comparable hierarchical levels together and to define their territorial
responsibilities. The restructuring had as main objectives the following
(Beato et al. 2007):

• promote greater interaction and integration between the Civil and
Military Police forces;
• allow exchange of information in the area of public safety;
• provide flexibility to police procedures;
• improve the performance of police activities;
• monitor the behavior of the criminal phenomenon;
• promote community participation in fighting crime;

- increase police actions in the areas of greatest risk; and
- decentralize strategic decisions in fighting crime.

10.4   Geographic Reorganization of the Police Forces

In practical terms, the integration of police activities required, ultimately, that the two most disaggregated units of the two police forces—the Military Police companies and the Civil Police stations—be assigned in pairs to the same territorial jurisdictions. The areas of action of the Military Police companies and the Civil Police stations, which represented the area where the integration effectively took place, were termed Integrated Areas of Public Safety (Áreas Integradas de Segurança Pública).

But the creation of the Integrated Areas of Public Safety demanded also of both police forces a spatial readjustment of the upper levels of the hierarchical structure throughout the state of Minas Gerais, to ensure again joint actions and planning by the superior levels in the command chain. The state was therefore divided into subsequently smaller jurisdictions, corresponding to different hierarchical levels, starting with Integrated Regions of Public Safety (Região Integrada de Segurança Pública, or RISP), corresponding to regional commands of the Military Police and departments of the Civil Police, and culminating with the Integrated Areas of Public Safety mentioned above, corresponding to companies of the Military Police and stations of the Civil Police. This geographic subdivision took into account the socioeconomic, cultural, political, and criminal characteristics of each subdivision, as well as the presence of analogous hierarchical units within the two police organizations. The diagram in figure 10.2 illustrates the hierarchical levels affected by the restructuring of the police forces.

In effect, the state was divided into sixteen Integrated Regions of Public Safety (RISPs), each with a regional command of the Military Police and a Civil Police department. The Integrated Regions of Public Safety were then subdivided into Areas of Coordinated Integration in Public Safety (Áreas de Coordenação Integrada de Segurança Pública, or ACISPs), combining a regional Civil Police station with a Military Police battalion. The Areas of Coordinated Integration in Public Safety were subdivided further into Integrated Areas of Public Safety (AISPs), which formed the actual areas of action of the Civil Police stations and Military Police units.

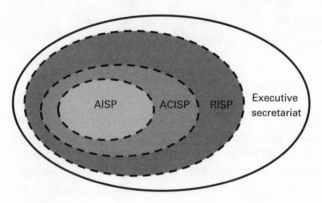

Figure 10.2
Representation of administrative division of integrated areas

Despite the fact that the geographic division of the state into Integrated Regions of Public Safety was made official only in 2008 (Joint Resolution 51, February 15, 2008), the operational concept was started de facto in 2005. In that year the state capital Belo Horizonte was defined as the first Integrated Region of Public Safety, in a pilot project for the implementation of the IGESP methodology. Subsequently municipalities in the metropolitan area of Belo Horizonte were divided into two more Integrated Regions of Public Safety: one headquartered in the city of Contagem and another in the city of Vespasiano. In following years new RISPs continued to be created and implemented within the state. Table 10.1 shows the division of the state into RISPs in the year 2008.

In 2010 a rearrangement led to the creation of two new Integrated Regions of Public Safety: the 17th, based in Pouso Alegre, and the 18th, based in Poços de Caldas. These new regions primarily include municipalities belonging to the previous 6th and 7th regions.

The coordination of the entire system of integrated areas is responsibility of the Executive Secretariat, composed by members of the State Secretariat of Social Defense and representatives of the Civil and Military Police forces. This Executive Secretariat coordinates the activities of the different policing agents across all levels of the integrated areas. The specific responsibilities and authority of each sphere in decision-making can be summarized as follows:

Executive Secretariat—Responsible for monitoring the RISPs, ACISPs, and AISPs, the behavior of crime, and overall police operations in the state. It oversees the expansion and implementation of the IGESP in

Table 10.1

Integrated regions of public safety (RISPs): Headquarter municipality and descriptive statistics (averages for 2000 to2008)

RISP	Headquarter municipality	Number of municipalities	Population	Area (km²)	Demographic density
1[a]	Belo Horizonte	1	2,338,766	332.1	7,043.0
2[a]	Contagem	17	1,646,941	4,380.1	376.0
3[a]	Vespasiano	22	918,785	8,427.5	109.0
4[a]	Juiz de Fora	86	1,499,313	21,493.1	69.8
5[a]	Uberaba	32	671,728	41,915.3	16.0
6[a]	Lavras	143	2,232,245	47,019.8	47.5
7[a]	Divinópolis	84	1,529,809	49,144.9	31.1
8[a]	Gov. Valadares	50	639,232	21,053.9	30.4
9[a]	Uberlândia	14	893,694	26,413.2	33.8
10[a]	Patos de Minas	25	498,299	32,095.8	15.5
11[a]	Montes Claros	76	1,365,527	100,451.3	13.6
12[a]	Ipatinga	101	1,682,115	32,893.0	51.1
13[a]	Barbacena	56	770,807	16,389.1	47.0
14[a]	Curvelo	68	1,004,653	70,322.4	14.3
15[a]	Teófilo Otoni	61	861,395	56,580.3	15.2
16[a]	Unaí	17	331,562	59,471.7	5.6

Source: Minas Gerais, 2008; SEDS, 2008; Datasus, 2008

Minas Gerais and the information flow between the Civil and Military Police forces and manages the crime data in the state. It also provides training for individuals hired to implement the IGESP in a given AISP.

Integrated Region of Public Safety (RISP)—Responsible for the strategic planning of the ACISPs and AISPs. This includes information exchange and strategies for fighting crime based on the coordination of Civil and Military Police forces. The RISP sets up meetings for monitoring and evaluating joint actions, establishes timelines for the meetings that are to take place at the ACISPs and AISPs levels, and produces yearly evaluation reports. Within a RISP, there exists a Group of Evaluation and Support (or Regional Executive Secretariat) that is responsible for a continuous evaluation of the IGESP, as well as for providing support and advice to the ACISPs and AISPs. This group is also responsible for recording the agenda and keeping minutes of the strategic meetings promoted by the RISP.

Integrated Area of Coordination in Public Safety (ACISP)—Handles AISPs' strategic planning by constant monitoring of the material conditions and performances of the joint activities of the Civil and Military Police forces. It contains a support group responsible for processing the demands of each AISP to the RISP, as well as for managing the implementation of the IGESP on the ground and for writing up its evaluation reports.

Integrated Area of Public Safety (AISP)—Geographic unit where the IGESP is implemented. It is responsible for the operational planning and promoting dialogue between Civil and Military Police forces on a routinely basis. It discusses and analyzes the goals and actions determined at the meetings taking place at higher levels (RISP and ACISP). Within this group is a data analysis group responsible for feeding, receiving, and extracting data from the information systems of the Civil and Military Police forces. Using this information, the data analysis group generates the indicators that guide actions at the AISP level. The group also organizes weekly meeting between Civil and Military Police forces, where the specific goals and actions to be implemented at each moment are determined.

Up to 2008, the state of Minas Gerais had 31 operational Integrated Areas of Coordination in Public Safety, responsible for 123 Integrated Areas in Public Safety, in 56 municipalities.

10.5   Managerial Changes and the Integration of the Police Forces

The Program of Integration and Management in Public Safety, or IGESP, is a method of police administration based on COMPSTAT, with adaptations to Brazilian reality. Its implementation required the development of a unified system of information and the geographic restructuring of the police forces, but essentially the IGESP is a management model of information-sharing and coordination of actions across the entire system of public safety.

According to the Secretariat of Social Defense, the IGESP introduced the following elements for integrated police management:

1. decentralization of planning and implementation of the units of integrated police action;
2. transparent and result-focused management;
3. emphasis on prevention and identification of crime hot spots;
4. intensive use of data and dissemination of information;
5. community involvement, with training in community policing;

6. fast, focused, and localized allocation of efforts, based on joint daily planning;

7. establishment of special task units to focus on specific issues (e.g., monitoring of gangs); and

8. ongoing assessment and monitoring of performance at different levels.

As this list makes clear, there is a close connection between the IGESP and the COMPSTAT methodology originally implemented by Commissioner William Bratton in 1994 in the New York City Police Department. Most of the NYPD objectives noted in Weisburd et al. (2003) as constituting key aspects of the COMPSTAT methodology— such as internal accountability, geographic organization of command, organizational flexibility, and data-driven problem identification and assessment—have immediate counterparts in the list above. In the Brazilian case, an obvious additional step in this direction was the coordination of planning and action across the Military Police, responsible for patrolling and ostensive policing, and the Civil Police, responsible for investigations. In this sense, the IGESP in Minas Gerais can be seen as a straightforward example of centralized decision of implementation of a a COMPSTAT methodology in a dual police system.

Thus, in practice, the IGESP aimed at implementing a methodology for the development, monitoring, and evaluation of the joint work between the Civil and Military Police forces, initially in the capital Belo Horizonte and later in other cities of Minas Gerais, and established planning mechanisms at the strategic, tactical, and operational levels. Through weekly meetings in the Integrated Areas of Public Safety (AISPs) and monthly meetings in the Integrated Areas of Coordination in Public Safety (ACISPs), criminal activities in these areas and problems related to public order and law enforcement are discussed and potential solutions are analyzed. Operationally, the Civil and Military Police forces must plan together, setting targets and objectives to be achieved in a period stipulated by the team and fully recorded for comparison of results. Participation in local communities is encouraged, although this was not an initial goal of the process.

Since its inception in 2005, the IGESP has been the most visible feature of the operational integration of the police forces. From its regular meetings IGESP produces key documents for analysis, reporting, and performance evaluation. At the AISP meetings participants exchange information in order to further police understanding of what motivates crime. Following, there are discussions of strategies for fighting crime and of future joint operation plans.

The meetings take place at predetermined dates and times. This is important both for the collection as well as for the consistency and reliability of data. Working sessions are conducted weekly at the AISPs level, with the presence of members from the Civil Police (district chief detective and operational staff) and the Military Police (company commander and operational staff). Polices share information and discuss actions and targets that might be used to solve and minimize the identified problems. The protocol followed to systematize the procedure and the outcomes of these meetings are consolidated in a document titled Report on Management of Public Safety (Documento de Gestão da Segurança Pública).

This document has a set format designed by the Secretariat of Social Defense and the Center for the Study of Crime and Public Safety from Federal University of Minas Gerais (CRISP/UFMG). It has an introduction plus six sections, each with several questions whose answers lead to the final structure of the Report on Management of Public Safety: (1) the introduction contains an analysis of crime patterns and trends; (2) the first section presents an evaluation of the results of actions taken, while the second section describes these results; (3) the third section consists of questions related to interactions with the local community; (4) the fourth section discusses issues of quality and adequacy of police work; (5) the fifth section addresses questions of material and human resources and cooperation with other entities; and (6) the final section deals with plans and targets set by the Integrated Areas of Public Safety (AISPs) to be evaluated at the next meeting.

At a higher level of the IGESP is a meeting where the AISPs present to teams from the Integrated Areas of Coordination in Public Safety (higher level units) the main issues identified and discussed in the weekly meetings. The frequency of these meetings is based on the schedules of the command areas, but usually they take place monthly. According to Beato et al. (2007, p. 5, transl. by the authors):

In these meetings, the main problems and occurrences identified in the weekly working meetings are presented, as well as the actions planned and/or implemented by the AISP and their effectiveness in crime prevention and control. Representatives from the Civil and Military Police forces, the public defense system, the penitentiary system, and the State Secretariat of Social Defense are present, together with a meeting facilitator responsible for handling and directing the discussion, recapping discussions from previous meetings, and raising questions about practical issues and actions. . . . Questions may be raised as to the potential crime generating factors in a given area, the personal characteristics of victims and their behavior, the motivation of the aggressors and their characteristics, the reasons why a certain strategy worked while another did not, the progress achieved, the resources used, and, finally, the plans for action and what is intended as next steps.

In summary, the presentation meetings take form as follows: (1) data on crime in the area are presented; (2) crime patterns, causes, and prevention actions are discussed; (3) a plan of strategic decisions to be taken in the future is proposed; (4) cooperation with other agencies and entities is analyzed; and (5) specific actions for the immediate future are planned and formalized.

Within this setting, the Military and Civil Police forces are challenged to achieve their goals through constant target-setting and evaluation of past performance. The meetings are coordinated by managers from the Secretariat of Social Defense, assisted by higher level officers from the police organizations who evaluate the fulfillment of goals agreed upon in the past, discuss potential solutions, and set new goals to be evaluated at the next meeting.

The meetings also reveal some important aspects of the new management technology in the area of public safety. Most meetings follow a pattern where Military and Civil Police representatives submit jointly a description of material and administrative resources available in their respective units, joint operations undertaken, and spatial patterns of crime data (identifying important locations, e.g., banks, shopping malls, slums, and escape routes). The meetings are also set up to identify the main types of offenses and the key offenders operating in an area.

In addition the meetings provide a way to improve communications between law enforcement agencies and other institutions, and include prosecutors, utilities and public transportation companies, and health units, among others. The meetings can be focused on specific themes, such as traffic accidents, violence against women and minorities, or the problem of juvenile offenders.

The higher level evaluation of policies and programs implemented takes place through weekly meetings of the Council of Social Defense, composed by members of the Secretariat of Social Defense, including the Office of Integration and the Undersecretariat of Penitentiary Affairs, the commanders of Police Organizations and Fire Brigade, and the Public Defensory.

10.6   A Descriptive Analysis of the IGESP Implementation

Early studies presented anecdotal evidence on the effect of IGESP implementation in the reduction of crime rates in Minas Gerais. According to Beato et al. (2007), eight months after the implementation of IGESP in the capital Belo Horizonte, crime rates fell by 17.3 percent. In Montes Claros, the reduction was of 45.2 percent according to the State Secretariat of Social Defense. Soares and Viveiros (2010) conduct a thorough analysis of the impact of the IGESP on crime rates, in an attempt to establish a causal relationship between IGESP implementation and reductions in crime. In this section we describe the program's expansion process, the changing dynamics of crime in the state, and revisit some basic results from Soares and Viveiros (2010). The interested reader—looking for a more complete impact assessment of the program using tests of robustness for specific alternative hypotheses—should refer to that paper.

For our descriptive analysis here we use data from 2000 to 2008 on homicides, violent crimes against the person, and violent crimes against property, and on the number of Military Police personnel dispatched from the Military Police of the state of Minas Gerais, and the population size and GDP from the Brazilian Census Bureau (Instituto Brasileiro de Georgafia e Estatística) and from the state of Minas Gerais statistical agency (Fundação João Pinheiro). Then we construct a dummy variable indicating whether a municipality is covered by the IGESP in a given year based on information related to the implementation of the program from the State Secretariat of Social Defense.

Table 10.2 presents a quick summary of the expansion process of the IGESP. The program started in 2005, within a single municipality

Table 10.2
Coverage of the IGESP in the state of Minas Gerais

Year	Number of municipalities	Percent of Municipalities	Population	Percent of population
Pre-2005	0	0.00%	0	0.0%
2005	1	0.12%	2,375,329	12.3%
2006	40	4.69%	5,855,519	30.1%
2007	44	5.16%	7,253,908	36.7%
2008	56	6.57%	8,508,737	43.0%

Source: Minas Gerais, 2008; SEDS, 2008; Datasus, 2008

through a pilot project implemented in the state capital (Belo Horizonte). In 2006 it was expanded to 40 municipalities, and then to 44 in 2007 and 56 in 2008. Given the large number of municipalities in the state of Minas Gerais (853), only a small fraction was eventually considered for the program before 2009 (6.57 percent). But these were all relatively large municipalities, so the fraction of population covered was indeed much larger than that of municipalities covered: by 2008, 43 percent of the population in the state lived in municipalities covered by the IGESP. So, despite being relatively small in terms of number of municipalities receiving coverage, the program is affecting a significant fraction of the population living in the state.

As the numbers in table 10.2 indicate, the municipalities that eventually received the IGESP were, on average, very different from those that did not. Table 10.3 demonstrates this by a breakdown of data by population, military police personnel (per 1,000 inhabitants), GDP per capita, and rates (per 100,000 inhabitants) of homicides, personal crimes, and property crimes. To aid the discussion, we set up the data by the year in which a municipality entered the program. As the data have municipalities entering the IGESP in every year between 2005 and 2008, this strategy generates five groups: municipalities that did not receive the IGESP up to 2008, those that received the IGESP in 2005, those that received it in 2006, and so on, up to 2008.

The first panel illustrates that, in 2005, the IGESP was implemented only in the state capital, with a population of more than 2 million inhabitants. In 2006, when it expanded to the remainder of the metropolitan area of the capital and other areas in the state, it incorporated municipalities of much smaller size, around 80,000 inhabitants (but rapidly growing during the period). Afterward, the program moved further into the state incorporating somewhat larger municipalities, with population around 300,000 inhabitants in 2007 and 100,000 in 2008. Regardless of the pattern of expansion of the IGESP during this period, the striking difference from municipalities that did not receive the program is that these tended to be much smaller, with populations of around 14,000 inhabitants. The reason behind this is that the program expansion from the state capital incorporated first municipalities that housed higher level hierarchical units of the Civil and Military Police forces, so that integration at the higher level could be developed before it was pushed down to the remainder of the command chain. Naturally these municipalities tended to be larger regional centers.

Table 10.3
Descriptive statistics by year of IGESP implementation and calendar year, state of Minas Gerais, Brazil, 2000 to 2008

year	Population					Military Police personnel per 1,000					GDP per capita (in 1,000R$)				
	IGESP 2005	IGESP 2006	IGESP 2007	IGESP 2008	No IGESP	IGESP 2005	IGESP 2006	IGESP 2007	IGESP 2008	No IGESP	IGESP 2005	IGESP 2006	IGESP 2007	IGESP 2008	No IGESP
2000	2,154,161	71,830	276,434	93,431	12,936	3.92	2.05	3.21	3.37	1.21	7.46	9.76	7.03	6.79	4.60
2001	2,258,857	76,387	286,242	95,963	13,291	3.70	1.90	3.02	3.19	1.17	8.06	10.91	8.01	7.80	4.95
2002	2,284,468	78,180	291,023	97,134	13,401	3.90	2.03	3.03	3.22	1.21	9.92	10.82	8.97	8.54	5.86
2003	2,305,812	80,105	295,840	98,316	13,501	3.79	1.92	2.87	3.02	1.18	11.54	13.01	10.75	10.68	7.26
2004	2,350,564	84,148	305,953	100,795	13,711	3.92	1.95	2.80	2.95	1.20	12.33	13.38	11.08	12.32	8.02
2005	2,375,329	86,385	311,550	102,168	13,828	3.92	1.92	2.67	2.79	1.16	12.95	14.57	11.38	13.16	8.68
2006	2,399,920	88,605	317,105	103,530	13,944	4.04	2.01	2.66	2.75	1.20	14.21	16.29	11.94	13.56	9.13
2007	2,424,292	90,807	322,036	104,881	14,058	4.09	2.15	2.70	2.77	1.29	15.23	16.82	13.31	15.24	10.46
2008	2,434,642	90,042	324,340	105,425	14,230	4.42	2.31	2.72	2.81	1.38	19.77	21.38	16.79	19.04	12.89

Table 10.3
(continued)

year	Homicides per 100,000					Personal crimes per 100,000					Property crimes per 100,000				
	IGESP 2005	IGESP 2006	IGESP 2007	IGESP 2008	No IGESP	IGESP 2005	IGESP 2006	IGESP 2007	IGESP 2008	No IGESP	IGESP 2005	IGESP 2006	IGESP 2007	IGESP 2008	No IGESP
2000	25.9	20.9	7.5	9.3	8.9	118.1	92.5	57.5	53.9	44.0	1,061.1	662.2	330.0	148.4	61.2
2001	25.6	24.6	7.9	9.6	9.3	109.4	100.1	58.6	59.3	46.9	1,005.6	635.9	335.8	184.4	71.7
2002	32.3	30.0	8.6	11.8	10.0	118.0	112.1	56.6	63.9	50.8	1,215.7	777.4	378.8	229.4	83.9
2003	42.4	35.9	8.3	12.7	10.5	138.6	123.2	56.4	70.6	49.7	1,775.6	892.2	443.5	269.5	98.3
2004	45.7	40.3	8.7	13.1	9.7	138.4	118.4	49.8	66.6	50.7	1,654.1	892.7	493.0	262.5	101.0
2005	35.9	38.1	9.9	12.2	12.0	120.6	112.2	58.7	68.4	56.2	1,410.5	810.2	630.6	296.0	121.7
2006	35.5	37.1	9.7	12.1	11.9	104.3	106.8	50.7	62.1	57.1	1,158.4	685.3	592.0	319.0	125.2
2007	36.3	32.8	12.7	11.5	11.9	99.9	97.9	46.0	61.2	54.5	1,017.5	576.7	582.2	335.1	128.8
2008	30.6	33.4	11.3	11.8	11.8	73.8	82.8	35.1	50.4	47.3	845.0	483.5	420.5	260.2	105.3

Source: Minas Gerais, 2008; SEDS, 2008; Datasus, 2008
Note: Group averages weighted by municipality population (for military personel per 1,000 inhabitants, income per capita, and crime rates)

Differences across municipalities receiving and not receiving the IGESP are also patent in other dimensions. Overall, municipalities that eventually received the IGESP were wealthier and had, even before implementation, relatively larger police forces. This last fact was probably explained by the pattern noticed in the lower panels of table 10.3: municipalities receiving the IGESP typically had also much higher crime rates.

The table paints a very simple picture: larger, wealthier, and more violent municipalities were those that received the IGESP. This pattern raises some challenges for any attempt at an impact evaluation of the program, since municipalities in the treatment and control groups are not really directly comparable. In one specific dimension, though, the data may be reassuring: there is no discrete jump on the number of Military Police personnel at the specific time of IGESP implementation in any of the cities, suggesting that the main innovation was indeed the integration of polices and change in practices, rather than increased resources or expanded manpower.[2]

In order to illustrate the crime patterns in the different municipalities around the time of implementation of the IGESP, we present in figure 10.3 the different rates (per 100,000 inhabitants) up to 2008 for homicides, crimes against the person, and crimes against property in municipalities that received the IGESP in a given year and municipalities that had not received the IGESP. For each municipality that received the IGESP, a point indicates the first year of implementation. As can be seen in figure 10.3, crime rates were particularly high in the first places where the program was implemented but became less so as the program expanded. In any case, the main issue still remains: these municipalities with higher levels of violence may also be intrinsically different and, because of that, may naturally have distinct dynamic behaviors of crime.

Figure 10.3 also suggests a time series correlation between the introduction of IGESP and reductions in crime rates. In some cases, the first year of implementation is clearly associated with lower crime rates, and in others it seems that there was a reduction in crime previous to entry into the program.

To better show the correlation of crime rates with the timing of IGESP implementation, we present in figure 10.4 the same crime data organized in a different way. In the figure we restrict the crime rates sample to municipalities that received the IGESP, and normalize the crime rates and years so that the groups of municipalities are aligned

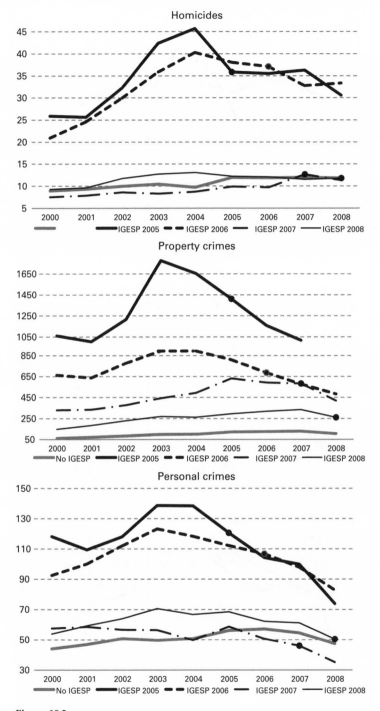

Figure 10.3
Crime rates by year of implementation of IGESP, state of Minas Gerais, Brazil, 2000 to 2008

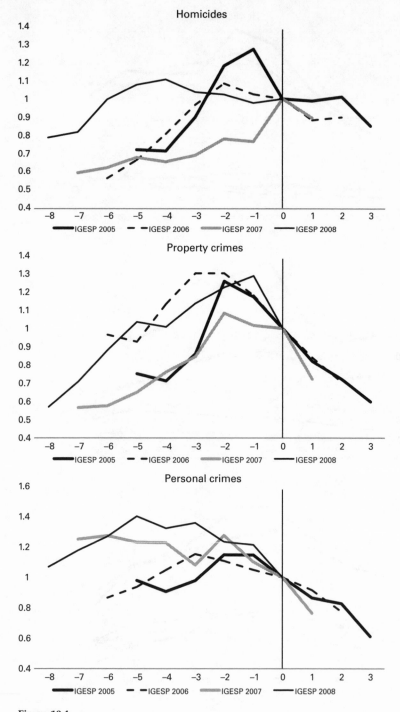

Figure 10.4
Crime rates normalized to 1 in the first year of IGESP implementation (year 0), state of Minas Gerais, Brazil, 2000 to 2008

according to the first year of IGESP implementation. In the figure, year zero indicates the first year of IGESP and all municipalities have their crime rates normalized to 1 in that year. The figure is therefore restricted to those municipalities that received the IGESP at some point in the sample period.

Note that in figure 10.4 homicide rates drop substantially in the year of implementation for the municipality that received the program in 2005 (the state capital). For municipalities receiving the program in other years, it is not clear that implementation is associated with any immediate reduction. For property crimes, there seems to be a clearer effect of IGESP on crime rates. In some cases, implementation marks the first year of reductions in crime rates, and in others it is associated with a marked acceleration in these reductions. For personal crimes, the figure is similar but a little less clear. Still, in all cases, post-IGESP crime rates show a declining trend, of similar slope, across different groups of cities.

In order to analyze the trends in crime rates before and after IGESP implementation a little more formally, we estimate a simple difference-in-differences specification. The estimated equation is the following:

$$y_{it} = \alpha + \beta \times IGESP_{it} + \delta_i + \tau_t + \varepsilon_{it}, \tag{10.1}$$

where y_{it} is the natural logarithm of crime rates (per 100,000 inhabitants) in municipality i and year t, $IGESP_{it}$ is a dummy variable assuming value 1 when municipality i in year t is covered by the program, δ_i is a municipality fixed-effect, τ_t is a year fixed effect, ε_{it} is a random term, and α and β are parameters.

This is the basic specification estimated by Soares and Viveiros (2010). Here we simply replicate their initial results and check the robustness of the basic results to some variations in the sample. For a detailed impact evaluation of the IGESP, including an explicit econometric analysis of the process of implementation of the program and robustness exercises related to municipality level controls, preexisting trends, other variations in the sample, and functional forms of the estimating equation, the reader should refer to Soares and Viveiros (2010). In that paper we further analyze the impact of the program on measures of police efficacy, such as seizures of weapons and arrests.

Table 10.3 gives a sample of the heterogeneity across municipalities that did and did not receive the IGESP program. To address this concern, we used equation (10.1) for the entire sample of municipalities in the state of Minas Gerais, and then also for subsamples that concentrate on a more homogeneous group of municipalities. We used the model, in sequence, (1) estimating the full sample; (2) excluding the state capital; (3) restricting municipalities only to those that received the IGESP at some point; (4) excluding the state capital and restricting municipalities to those that received the IGESP; (5) excluding the years before 2004; and (6) excluding the state capital, restricting municipalities to those that received the IGESP, and excluding the years before 2004. This way we have an increasingly restrictive sample, culminating with a set of observations that concentrates on the period of program expansion and focus on the set of more homogeneous municipalities that received the program (excluding the state capital, which is substantially larger than any other municipality in the state). The results are presented in table 10.4.

Note that in the full sample, the estimated coefficients indicate a negative and significant effect of IGESP implementation on property crimes and personal crimes, with no significant effect on homicides. In this first specification, the estimated effects are very large: using the approximation to the log-linear specification, IGESP implementation would be associated with reductions of 53 percent in property crimes and 20 percent in personal crimes. When we exclude the state capital from the analysis, the only noticeable change in the results is that the coefficient in the personal crimes regression changes from -0.197 to -0.16 (but remains statistically significant).

In the next three columns, when the sample is restricted only to those municipalities that received the IGESP, there are two noticeable changes. First, the coefficient in the personal crimes regression drops substantially in magnitude, coming close to zero and ceasing to be statistically significant. The coefficient in the property crimes regression drops in magnitude but remains statistically significant. In this specification, IGESP implementation would be associated with a reduction of 28 percent in property crime rates. The following specification simultaneously excludes the state capital and restricts the sample to municipalities that received the IGESP. In this case the coefficient on the regression for property crimes increases again to -0.407.

Finally, the last two sets of columns exclude from the sample the years before 2004 (the first year of IGESP implementation was 2005), first maintaining the entire set of municipalities, and then excluding the state capital and restricting to municipalities that received the

IGESP. In the first case, we estimate effects similar to those obtained in our initial specification with the full sample, even though slightly smaller in magnitude. When, in the second case, we look at the most restrictive sample, both in terms of years and municipalities covered, we estimate effects very similar to those obtained when we restricted the sample to municipalities that received the IGESP. In this case we still estimate that IGESP implementation is associated with a significant reduction of 25 percent in property crime rates.

Overall, it seems fair to say that there is a robust correlation between IGESP implementation and reduction in property crimes. As we demonstrate in Soares and Viveiros (2010), this correlation survives a wide range of robustness tests and indeed seems to confirm a causal impact of the program on crime rates.

10.7   Concluding Remarks

The dual structure of Brazilian police, with a uniformed Military Police responsible for ostensive patrolling and a Civil Police dealing with investigations, has often been identified as one of the reasons behind the country's historic inability to deal with increasing levels of crime and violence. This chapter analyzes a unique episode involving the coordination of operations of the Civil and Military Police forces that took place in the state of Minas Gerais in the mid-2000s.

Operations of the two police forces were centralized by a decision to implement a COMPSTAT like methodology, called IGESP. The IGESP program was implemented in the state capital in 2005 and progressively expanded to the rest of the state, reaching more than 50 municipalities by 2008. The program involved an organizational restructuring of the Civil and Military Police forces, as well as coordination of their operations with other agents in the public security arena, and the development of a unified system of information.

The municipality level evidence available from Minas Gerais suggests that the IGESP had a significant impact on property crimes. The most conservative estimates presented here indicate that implementation of the program resulted in reductions of 25 percent in property crimes. There is also some evidence of impacts on person crimes, but these results are less robust and may vary depending on the sample of municipalities used. Evidence from elsewhere (Soares and Viveiros 2010) suggests that the reduction in crime rates was achieved through

Table 10.4
IGESP and crime rates (ln), difference-in-difference (OLS), various samples: Municipalities in Minas Gerais, 2000 to 2008

Variables	Full sample			Excluding state capital			Only municipalities that received IGESP		
	Homicides	Property	Personal	Homicides	Property	Personal	Homicides	Property	Personal
igesp	-0.0426	-0.531**	-0.197**	0.0206	-0.533**	-0.160**	0.038	-0.278**	-0.055
	[0.0586]	[0.0534]	[0.0366]	[0.0610]	[0.0847]	[0.0406]	[0.0888]	[0.0729]	[0.0365]
const	2.094**	4.548**	3.815**	1.930**	4.207**	3.680**	2.688**	6.173**	4.372**
	[0.0345]	[0.0310]	[0.0247]	[0.0380]	[0.0322]	[0.0241]	[0.0579]	[0.0425]	[0.0418]
Obs	7677	7677	7677	7,668	7,668	7,668	504	504	504
R^2	0.661	0.867	0.668	0.608	0.832	0.635	0.861	0.898	0.838

Table 10.4
(continued)

Variables	Only municipalities that received IGESP, excluding state capital			Full sample, excluding years before 2004			Only municipalities that received IGESP, excluding state capital, and years before 2004		
	Homicides	Property	Personal	Homicides	Property	Personal	Homicides	Property	Personal
igesp	0.160	-0.407**	-0.0346	-0.141	-0.390**	-0.176**	0.0708	-0.244**	-0.0659
	[0.0940]	[0.0868]	[0.0571]	[0.0811]	[0.0522]	[0.0407]	[0.0975]	[0.0640]	[0.0569]
const	2.453**	5.845**	4.206**	2.331**	5.085**	3.975**	2.813**	6.064**	4.106**
	[0.0805]	[0.0584]	[0.0411]	[0.0421]	[0.0290]	[0.0250]	[0.0892]	[0.0803]	[0.0626]
Obs	495	495	495	4,265	4,265	4,265	275	275	275
R^2	0.841	0.853	0.814	0.736	0.888	0.719	0.903	0.922	0.88

Note: Robust standard errors in brackets (clustering at municipality); **$p < 0.01$, *$p < 0.05$. Dependent variables are logs of crime rates (per 100,000 inhabitants). All regressions include municipality and year dummies, and are weighted by municipality population. The full sample contains 853 municipalities.

the increased effectiveness of the police, not through increased resources or personnel.

Notes

This chapter benefited from comments by Ben Vollaard and seminar participants at the CESifo Summer Institute Conference "Lessons from the Economics of Crime: What Works in Reducing Offending?" (July 2011, Venice). The authors gratefully acknowledge the essential help, throughout this project, from Fundação João Pinheiro (in particular, Afonso Henriques Borges Ferreira, Cláudio Santiago, Ricardo Candea de Sá Barreto, Délio Cunha, Rútila Gazzinelli, Sálvio Lemos, Valeska Drummond, Betânia Peixoto Lemos, and Marcus Vinicius Gonçalves da Cruz) and from Estado para Resultados and the Secretaria de Defesa Social from the state of Minas Gerais (in particular, Florence Fiuza de Carvalho, Helger Marra Lopes, Eder Sá Alves Campos, and Murillo Marschner Alves de Brito). Contact information: *soares@econ.puc-rio.br* and *igorviveiros@gmail.com*.

1. This discussion ignores the Federal Police, which is responsible intelligence and investigation of federal crimes, similar to the American FBI, as well as the Federal and State Highway Polices. These are smaller and specialized police forces that do not interfere in the usual business of crime control in the country.

2. Since the Civil Police has the status of a judiciary police and is mainly responsible for investigation, its numbers are much lower than that of the Military Police. This is the main reason why we concentrate the discussion on Military Police personnel.

References

Bayley, David H. 1999. The contemporary practices of policing: A comparative view. In *Research Forum*, ed., *Civilian Police and Multinational Peacekeeping: A Role for Democratic Policing*. Washington, DC: National Institute of Justice.

Beato, Cláudio. 1999. Políticas públicas de segurança e a questão policial. *São Paulo em Perspectiva* 13 (4): 13–27.

Beato, Cláudio, Elenice de Souza, Karina Leite, Bráulio da Silva, Rodrigo Fernandes, Andréa Maria Silveira and Róbson Sávio Reis Souza. 2007. IGESP—Uma solução viável e eficiente na execução da política pública de segurança. *Informativo CRISP* 5 (7).

Bicudo, Hélio. 2000. A unificação das polícias. *Estudos Avançados* 14 (40): 91–106.

Brasil, Glaucíria, and Domingos Abreu. 2002. Uma experiência de integração das polícias civil e militar: Os distritos-modelo em fortaleza. *Sociologias* 4 (8): 318–55.

Chesnais, Jean Claude. 1999. A violência no Brasil. Causas e recomendações políticas para a sua prevenção. *Ciencia e Saude Coletiva* 4 (1): 53–69.

Muniz, Jacqueline. 2001. A crise de identidade das polícias militares Brasileiras: Dilemas e paradoxos da formação educacional. *Security and Defense Studies Review* 1 (1):177–98.

Rocha, Geórgia R., and Jésus T. Barreto Jr, and Ricardo F. Gontijo. 2008. Modelo de Gestão Integrada do Sistema de Defesa Social de Minas Gerais. I Congresso Consad de Gestão Pública, Brasília-DF.

Soares, Rodrigo R., and Igor Viveiros. 2010. Organization and information in the fight against crime: An evaluation of the integration of police forces in the state of Minas Gerais, Brazil. Discussion paper 5270. IZA, Bonn.

Weisburd, David, Stephen D. Mastrofski, Ann Marie McNally, Rosann Greenspan, and James J. Willis. 2004. Reforming to preserve: COMPSTAT and strategic problem solving in America policing. *Criminology and Public Policy* 2 (3): 421–56.

Contributors

Brian Bell London School of Economics

Paolo Buonanno University of Bergamo

Philip J. Cook Duke University

John J. Donohue III Stanford Law School

Jeffrey R. Kling United States Congressional Budget Office

Jens Ludwig University of Chicago

Stephen Machin University College London

Olivier Marie Maastricht University

Giovanni Mastrobuoni Collegio Carlo Alberto

Sendhil Mullainathan Harvard University

Aurélie Ouss Harvard University

Emily Greene Owens Cornell University

Stefan Pichler TU Darmstadt and Goethe University Frankfurt

Paolo Pinotti Bocconi University and DONDENA

Mikael Priks Stockholm University

Daniel Römer Heidelberg University

Rodrigo R. Soares Pontifical Catholic University of Rio de Janeiro and IZA

Igor Viveiros Federal University of Minas Gerais and Federal University of Ouro Preto

Index